Italian

Oxford   New York
Oxford University Press
2002

OXFORD
UNIVERSITY PRESS

Great Clarendon Street, Oxford OX2 6DP

Oxford University Press is a department of the University of Oxford.
It furthers the University's objective of excellence in research, scholarship,
and education by publishing worldwide in

Oxford New York

Auckland Cape Town Dar es Salaam Hong Kong Karachi Kuala Lumpur
Madrid Melbourne Mexico City Nairobi New Delhi Taipei Toronto
Shanghai

With offices in
Argentina Austria Brazil Chile Czech Republic France Greece
Guatemala Hungary Italy Japan South Korea Poland Portugal
Singapore Switzerland Thailand Turkey Ukraine Vietnam

Oxford is a registered trade mark of Oxford University Press
in the UK and in certain other countries

Published in the United States
by Oxford University Press Inc., New York

© Oxford University Press 2002

First published 2002

British Library Cataloguing in Publication Data
Data available

Library of Congress Cataloging in Publication Data
Data available
ISBN-13: 978-0-19-860381-8

13

Typeset in Slimbach and Trade Gothic
by Read Setter
Printed in Great Britain by
Clays Ltd, Bungay, Suffolk

Contents

Preface

The *Italian Grammar and Verbs* is part of a series of Oxford grammars of modern languages. It is designed for students learning Italian at school or university and adults studying the language on their own or at evening classes. It contains everything that is essential up to A level standard.

The text is divided into chapters dealing with the main parts of speech, like nouns and verbs, and functional and notional topics, like time and place. A list of all the regular verb patterns and all the irregular verbs in common use in modern Italian is given at the back of the book. A separate glossary explains the grammatical terms used in the book and an index allows the user to look up points of grammar and Italian words. The verb list and the glossary of grammatical terms have a grey tint to the outside edge of the pages to enable quick reference.

The explanatory style of the book has been kept simple, and specialist grammatical terminology has been avoided wherever possible. Numerous examples illustrate each area of grammar, and these too have been kept simple and at the same time natural-sounding.

Acknowledgements

The author would like to thank Francesca Logi, Francesca Moy, and Flavio Pernassi for their advice on Italian usage and for reading and checking the text. Thanks are also due to Dr Richard Ingham, Series Adviser, and to Professor Giulio Lepschy for their valuable comments on the text.

Colin McIntosh

Proprietary terms

The inclusion in this book of any words which are, or are asserted to be, proprietary names or trademarks does not imply that they have acquired for legal purposes a non-proprietary or general significance, nor is any other judgement implied concerning their legal status.

Spelling

I The Italian alphabet

The Italian alphabet has 21 letters:

letter	pronunciation	telephone alphabet
A	a	Ancona
B	bi	Bologna
C	ci	Como
D	di	Domodossola
E	e	Empoli
F	effe	Firenze
G	gi	Genova
H	acca	Hotel
I	i	Imola
L	elle	Livorno
M	emme	Milano
N	enne	Napoli
O	o	Otranto
P	pi	Padova
Q	cu	Quarto
R	erre	Roma
S	esse	Savona
T	ti	Torino
U	u	Udine
V	vu	Venezia
Z	zeta	Zara

When speaking on the telephone it is common to give spellings using the standardized telephone alphabet:

Harpes Road: **H**otel **A**ncona **R**oma **P**adova **E**mpoli **S**avona

The other letters are used to spell words from other languages:

letter	pronunciation	telephone alphabet
J	i lunga	Jersey
K	cappa	Kursaal
W	doppia vu *or* vu doppia	Washington
X	ics	Xeres
Y	ipsilon	York

The letters **vu** and **doppia vu** (or **vu doppia**) have the alternative pronunciations **vi** and **doppia vi** (or **vi doppia**).

> **!** **Note:** The names of the letters can be feminine or masculine: both genders are commonly used. **Una** and **la** are not normally shortened to **un'** and **l'** before those beginning with a vowel.

I Spelling rules

The letters *c* and *g* can have a soft sound (as in **cinque**, **Genova**) or a hard sound (as in **Carlo**, **Gabriele**). The pronunciation depends on the letter which follows. When *c* or *g* is followed by an *e* or an *i*, the pronunciation is soft; when it is followed by an *a*, an *o*, or a *u*, it is hard.

In order to represent the hard sound when *c* or *g* is followed by an *e* or an *i*, *h* is inserted. Note that *ch* is always pronounced *k*, never as in English:

chianti, ghetto

In order to represent the soft sound when *c* or *g* is followed by an *a*, an *o*, or a *u*, *i* is inserted. Note that this extra letter is not pronounced as a syllable; it is there only to make the sound soft:

ciao, Giovanni

Italian words often have different endings, depending on whether they are singular or plural, masculine or feminine, etc. The above rule should be kept in mind when adding these endings, so that a hard pronunciation remains hard and a soft pronunciation remains soft:

un fungo, due funghi   *one mushroom, two mushrooms*
poco tempo, pochi giorni   *not much time, not many days*
tu mangi, lui mangia   *I eat, he eats*
tu cominci, lui comincia   *you start, he starts*

| Stress and accents

It is not always easy to tell where the stress falls in an Italian word. If the stress is on the last syllable of the word, a written accent is added (**così**, **università**), but otherwise the stress can fall on the second-last syllable (**pizzeria**) or the third-last syllable (**telefono**), or, in rare cases, on the fourth-last or fifth-last syllable.

In some words of one syllable, a written accent is used to distinguish between words which would otherwise be spelt the same:

da	from	dà	(he, she, it) gives
di	of	dì	day
e	and	è	(he, she, it) is
la	the, her, it	là	there
li	them	lì	there
ne	of it	né	neither/nor
se	if	sé	himself, herself, etc.
si	himself, herself, etc.	sì	yes
te	you	tè	tea

The accent is usually a grave accent. The main exception to this, apart from **né** and **sé**, is when the word ends in **-ché**, when it is acute:

   perché, finché because, until

When you are typing emails or when accented characters are not available, the accents are sometimes replaced with apostrophes:

   E' vero! It's true!

   Incontriamoci in citta' Let's meet in town

This should only be done when absolutely necessary, as it is not usually considered good style.

! Note: Po' is always written with an apostrophe because it is short for **poco**.

Nouns

What is a noun?

A noun is a word that names a person, place, or thing:

Fellini
granny
Rome
tree

It can also name things like abstract qualities, emotions, or actions:

health
happiness
intelligence
departure

Gender

If you use a bilingual dictionary you will see that some Italian words are marked *noun, masculine* or *noun, feminine*, often abbreviated to *nm* or *nf*. Unlike English nouns, every Italian noun has one of two genders: it is either masculine or feminine. For example, the Italian words for 'office', 'tree', and 'roof' are masculine (**un ufficio**, **un albero**, **un tetto**), and the words for 'car', 'house', and 'wing' are feminine (**una macchina**, **una casa**, **un'ala**). It is important to know the gender of an Italian noun because the ending of many words that go with it (such as articles and adjectives) will depend on whether the noun is masculine or feminine. You may find it helpful to remember genders by learning new words together with their article, i.e. preceded by **un/una**, etc. or **il/la**, etc. Your dictionary will tell you the gender of a word you are not sure about.

Masculine

In Italian masculine nouns usually end in **–o** or **–e**:
un ragazz**o**   *a boy*
un bicchier**e**   *a glass*

Occasionally masculine nouns have another ending:
un problem**a**   *a problem*

Feminine

In Italian feminine nouns usually end in **–a** or **–e**:
una donn**a**   *a woman*
una stazion**e**   *a station*

Occasionally feminine nouns have another ending:
una radi**o**   *a radio*
una cris**i**   *a crisis*

! **Note:** A noun which ends in *-e* may be either masculine or feminine.

As there are only two genders in Italian, words for inanimate objects and abstract concepts must be either masculine or feminine, although clearly they have no sex.

Inanimate objects and concepts

Trees and fruit

Words for trees are often masculine. Words for their fruit are often feminine:
un per**o**   *a pear tree*
una per**a**   *a pear*

Rivers, lakes, and seas

Names of rivers, lakes, and seas are usually masculine:
il Tamigi   *the Thames*
il Mediterraneo   *the Mediterranean*

A few rivers are feminine:
la Senna   *the Seine*
la Loira   *the Loire*

Cities

Names of cities are usually feminine, even if they end in **-o**:
  la bella Palermo   *beautiful Palermo*

Companies

Names of companies are always feminine:
  la Fiat   *Fiat*
  la BBC   *the BBC*

Cars

Names of cars are always feminine:
  una Ferrari   *a Ferrari*

Days of the week and months of the year

Days and months are masculine:
  lunedì prossimo   *next Monday*

  ! **Note:** The only exception is **domenica**: la domenica   *on Sundays*

Abstract nouns

Abstract nouns are usually feminine, including all nouns ending
in **-tà**, **-zione**, **-sione** and **-ssione**:
  la felicità   *happiness*
  la televisione   *television*

I Male and female

People

Usually words for male and female people are masculine and feminine respectively:

un uomo   *a man*
una donna   *a woman*
un amico   *a (male) friend*
un'amica   *a (female) friend*

There are exceptions, however. These words are always feminine, but can refer to males:

una vittima   *a victim*
una guida   *a guide*
una spia   *a spy*

These words are masculine, but can refer to females:

un politico   *a politician*
un soprano   *a soprano*

Often a word that refers to a person can have both masculine and feminine forms. Nouns ending in **-o** usually change to **-a** in the feminine:

un ragazz**o**, una ragazz**a**   *a boy, a girl*
il nonn**o**, la nonn**a**   *the grandfather, the grandmother*

To refer to a group consisting of males and females, the masculine plural is used:

i ragazzi   *the children*
i nonni   *the grandparents*

Some nouns ending in **-e** remain the same. whilst others change to **-a**:

un cantant**e**, una cantant**e**   *a (male) singer, a (female) singer*
un infermier**e**, un'infermier**a**   *a (male) nurse, a (female) nurse*

Sometimes other endings are added:

un professor**e**, una professor**essa**   *a (male) teacher, a (female) teacher*

Nouns ending in –**tore** change to –**trice**:

uno scrit**tore**, una scrit**trice**   *a (male) writer, a (female) writer*

> **!** **Note:** Italian uses these feminine forms for jobs much more than English, but
> there are still some jobs where only the masculine form is used:
> un architetto *an architect (male or female)*

Some words which refer to people end in **–a**. They can be
masculine or feminine, depending on the sex of the person:
  un artista, un'artista *a (male) artist, a (female) artist*
  un pediatra, una pediatra *a (male) paediatrician, a (female)
  paediatrician*

Animals

Words for animals can be masculine or feminine. The gender does
not necessarily depend on the sex of the animal:
  un panda *a panda*
  una volpe *a fox*

To specify the sex of the animal, Italian uses the words **maschio**
(male) and **femmina** (female):
  un panda femmina *a female panda*
  una volpe maschio *a dog fox*

Sometimes the ending changes:
  un gatt**o**, una gatt**a** *a male cat, a female cat*
  un leon**e**, una leon**essa** *a lion, a lioness*

In some cases there is a specific term for a female animal:
  una cagna *a bitch*

I Plural

As in English, most nouns in Italian can be singular or plural. Plural nouns are used to refer to more than one example of that object. In Italian nouns usually change their ending to show that they are plural. Most form their plurals in a regular way, but there are many exceptions to the rules, which are mentioned below.

Regular plurals

Nouns ending in **-o** or **-e** in the singular usually end in **-i** in the plural, and feminine nouns ending in **-a** in the singular usually end in **-e** in the plural:

un lib**ro**, due lib**ri**   *one book, two books*
un fio**re**, due fio**ri**   *one flower, two flowers*
una stazio**ne**, due stazio**ni**   *one station, two stations*
una cas**a**, due cas**e**   *one house, two houses*

A large group of words are basically regular, but require adjustments to the spelling in the plural.

Nouns ending in *-io* / *-ia*

When the *i* is stressed, **-io** becomes **-ii**:
uno <u>zi</u>o, due zi**i**   *one uncle, two uncles*

When the syllable before the *i* is stressed, **-io** becomes **-i**:
un ar<u>ma</u>d**io**, due arma**di**   *one cupboard, two cupboards*

Nouns ending in **-ia** always keep the *i* in the plural if it is pronounced as a syllable (for nouns ending in **-cia**, **-gia**, and **-glia**, see below):
una pizzer**ia**, due pizzer**ie**   *one pizzeria, two pizzerias*

Nouns ending in *-co*/*-ca* or *-go*/*-ga*

For nouns which end in **-co**/**-ca** or **-go**/**-ga**, an *h* is usually inserted to preserve the hard sound (*see p. 2*):

   una bar**ca**, due bar**che**   *one boat, two boats*

   un a**go**, due a**ghi**   *one needle, two needles*

But some masculine nouns ending in **-co** or **-go** actually change their pronunciation in the plural. The *c* or *g* changes to a soft sound, which means that no *h* is inserted:

   un ami**co**, due ami**ci**   *one friend, two friends*

   un biolo**go**, due biolo**gi**   *a biologist, two biologists*

> **! Note:** The feminine form of these words always keeps the hard sound:
> un'ami**ca**, due ami**che**   *one friend, two friends*
> una biolo**ga**, due biolo**ghe**   *one (female) biologist, two (female) biologists*

Nouns ending in *-cio*/*-cia* or *-gio*/*-gia*

If a noun ends in **-cio**/**-cia** or **-gio**/**-gia**, the *i* may be there simply to make the *c* or *g* sound soft and is not pronounced as a syllable. When these nouns are made plural, the *i* is no longer necessary and is dropped:

   un orolo**gio**, due orolo**gi**   *one clock, two clocks*

   una fac**cia**, due fac**ce**   *one face, two faces*

> **! Note:** There are some exceptions:
> una cami**cia**, due cami**cie**   *one shirt, two shirts*
> una vali**gia**, due vali**gie** *or* due vali**ge**   *one suitcase, two suitcases*

Sometimes, however, the *i* is pronounced as a stressed syllable. When this is the case, the *i* remains in the plural:

   una farma**cia**, due farma**cie**   *one chemist's, two chemists*

Nouns ending in *-glio*/*-glia*

Masculine nouns ending in **-glio** take the ending **-gli** in the plural:

   un ta**glio**, due ta**gli**   *one cut, two cuts*

Feminine nouns ending in **-glia** always keep the *i* in the plural:

   una ta**glia**, due ta**glie**   *one size, two sizes*

Plurals which remain the same

Nouns of one syllable do not change in the plural:
  un re, due re   *one king, two kings*

All nouns which end in an accented syllable (**-à**, **-è**, **-ì**, **-ò**, **-ù**) remain the same in the plural:
  una città, due città   *one city, two cities*
  un caffè, due caffè   *one coffee, two coffees*

Some nouns which come from English or other languages do not change in the plural:
  un computer, due computer   *one computer, two computers*
  un autobus, due autobus   *one bus, two buses*
  una radio, due radio   *one radio, two radios*

Abbreviations do not change in the plural:
  una foto, due foto   *one photo, two photos*
  un CD, due CD   *one CD, two CDs*

Words ending in **-i** in the singular do not change in the plural:
  una tesi, due tesi   *one thesis, two theses*

Words ending in **-ie** in the singular do not change in the plural:
  una specie, due specie   *one species, two species*

! **Note:** There is one exception:
  una moglie, due mogli   *one wife, two wives*

Compound nouns

The majority of compound nouns (formed from two or more words) form their plural in the same way as normal nouns:

un francobollo, due francobolli   *one stamp, two stamps*
una banconota, due banconote   *one banknote, two banknotes*

Compound nouns formed from a verb plus a singular masculine noun also change in the plural:

un passaporto, due passaporti   *one passport, two passports*

But if the second element is feminine or plural, the noun does not change in the plural:

un cacciavite, due cacciavite   *one screwdriver, two screwdrivers*
un apriscatole, due apriscatole   *one tin-opener, two tin-openers*

Compound nouns formed from an adjective plus a noun mostly change both parts in the plural:

una cassaforte, due casseforti   *one safe, two safes*

Compounds formed from **capo** plus a noun form their plurals in three different ways.

● Those which refer to objects change only the ending:

un capolavoro, due capolavori   *one masterpiece, two masterpieces*

● Those which refer to males change the first element only:

un capovendite, due capivendite   *one head of sales, two heads of sales*

● Those which refer to females do not change in the plural:

una caposquadra, due caposquadra   *one team captain, two team captains*

Where the compound is formed from two separate nouns, only the first noun changes:

un divano letto, due divani letto   *one sofa bed, two sofa beds*

! **Note:** There are some exceptions to the above rules:
un asciugamano, due asciugamani   *one towel, two towels*
un senzatetto, due senzatetto   *one homeless person, two homeless people*
un palcoscenico, due palcoscenici   *one stage, two stages*
un purosangue, due purosangue   *one thoroughbred, two thoroughbreds*

Irregular plurals

These plurals are irregular:
  un uomo, due uomini *one man, two men*
  un dio, due dei *one god, two gods*
  un tempio, due templi *one temple, two temples*

Feminine in the plural

Some masculine nouns have a plural which is feminine:
  un braccio, due braccia *one arm, two arms*
  un centinaio, due centinaia *one hundred, two hundreds*
  un corno, due corna *one horn, two horns*
  un dito, due dita *one finger, two fingers*
  un ginocchio, due ginocchia *one knee, two knees*
  un grido, molte grida *a shout, many shouts*
  un labbro, le labbra *a lip, lips*
  un lenzuolo, le lenzuola *a sheet, the sheets*
  un migliaio, due migliaia *one thousand, two thousands*
  un miglio, due miglia *one mile, two miles*
  un osso, le ossa *one bone, the bones*
  un paio, due paia *one pair, two pairs*
  un uovo, due uova *one egg, two eggs*
  un urlo, molte urla *a scream, many screams*

> **!** Note: If these nouns are used with an adjective, the adjective too must be
> masculine in the singular and feminine in the plural:
>   un uovo sodo, due uova sode *one boiled egg, two boiled eggs*

Variable plurals

The plural of **osso** is **ossi** when it refers to non-human bones. The
plural of **corno** is **corni** when it refers to musical instruments.
Ginocchio, **grido**, **lenzuolo**, and **urlo** also have the regular plurals
ginocchi, **gridi**, **lenzuoli**, and **urli**, but these are less common.
  The plural of **muro** is **muri** when it refers to the walls of a
building and **mura** (feminine) when it refers to the walls of a city:
  le mura della città *the city walls*

Irregular feminine nouns

Mano is a feminine noun, despite its appearance. The plural is
mani, also feminine:

una mano, due mani   *one hand, two hands*

The plurals of **arma** and **ala** are also irregular:

un'arma, due armi   *one weapon, two weapons*

un'ala, due ali   *one wing, two wings*

Masculine nouns ending in -*a*

Masculine nouns ending in **-a** have their plural in **-i**:

un problem**a**, due problem**i**   *one problem, two problems*

Nouns ending in **-a** which refer to people have their plural in **-i**
when they are masculine and **-e** when they are feminine:

un astronaut**a**, due astronaut**i**   *one (male) astronaut, two (male)*
astronauts

una tennist**a**, due tennist**e**   *one (female) tennis player, two*
(female) tennis players

> **!** **Note:** Sometimes an *h* needs to be inserted to preserve the hard pronunciation
> of a *c* or a *g* (*see p. 2 for more information*):
> un colle**g**a, due colle**ghi**   *one colleague, two colleagues*

Singular and plural

Some nouns only have a singular form:

il latte   *milk*

and some only have a plural form:

le forbici   *scissors*

Some nouns which are singular in English are plural in Italian:

i soldi   *money*

and some nouns which are plural in English are singular in
Italian:

la gente   *people*

> **!** **Note:** Types of pasta are plural in Italian:
> Gli spaghetti erano scotti   *The spaghetti was overcooked*

A noun which refers to a group of people is singular in Italian, and
takes a singular verb:

Il personale non è contento   *The staff are not happy*

I The definite article

What is the definite article?

The definite article (**the** in English) is used to indicate something which has already been mentioned, or whose identity is obvious:

the present which we chose

The sun was shining

Forms of the definite article

In Italian the form of the definite article varies according to the gender and the first few letters of the noun which follows it.

● **lo** before a masculine singular beginning with *z*, *ps*, *gn*, or *s* + another consonant:

lo zucchero   the sugar

lo sciopero   the strike

● **il** before a masculine singular beginning with any other consonant:

il cane   the dog

● **la** before a feminine singular beginning with a consonant:

la città   the city

● **l'** before a masculine or feminine singular beginning with a vowel:

l'est   the east

l'aria   the air

● **gli** before a masculine plural beginning with a vowel or with *z*, *ps*, *gn*, or *s* + another consonant:

gli abitanti   the inhabitants

gli zii   the aunts and uncles

● **i** before a masculine plural beginning with any other consonant:

i pasti   the meals

● **le** before a feminine plural:

le tazze   the cups

> **!** **Note:** If another word comes between the article and the noun, the form of the article depends on the first few letters of the word which follows the article:
> i miei zii   my aunts and uncles

Uses of the definite article

The definite article in Italian usually corresponds to **the** in English:

il sole   *the* sun
il presidente della Repubblica   *the President of the Republic*
mi passi **il** sale?   *Can you pass* **the** *salt?*

There are some exceptions, however.

Talking in general

The most important exception is that Italian uses the definite article when talking about things in general, where English uses no article:

Mi piace **il** gelato   *I like ice cream*
Le sigarette fanno male   *Cigarettes are bad for you*

Countries and cities

Names of countries, states, regions, and continents have the definite article in Italian:

l'Italia   *Italy*
il Giappone   *Japan*
gli Stati Uniti   *the United States*
la California   *California*

But the article is not used after **in**:

in Italia   *in Italy*

A few names of cities have an article:

la Spezia   *La Spezia*
l'Aia   *the Hague*
il Cairo   *Cairo*

See p. 186 for more information about countries, cities, etc.

Languages

Names of languages have an article (they are always masculine). The article is dropped, however, when used with the verb **parlare** or after **in**:

Il cinese è una lingua difficile   *Chinese is a difficult language*
Parlo italiano   *I speak Italian*
Parlavano in albanese   *They were speaking Albanian*

Illnesses

Illnesses generally have the definite article:
  Ho già avuto **la** varicella   I've already had chickenpox

! **Note:** Ho **un** brutto raffreddore   I've got **a** nasty cold

Sport

The definite article is used with the names of sports:
  È fissata con **il** calcio   She's mad about football

but not when they are used with **giocare**:
  Gioco a calcio   I play football

Titles

The article is used before titles like **signore**, **signora**, **dottore**, etc. when speaking about the person:
  Ho parlato con **il** signor Carli   I spoke to Mr Carli

but it is not used when addressing the person directly:
  Buongiorno, **signorina** Simoni!   Hello, **Miss** Simoni!

Parts of the body

The definite article is used with parts of the body where English uses **my**, **your**, etc:
  Chiudi **gli** occhi!   Close **your** eyes!

Possessions

When it is clear who the owner is, the definite article tends to be used with possessions where English uses **my**, **your**, etc:
  Dove ho messo **gli** occhiali?   Where did I put **my** glasses?

Colours

Names of colours have the definite article:
  Il blu ti dona   Blue suits you

Dates and times

The definite article is used in many expressions referring to time:

il 13 febbraio   *on 13 February*
Sono **le** nove   *It's nine o'clock*

For more information about time expressions, *see p. 170.*

Names

In English the definite article is never used with people's names. In Italian, however, it is sometimes used.

It is sometimes used in speech before first names (females only):

Ho parlato con **la** Carla.   *I spoke to Carla.*

! Note: The article is not used with first names in standard Italian.

It is commonly used before surnames:

il Leopardi   *Leopardi*
la Callas   *Callas*

The definite article is used to talk about all the members of a family:

i Borgia   ***the** Borgias*
gli Smith   ***the** Smiths*

Names of companies are always used with the definite article:

la Mondadori   *Mondadori*

When the company name begins with a vowel, **la** is not shortened to **l'**:

la Oxford University Press   *Oxford University Press*
la IBM   *IBM*

The definite article is also used with the names of geographical features such as rivers, lakes, seas, and mountains:

il lago Maggiore   *Lake Maggiore*
il monte Bianco   *Mont Blanc*
l'Everest   *Mount Everest*
il Mediterraneo   ***the** Mediterranean*
il Tevere   ***the** Tiber*

I The indefinite article

What is the indefinite article?

The indefinite article (**a** or **an** in English) is used to introduce a new topic or to indicate just one thing when several exist:

A man approached me

Would you like **a** chocolate?

Forms of the indefinite article

In Italian the form of the indefinite article varies according to the gender of the noun which follows it, and also according to the first few letters of the noun. It is only used in the singular.

● **uno** before a masculine singular beginning with *z, ps, gn,* or *s* + another consonant:

uno zio   an uncle

uno squalo   a shark

● **un** before a masculine singular beginning with any other consonant:

un gatto   a cat

● **una** before a feminine singular beginning with a consonant:

una macchina   a car

● **un'** (or **una**) before a feminine singular beginning with a vowel:

un'intervista   an interview

> **!** **Note:** If another word comes between the article and the noun, the form of the article depends on the first few letters of the word which follows the article:
> una lunga attesa   a long wait

Uses of the indefinite article

The indefinite article in Italian usually corresponds to **a** or **an** in English:

Conosco **un** bravo dentista   I know **a** good dentist

un'opera di Rossini   **an** opera by Rossini

There are some exceptions, however.

Jobs

In Italian the indefinite article **un**/**una** is never used when specifying what job someone does:

Sono insegnante   I'm a teacher

Fa il tassista   He's a taxi-driver

Voglio fare l'avvocato   I want to be a lawyer

However, it may be used when describing what kind of teacher/taxi-driver/lawyer a person is:

È **un'**insegnante molto brava   She's a very good teacher

I Diminutive and other endings

Italian has a word for 'little', **piccolo**/**piccola**:
  una macchina **piccola**   *a* **little** *car*

But Italians often express the idea of 'smallness' by adding an ending to the noun. There are two very common ones: **-ino**/**-ina** and **-etto**/**-etta**. These also tend to express an affectionate attitude towards the person or thing, and can be used humorously:
  un fratell**ino**/una sorell**ina**   *a little brother/sister*
  un lavor**etto**   *a little job*
  un problem**ino**   *a little problem*

Sometimes these endings change the meaning of the word in unexpected ways. In addition, the gender sometimes changes from feminine to masculine:
  una sella   *a saddle (for a horse)*
  un sell**ino**   *a saddle (for a bicycle)*
  un disco   *a disc, a disk*
  un disch**etto**   *a floppy disk*

Italian also has an ending **-one**/**-ona** to express the idea of bigness:
  una cas**ona**   *a barn of a house*
  un problem**one**   *a hell of a problem*

Another common ending is **-accio**/**-accia**, which expresses the idea of 'horrible, nasty':
  un lavor**accio**   *a horrible job*
  gent**accia**   *nasty people*

Adjectives

What is an adjective?

An adjective is used to add extra information to a noun. It can be used to describe the noun it modifies, or it can be used to identify what is being referred to:

an **honest** politician
heavy books
the **black** cat

Note that in English the adjective usually comes before the noun, whereas in Italian it usually comes after.

Sometimes, of course, the adjective is separated from its noun by a verb:

The flowers are **beautiful**

Agreement

All nouns in Italian have a gender, and most can also be either singular or plural. Any adjective which describes a noun must 'agree' with it in both gender (masculine or feminine) and number (singular or plural). In other words, the adjective must always be masculine or feminine, singular or plural. For this reason it is important to learn the gender of any noun that you learn.

Adjectives ending in *-o / -a*

Adjectives which end in **-o** have their feminine in **-a**. The masculine plural ends in **-i** and the feminine plural in **-e**:

masculine singular	un ragazzo italiano an Italian boy
	uno studente italiano an Italian (male) student
feminine singular	una ragazza italiana an Italian girl
	una cantante italiana an Italian (female) singer
masculine plural	ragazzi italiani Italian boys
	film italiani Italian films
feminine plural	ragazze italiane Italian girls
	cantanti italiane Italian (female) singers

Adjectives ending in *-e*

Another group of adjectives ends in **-e** in the singular, both masculine and feminine. The plural of these adjectives ends in **-i** (both masculine and feminine):

masculine singular	un ragazzo inglese an English boy
	uno studente inglese an English student
feminine singular	una ragazza inglese an English girl
	la televisione inglese English TV
masculine plural	ragazzi inglesi English boys
	film inglesi English films
feminine plural	ragazze inglesi English girls
	madri inglesi English mothers

If the adjective goes with more than one noun, it takes the feminine plural ending if all the nouns are feminine. In all other cases it takes a masculine plural ending:

all masculine	cani e gatti randagi stray cats and dogs
all feminine	una professoressa e una dottoressa italiane an Italian (female) teacher and an Italian (female) doctor
masculine and feminine	giornali e riviste italiani Italian newspapers and magazines

Adjectives ending in -a

Some adjectives (usually applicable to people) end in **-a** in the
masculine singular and do not change in the feminine. These
adjectives include those in **-ista**, but note **belga** 'Belgian', which
is also irregular in the plural:

masculine singular	un monaco buddista an Buddhist monk
	un politico belga a Belgian politician
feminine singular	una persona ottimista an optimistic person
	la televisione belga Belgian TV
masculine plural	atteggiamenti maschilisti sexist attitudes
	politici belgi Belgian politicians
feminine plural	idee razziste racist ideas
	suore belghe Belgian nuns

Adjectives ending in -tore

Adjectives which end in **-tore** in the masculine change to **-trice** in
the feminine:

masculine singular	il cantante vincitore the winning singer
feminine singular	la canzone vincitrice the winning song
masculine plural	i cantanti vincitori the winning singers
feminine plural	le canzoni vincitrici the winning songs

Adjectives which never change

Some adjectives remain the same in the feminine and in the
plural. These are often nouns or other words which are being
used as adjectives, and include a number of colours (**blu**, **rosa**,
viola):

  una camicia blu   a blue shirt
  rose rosa   pink roses

The plural of **marrone** can be either **marrone** or **marroni**:

  scarpe marrone / scarpe marroni   brown shoes

Note also **pari** and **dispari**:

  un numero pari   an even number
  un numero dispari   an odd number

Spelling changes in the plural

Rules for the formation of the plural of adjectives are the same as for the formation of noun plurals.

Adjectives ending in *-co/-ca* or *-go/-ga*

Adjectives ending in **-go / -ga** generally keep the hard sound in the plural and an *h* must be added in the spelling to show this.

Adjectives ending in **-co / -ca** vary in their behaviour. In cases where the second-last syllable is stressed (e.g. **stanco**), the *c* remains hard and an *h* must be added in the spelling to show this. In cases where the third-last syllable is stressed (e.g. **allergico**), the *c* becomes soft in the masculine plural but remains hard in the feminine plural.

	masculine plural	*feminine plural*
lungo	lun**ghi**	lun**ghe**
stanco	stan**chi**	stan**che**
allergico	allergi**ci**	allergi**che**

piedi lun**ghi**   *big feet*
persone cie**che**   *blind people*
va**ghi** ricordi   *vague memories*
voci criti**che**   *critical voices*

> **!** **Note: Carico** has a hard sound in the masculine plural:
> treni cari**chi** di pendolari   *trains packed with commuters*

Adjectives with *qualcosa* and *niente*

Adjectives with **qualcosa** and **niente** are preceded by **di**. There is no agreement:

Ci hai preparato qualcosa **di** buono?   *Have you made something tasty for us?*
Non è niente **di** grave   *It's nothing serious*

The position of adjectives

Before or after?

As stated above, most adjectives are placed after the noun they
modify. But a number of very common adjectives can come
before their noun. These include **bello**, **brutto**, **buono**, **cattivo**,
piccolo, **grande**, **vecchio**, **nuovo**, **giovane**, and **povero**. The position
of these adjectives has an effect on the meaning: sometimes the
meaning changes completely, sometimes the difference is more
subtle. In general, when the adjective comes after the noun the
meaning is more concrete, and when it comes before it is more
abstract or figurative:

un appartamento piccolo   *a small flat*
un piccolo problema   *a small problem*

Sometimes an adjective placed after the noun can have the
function of identifying which person or object is being referred to,
whereas an adjective placed before is simply descriptive:

la strada vecchia per Pisa   *the old road to Pisa (i.e. not the new
one)*
quel vecchio armadio   *that old wardrobe*

These are the most important changes in meaning that you should
know about:

	meaning before the noun	*meaning after the noun*
buono	good	well-behaved, tasty
	buone idee *good ideas*	una bambina buona *a well-behaved girl*
caro	dear (person)	dear, expensive
	un caro amico *a dear friend*	prodotti cari *expensive products*
certo	certain, some	sure, definite
	certe scuole *some schools*	una risposta certa *a definite answer*
povero	poor (expressing sympathy)	poor (not rich)
	il povero Dino! *poor Dino!*	famiglie povere *poor families*
unico	only	unique, single
	l'unico problema *the only problem*	un'occasione unica *a unique occasion*
vero	real	true
	il suo vero nome *his real name*	una storia vera *a true story*

Changes to adjectives before nouns

When some adjectives come before the noun, they take slightly
different endings from normal adjectives. **Bello**, **buono**, **grande**,
and **santo** change their forms depending on which noun they
precede.

bello

● **bell'** before a singular noun (masculine or feminine) beginning
with a vowel:

un bell'appartamento   *a nice flat*
una bell'attrice   *a beautiful actress*

● **bello** before a masculine singular noun beginning with *z*, *ps*, *gn*,
or *s* + another consonant:

un bello scherzo   *a great joke*

● **bel** before a masculine singular noun beginning with any other
consonant:

un bel film   *a good film*

● **bella** before a feminine singular noun beginning with any
consonant:

una bella zona   *a nice area*

● **begli** before a masculine plural noun beginning with a vowel or
z, *ps*, *gn*, or *s* + another consonant:

begli occhi   *beautiful eyes*

● **bei** before a masculine plural noun beginning with any other
consonant:

bei ragazzi   *good-looking boys*

● **belle** before any feminine plural noun:

belle ragazze   *good-looking girls*

buono

● **buono** before a masculine singular noun beginning with *z*, *ps*, *gn*, or *s* + another consonant:

   un buono spazzolino   *a good toothbrush*

● **buon** before a masculine singular noun beginning with any other consonant or with a vowel:

   un buon prezzo   *a good price*
   un buon odore   *a nice smell*

● **buona** before a feminine singular noun:

   una buona occasione   *a good opportunity*

● **buoni** before a masculine plural noun:

   buoni risultati   *good results*

● **buone** before a feminine plural noun:

   buone maniere   *good manners*

grande

● **grand'** or **grande** before a singular noun (masculine or feminine) beginning with a vowel:

   un grande amico   *a great friend*
   un grand'uomo   *a great man*
   una grande azienda   *a big company*

● **grande** before a masculine singular noun beginning with *z*, *ps*, *gn*, or *s* + another consonant:

   un grande sbaglio   *a big mistake*

● **gran** or **grande** before a singular noun (masculine or feminine) beginning with any other consonant:

   un gran / grande nome   *a great name*
   una gran / grande paura   *a great fear*

● **grandi** before any plural noun (masculine or feminine):

   grandi ambizioni   *great ambitions*
   grandi cambiamenti   *big changes*

santo

● **santo** before a masculine name beginning with *s* + another consonant:

santo Stefano   St Stephen

● **san** before a masculine name beginning with any other consonant:

san Francesco   St Francis

● **sant'** before a name (masculine or feminine) beginning with a vowel:

sant'Antonio   St Anthony
sant'Anna   St Anne

● **Santa** before a feminine name beginning with a consonant:

santa Chiara   St Clare

| Adjectives used as nouns

As in English, adjectives can be used as nouns:
un (telefono) cellulare   a mobile (phone)

In Italian the adjective takes the number and gender of the noun that it replaces:
una (macchina) decappottabile   a convertible (car)

Adjectives can also be used to refer to people:
una bionda   a blonde
un tossicodipendente   a drug addict

Used in the masculine plural, an adjective can refer to a group of people in society:
i ciechi   the blind
i giovani   young people

> **!** Note: For information about nationality, *see p. 188.*

| Comparative and superlative

The comparative

The comparative, as its name indicates, is the form of the adjective which enables us to compare two or more people or things. In English this is usually done by putting **more** before the appropriate adjective. Some shorter English adjectives have a special comparative ending in *-er* (for example *bigger, smaller, happier*):

a **more interesting** programme
a **clearer** answer

The Italian equivalent of **more** is **più**, which is placed before the adjective:

Voglio un taglio **più corto**   I want a **shorter** haircut

Note that 'than' is expressed in Italian by **di**. This is used before nouns, pronouns, and adverbs:

Il nuovo appartamento è **più grande** di quello vecchio   *My new flat is **bigger** than the old one*
Sono più stanco **di** prima   *I'm more tired **than** before*

But before prepositions, or if the comparison is between two adjectives, two adverbs, or two verbs, **che** is used:

È più famosa oggi **che** negli anni sessanta   *She's more famous today **than** she was in the 60s*
È più largo **che** lungo   *It's wider **than** it is long*

To say that someone or something is **less** intelligent, tall, etc., **meno** is used instead of **più**:

È **meno** caldo oggi   *It's **not so** hot today*

The superlative

The superlative is the form of the adjective which is used to express the highest degree. In English the adjective is usually preceded by **most**. Some English adjectives have forms ending in -est (*slowest, biggest*):

  the **most intelligent** animal
  the **tallest** building

The Italian equivalent of **most** is **più**, which is placed before the adjective. The superlative is always used with the definite article **il** / **la**, etc.:

  il serpente **più pericoloso** del mondo   the **most dangerous** snake in the world

! **Note:** 'In' with superlatives is expressed in Italian by **di**.

To say that someone or something is the **least** intelligent, tall, etc., **meno** is used instead of **più**:

  la persona meno adatta   the least suitable person

Irregular comparatives and superlatives

In English a few adjectives have an irregular comparative and superlative form: **good** (comparative **better**, superlative **best**), **bad** (comparative **worse**, superlative **worst**). In Italian the adjectives which have irregular comparative and superlative forms are **buono** and **cattivo**:

	comparative		*superlative*	
	singular	*plural*	*singular*	*plural*
buono	migliore	migliori	il/la migliore	i/le migliori
cattivo	peggiore	peggiori	il/la peggiore	i/le peggiori

  Non poteva succedere in un momento **peggiore**   It couldn't have come at a **worse** time
  il **miglior** atleta del mondo   the **best** athlete in the world

Migliore and **peggiore** can come before or after the noun. When they come before they are often shortened to **miglior** and **peggior**:

  la peggior cuoca d'Italia   the worst cook in Italy

! **Note:** Più buono rather than **migliore** is used when talking about food:
  Gli spaghetti della mia mamma erano più buoni   My mother's spaghetti was better

(*tanto*) *quanto*

To say that two things are equally big, small, etc., Italian uses **tanto quanto**. **Tanto** is often omitted, especially when speaking:

Mio figlio è alto (**tanto**) **quanto** me   My son's **as** tall **as** me

È grande **quanto** una casa   It's **as** big **as** a house

An alternative is to use **come**:

È alto **come** me   He's **as** tall **as** me

Come is also used in many common similes:

nero **come** il carbone   **as** black **as** coal

liscio **come** la seta   **as** smooth **as** silk

| Making an adjective stronger or weaker

The absolute superlative

The absolute superlative is a form of the adjective which has no equivalent in English. It intensifies the meaning of an adjective. To form the absolute superlative, the final vowel of the adjective is replaced with the ending **-issimo** / **-issima** (**-issimi** / **-issime** in the plural):

stupid**issimo**   *really stupid*
fredd**issimo**   *freezing cold*

Buono and **cattivo** have the irregular absolute superlatives **ottimo** and **pessimo**, as well as the regular forms **buonissimo** and **cattivissimo**:

un **ottimo** albergo   *an **excellent** hotel*
condizioni **pessime**   ***terrible** conditions*

Other ways of making an adjective stronger or weaker

The absolute superlative is one way to make an adjective stronger, but there are also other ways. As in English, an adverb or a phrase can be used to strengthen or weaken the meaning of the adjective:

molto veloce   ***very** fast*
estremamente utile   ***extremely** useful*
proprio stanco   ***really** tired*
noioso **da morire**   ***deadly** boring*
poco simpatico   ***not very** friendly*
un po' tardi   ***a bit** late*
piuttosto vecchio   ***rather** old*

Certain idiomatic combinations also exist:

stanco morto   *dead tired*
ricco sfondato   *filthy rich*

Describing feelings

One way to describe how you feel in Italian is to use **essere** followed by an adjective:

Sono stanco   I'm tired

The reflexive verb **sentirsi** is also used:

Mi sento sollevato   I feel relieved

Some fixed expressions use **avere** followed by a noun:

aver fame	to be hungry
aver sete	to be thirsty
aver freddo	to be cold
aver caldo	to be hot, to be warm
aver sonno	to be sleepy
aver paura	to be scared

There is no agreement with these expressions:

Abbiamo freddo   We're cold

Non avevate paura dei ragni?   Weren't you scared of the spiders?

Aver freddo and **aver caldo** are only used when talking about people. When talking about the temperature of objects, use **essere**. Note that the adjective agrees with the subject:

La minestra è fredd**a**   The soup's cold

I termosifoni sono ancora cald**i**   The radiators are still warm

When talking about the temperature of the air, **fare** or **essere** can be used:

Fa caldo / È caldo oggi   It's hot today

Note these other common expressions with **avere**:

aver voglia di	to feel like
aver ragione	to be right
aver torto	to be wrong
aver fretta/furia	to be in a hurry

Vuoi aver sempre ragione!   You think you're always right!

Non ho voglia di andare a letto   I don't feel like going to bed

Pronouns

What is a pronoun?

A pronoun is a word that is used instead of a noun to avoid repeating it unnecessarily:

Tracey said **she** was tired
The keys weren't where I left **them**

Subject pronouns

The subject of a sentence is generally the noun or pronoun that causes the action of the verb:

The minister resigned
The volcano is going to erupt
He's converting the attic

In English all verbs must have an explicit subject. In Italian this is not necessary because the ending of the verb does a lot of the work of showing what the subject is: **I** or **we** (*first person*), **you** (*second person*), or somebody or something else (*third person*):

Studio italiano   I study Italian
Piangeva   **He/she** was crying

Of course it is also possible to identify or name the subject:

Federico piangeva   Federico was crying

The subject pronouns in Italian are used for emphasis or to underline a contrast.

These are the subject pronouns in Italian:

first person singular	io
second person singular	tu, lei
third person singular	lui/lei, egli/ella, esso/essa
first person plural	noi
second person plural	voi
third person plural	loro, essi/esse

All of these pronouns must be used with the appropriate form of the verb: first, second, or third person, singular or plural (see the chapter on verbs on *p. 56* for more information).

io, noi

Io corresponds to **I** in English, **noi** to English **we**:

   Io rimango a casa   *I'll stay at home*
   Noi vogliamo andare a sciare   *We want to go skiing*

but, as stated above, they are often omitted:

   Vengo volentieri   *I'd love to come*
   Siamo in ritardo   *We're late*

In addition, they should also be used when identifying yourself:

   Sono **io**   *It's* **me**
   Siamo **noi**   *It's* **us**
   'Chi vuole provare?' '**Io**!'   *'Who wants to try?' '*Me!'

tu, lei, voi

In English **you** is used to address everybody, whereas Italian has various forms.

The informal pronoun **tu** is used between friends and family members. It is always used to address children and animals, and young people generally address each other as **tu**:

Serena, **tu** parli inglese?   Do **you** speak English, Serena?

The usual form for addressing someone you do not know particularly well is **lei**, which must be followed by a verb in the *third* person singular:

Lei è il signor Carli?   Are **you** Mr Carli?

In formal correspondence, **lei** is often written with a capital letter.

> **Note:** Italians are careful about who they use **tu** and **lei** to. While Italians are not likely to be offended if you use an inappropriate pronoun, it is worth getting right. In general, if you are not sure which pronoun to use, it is better to err on the side of caution and use the more formal **lei**. If the person you are talking to feels that this is unnecessarily formal they will say **dammi del tu** or **diamoci del tu**, which means 'let's use the pronoun **tu** to each other'.

Voi is used as the plural of **lei** and **tu**, and is used when addressing two or more people:

Voi avete mangiato?   Have **you** had dinner?

The subject pronoun is frequently omitted:

Hai preso le chiavi? (informal)   Did you get the keys?
Ha dimenticato l'ombrello (formal)   You forgot your umbrella
Come state? (plural)   How are you all?

Loro may occasionally be encountered meaning 'you'. It is used when addressing more than one person as the plural of **lei**, and is followed by the third person plural form of the verb. It is extremely formal and in most circumstances is replaced by **voi**.

lui/lei, egli/ella, esso/essa

There are various ways of expressing the third person in Italian.
In most cases the pronoun is omitted:

Mi ha detto che si sentiva male   *He told me he didn't feel well*

In order to underline a contrast, Italian uses **lui** 'he' and **lei** 'she':

Lui vuole vivere in campagna ma **lei** non è d'accordo   *He
wants to live in the country but **she** doesn't agree*

The forms **egli** 'he' and **ella** 'she' also exist, but they are used in
the written language and hardly ever encountered in normal
conversation:

Egli indossava un cappotto lungo e nero   *He wore a long black
coat*

Esso and **essa** are used to refer to things (**esso** is masculine and
essa is feminine), but they are also restricted to the written
language. In speech there is no direct equivalent of 'it', and the
verb is almost always used on its own:

il computer e ciò che (**esso**) rappresenta per noi   *the computer
and what **it** represents for us*

Esso and **essa** can also be used to refer to people, but only in the
written language.

loro, essi/esse

Loro means 'they'. Again, it is normally omitted, and is used mainly for emphasis:

Loro non sanno chi siamo   **They** don't know who we are

Loro is only used for people, never for things. When referring to things, the subject is almost always omitted in speech:

Girano ad alta velocità   They turn at high speed

In more formal language **essi** (masculine) and **esse** (feminine) are used:

Esse girano ad alta velocità   **They** turn at high speed

They can also be used to refer to people in the written language.

stesso/stessa

Stesso/stessa (**stessi/stesse** in the plural) can be added to the subject pronouns for emphasis:

Tu stessa me l'hai detto   **You** told me **yourself**

Direct object pronouns

The direct object of a sentence is the word or group of words which is immediately affected by the action indicated by the verb:

The waiter brought **the bill**
Can you hear **me**?

These are the direct object pronouns in Italian:

first person singular	mi
second person singular	ti, la
third person singular	lo/la
first person plural	ci
second person plural	vi
third person plural	li/le

In Italian object pronouns come immediately before the verb, not after, as in English:

Mi criticano sempre   They always criticize **me**

Exceptions to this rule are when the pronoun is used together with an infinitive, an imperative, or a gerund (*see p. 51* for more information).

ti, la, vi

Ti, **la**, and **vi** can all mean 'you'. The differences between them are the same as the differences between **tu**, **lei**, and **voi**, which are explained in more detail on *p. 37*.

Ti and **la** are the object pronoun forms of the subject pronouns **tu** (informal) and **lei** (formal) respectively:

Ti ho sentito la prima volta   I heard **you** the first time
La conosco?   Do I know **you**?

Vi is the object pronoun form of the subject pronoun **voi**, and is used when addressing more than one person:

Vi aspetto qui   I'll wait for **you** here

lo/la, li/le

Lo, **la**, **li**, and **le** are used for things as well as people:

masculine singular	lo
feminine singular	la
masculine plural	li
feminine plural	le

Lo conosco da anni   I've known **him** for years
La vediamo tutti i giorni   We see **her** every day
Li aggiusto domani   I'll fix **them** tomorrow
Le cucino in acqua bollente   I cook **them** in boiling water

Lo and **la** are usually shortened to **l'** before forms of the verb **avere**:

L'ho comprato al mercato   I bought **it** at the market

! **Note:** When direct object pronouns are used with compound tenses, the past participle may change its form to agree with the gender and number of the pronoun. For more information see p. 94.

Indirect object pronouns

There may also be another object in the sentence: an *indirect* object. In general terms, the indirect object indicates the person or thing which 'benefits' from the action of the verb upon the direct object:

I gave **the tortoise** some lettuce

These are the indirect object pronouns in Italian:

first person singular	mi
second person singular	ti, le, gli
third person singular	gli/le
first person plural	ci
second person plural	vi
third person plural	loro, gli

In Italian indirect object pronouns come immediately before the verb, not after, as in English:

Mi ha dato un passaggio   He gave **me** a lift

Le spiego come funziona   I'll explain **to you** how it works

An exception to this is **loro**. **Loro** always follows the verb:

Offrì **loro** un caffè   He offered **them** a coffee

Deve dire **loro** la verità   You have to tell **them** the truth

Other exceptions to the rule are when the pronoun is used together with an infinitive, an imperative, or a gerund (*see p. 51* for more information).

ti, le, vi

Ti, **le**, and **vi** can all mean '(to) you'. The differences between them are the same as the differences between **tu**, **lei**, and **voi**, which are explained in more detail on *p. 37*.

Ti and **le** are the indirect object pronoun forms of the subject pronouns **tu** (informal) and **lei** (formal) respectively:

Ti ho portato dei fiori   I've brought **you** some flowers

Le darò la ricetta   I'll give **you** the recipe

Vi is the indirect object pronoun form of the subject pronoun **voi**, and is used when addressing more than one person:

Vi insegno il trucco   I'll teach **you** the trick

gli, le, loro

Gli means 'to him', **le** 'to her':

Gli ho dato un bacio   I gave **him** a kiss

Le ho spiegato la situazione   I explained the situation **to her**

Gli is also commonly used in place of **loro**, which is becoming rare as an indirect object pronoun in speech:

Gli hai detto che possono stare qui?   Did you tell **them** they can stay here?

In addition, **gli** is used in place of **le** in colloquial speech. This should be avoided in writing:

Gli ho detto di stare calma   I told her to stay calm

Strong pronouns

The strong pronouns are used after prepositions and in certain other situations. They have the following forms:

first person singular	me
second person singular	te, lei
third person singular	lui/lei, esso/essa
first person plural	noi
second person plural	voi
third person plural	loro, essi/esse

te, lei, voi

Te, **lei**, and **voi** can all mean 'you'. The differences between them are explained in more detail on *p. 37*.

Te and **lei** are the strong pronoun forms of the subject pronouns **tu** (informal) and **lei** (formal) respectively:

Posso venire con **te**? *Can I come with you?*

C'è una lettera per **lei** *There's a letter for you*

The strong pronoun form of the subject pronoun **voi** is also **voi**. It is used when addressing more than one person:

Ho comprato qualcosa per **voi** *I bought something for you*

lui/lei, esso/essa

Lui and **lei** are used for people only:

È per **lui** o per **lei**? *Is it for him or for her?*

To refer to things, **esso/essa** is used in the written language. There is no equivalent in the spoken language, and **ci** and **ne** are often used as the equivalent to preposition + **it** (*see p. 46* for more information about **ci** and **ne**):

Il gatto **ci** giocava *The cat was playing with it*

Ne sono stanco *I'm tired of it*

Other uses of the strong pronouns

The strong pronouns can also be used instead of the direct object pronouns for emphasis:

Non potresti portare anche **me**?   *Couldn't you take* ***me*** *too?*

Similarly, the indirect object pronoun can also be replaced by **a** + the strong pronoun:

A me non sembra tanto utile   *It doesn't seem very useful* ***to me***

And in the spoken language, the two can appear together:

A me non **mi** dice nulla   *It doesn't say anything* ***to me***

Other pronouns

ne

The basic meaning of the pronoun **ne** is 'of it' or 'of them'. It takes the place of a phrase beginning with **di**, and cannot be omitted, as the corresponding English expressions often are:

'Sei sicuro di questo fatto?' '**Ne** sono sicuro.'   'Are you sure of this fact?' 'I'm sure (**of it**).'

In this example, **ne** stands for **di questo fatto**.

Che **ne** pensi?   What do you think **of it**?

Ne parliamo domani   We'll speak **about it** tomorrow

If a verb takes the preposition **di** (for example **servirsi di...** 'to use'), **ne** is used to replace the phrase with **di**:

Me **ne** sono servito   I used **it**

It must be used when talking about numbers and quantities when the thing that is being counted or measured is not directly mentioned in the sentence:

Quanto **ne** hai?   How much (**of it**) have you got?

Ne abbiamo una ventina   We've got about twenty (**of them**)

Ce **ne** sono migliaia   There are thousands (**of them**)

It can mean 'some' or 'any':

'Avete dei biscotti?' 'Sì, **ne** abbiamo.'   'Have you got any biscuits?' 'Yes, we've got **some**.'

'Hai dell'acqua?' 'No, non **ne** ho.'   'Have you got any water?' 'No, I haven't got **any**.'

Ne can become **n'** before **è**, **era**, and **erano**:

Quanto ce **n'è**?   How much (**of it**) is there?

ne referring to people

Ne can also be used to mean 'of him' or 'of her':

Ti piace Marta? **Ne** parli sempre!   *Do you like Marta? You're always talking about her!*

ne as an adverb

Ne can be used as an adverb with verbs of motion to express the idea of 'from there':

È difficile uscir**ne**   *It's difficult to get out of there*

In particular, it is used in the verb **andarsene**, 'to go away'. This is the reflexive form of the verb **andare** combined with **ne**:

Me **ne** vado   *I'm leaving*

Se **n'**è andato subito   *He went away immediately*

> **!** **Note:** *See p. 103* for more information about reflexive verbs.

ci, vi

Ci and **vi** are the direct and indirect object forms of **noi** and **voi** respectively, as shown above.

Ci can also mean 'to it' or 'to them'. It takes the place of a phrase beginning with **a**:

'Hai pensato alle conseguenze?' '**Ci** ho pensato.' *'Have you thought about the consequences?' 'I've thought **about them**.'*

In this example, **ci** stands for **alle conseguenze**.

ci as an adverb

Ci can also be used as an adverb to mean 'here' or 'there':

Ci veniamo ogni anno *We come **here** every year*
Non **ci** sono mai stato *I've never been **there***

c'è

Ci is used with **essere** in the third person to mean 'there is', 'there are', etc. **C'è** means 'there is', **ci sono** means 'there are'. Before **è**, **era**, and **erano**, **ci** is shortened to **c'**:

C'è un problema *There's a problem*
Ci sono troppe macchine *There are too many cars*

Other tenses are also common:

Ci sarà molto da fare *There will be a lot to do*
Non **c'era** niente da mangiare *There was nothing to eat*

This structure can be used in the infinitive:

Ci deve essere una perdita *There must be a leak*

> **!** Note: Before **ne**, **ci** becomes **ce**:
> **Ce n'erano** troppe *There were too many (of them)*

Essere forms its compound tenses with the auxiliary **essere**, which means that the past participle must agree with the subject:

Ci sono state delle difficoltà *There have been difficulties*

ci with avere

Ci is frequently used with **avere** in the spoken language, especially before direct object pronouns and **ne**, when it becomes **ce**:

Non **ce** l'ho *I haven't got it*

> **!** Note: **Vi** is sometimes used as an alternative to **ci**. It is much less common, however, and is best avoided.

Reflexive pronouns

Reflexive pronouns are used when the subject and the object (direct or indirect) of a verb are the same. In English they are **myself, yourself**, etc.

I could have kicked **myself**!

Reflexive verbs are also used in Italian, but a reflexive verb in Italian may not necessarily be translated by a reflexive verb in English:

Non **ti** preoccupare!   Don't worry!

The reflexive pronouns in Italian are the same as the object pronouns for the first person (**mi** and **ci**) and the second person (**ti** and **vi**). These are both direct and indirect object forms:

Ci consideriamo i migliori   We consider **ourselves** the best

Mi faccio la stessa domanda   I ask **myself** the same question

The reflexive pronoun for the third person (and also for the **lei** form of the second person) is **si**. **Si** is used for both singular and plural:

Si è buttata nell'acqua   She threw **herself** into the water

Si esprimono bene   They express **themselves** well

Si è fatta male, signora?   Did you hurt **yourself**, madam?

Strong forms of the reflexive pronouns

The reflexive pronouns have strong forms which are used after prepositions and in certain other situations. The strong forms of the reflexive pronouns are the same as the strong pronouns described on *p. 44*, with the addition of **si**, whose strong form is **sé**.

L'ho portato con **me**   I brought it with **me**

È molto sicuro di **sé**   He's very sure of **himself**

The strong forms of the reflexive pronouns can be followed by **stesso/stessa** (**stessi/stesse** in the plural) for emphasis. When **sé** is followed by **stesso/stessa**, there is no acute accent:

L'ha fatto per **se stessa**   She did it for **herself**

! Note: For more information about reflexive verbs, *see p. 103.*

| Combinations of pronouns

When a direct object pronoun and an indirect object pronoun are used with a verb, the general rule is that the indirect object precedes the direct object. When **ne** is involved, **ne** comes second. The first pronoun changes its form slightly when followed by another:

mi + lo:	me lo	ti + lo:	te lo
mi + la:	me la	ti + la:	te la
mi + li:	me li	ti + li:	te li
mi + le:	me le	ti + le:	te le
mi + ne:	me ne	ti + ne:	te ne

gli + lo:	glielo	le + lo:	glielo	si + lo:	se lo
gli + la:	gliela	le + la:	gliela	si + la:	se la
gli + li:	glieli	le + li:	glieli	si + li:	se li
gli + le:	gliele	le + le:	gliele	si + le:	se le
gli + ne:	gliene	le + ne:	gliene	si + ne:	se ne

ci + lo:	ce lo	vi + lo:	ve lo
ci + la:	ce la	vi + la:	ve la
ci + li:	ce li	vi + li:	ve li
ci + le:	ce le	vi + le:	ve le
ci + ne:	ce ne	vi + ne:	ve ne

Te lo do domani   I'll give **it to you** tomorrow
Me ne dà un altro?   Can you give **me** another one (**of them**)?

! **Note:** Combinations with **gli** and **le** are written as one word:
Gliel'ho già chiesto   I've already asked **him for it**

Verb + pronoun combinations

Infinitive + pronoun

When a direct or indirect object pronoun (**mi**, **ti**, **lo**, **la**, **si**, **ci**, **vi**, **li**, **le**, **gli**, or **ne**) is used with an infinitive, the final **-e** of the infinitive is dropped and the pronoun is attached to the end of the infinitive. If the infinitive ends in **-rre**, the final **-re** is dropped. Here are some examples:

amare + lo: amarlo
vendere + la: venderla
finire + li: finirli
cercare + le: cercarle
produrre + ne: produrne

> Non ho potuto far**lo**   I wasn't able to do **it**
> Dovresti telefonar**gli**   You should phone **him**
> Smetti di interrompor**mi**!   Stop interrupting **me**!

The same rule applies to the adverbs **ci**, **vi**, and **ne**:
> Non ho voglia di andar**ci**   I don't feel like going **there**
> Era difficile uscir**ne**   It was difficult to get out **of it**

Infinitive + two pronouns

When two pronouns are used together, they are also added on to the end of the infinitive and the whole thing is written as one word. Usually a change must be made to the first pronoun, in accordance with the rules affecting pronouns described above.

dare + mi + ne: darmene
spiegare + ci + lo: spiegarcelo
togliere + gli + lo: toglierglielo

> Puoi dar**mene**?   Can you give **me some**?
> Vuoi spiegar**celo**?   Will you explain **it to us**?
> Dovresti toglier**glielo**   You should take **it from him**

Reflexive pronouns with the infinitive

The reflexive pronouns are also used with infinitives. The dictionary form of the infinitive of a reflexive verb always ends in **-arsi**, **-ersi**, etc. Note, however, that the actual form used in a sentence depends on the subject of the main verb:

prepararsi *to get ready*
Devo prepararmi *I have to get ready*
Devi prepararti *You have to get ready*
Deve prepararsi *He/she has to get ready*
Dobbiamo prepararci *We have to get ready*
Dovete prepararvi *You have to get ready*
Devono prepararsi *They have to get ready*

The reflexive pronoun can be combined with another pronoun:

Lui vuole tener**selo** *He wants to keep **it for himself***
Voglio disfar**mene** *I want to get rid of it*

Pronouns with *dovere*, *potere*, and *volere*

In spoken Italian it is also possible for the pronoun to come before the main verb instead of being attached to the infinitive. This is possible when the main verb is a form of **dovere**, **potere**, or **volere**. It is best to avoid this style in writing as it can be quite informal, and you may find it easier to use the combined forms mentioned above in all cases:

Non **l'**ho potuto fare *I wasn't able to do **it***
Gli dovresti telefonare *You should phone **him***
Mi devo preparare *I have to get ready*

Imperative + pronoun

Pronouns (and the adverbs **ci**, **vi**, and **ne**) are attached to the imperative form of the verb. This applies to the **tu** form, the **voi** form, and the **noi** form of the imperative:

Aiuta**mi**! *Help **me**!*
Andiamo**ci**! *Let's go **there**!*

It is not added to the **lei** form:

Mi dica tutto! *Tell **me** everything!*

Combinations of pronouns can be added:

Date**melo**! *Give **it to me**!*

When the imperative is a single syllable (**va'!**, **da'!**, **di'!**, **fa'!**, and **sta'!**), the first letter of the pronoun (or adverb) is doubled:

Di**mmi** tutto!   Tell **me** everything!

Fa**llo** subito!   Do **it** at once!

Va**cci** e sta**cci**!   Go **there** and stay **there**!

The same applies with combinations of pronouns:

Da**mmelo**!   Give **it to me**!

Reflexive pronouns with the imperative

Reflexive pronouns are attached to the end of imperatives of reflexive verbs in the same way as normal object pronouns are attached to normal verbs:

Alza**ti**!   Stand up!

Servite**vi**!   Help **yourselves**!

Spostiamo**ci**!   Let's move!

Two pronouns can be added, an indirect object and a direct object:

Tieni**telo**!   Keep **it for yourself**!

Pronouns are not added on to the end of the **lei** form of the imperative:

Si accomodi, prego!   Sit down, please!

> **!** **Note:** The **tu** imperative of **andarsene**, 'to go away':
> Vattene!   Get lost!

ecco + pronoun

Ecco means 'here!'. Pronouns can be added to **ecco** as if it were
an imperative:

Ecco**lo**!   Here it is!
Ecco**mi**!   Here I am!

Gerund + pronoun

When object pronouns (and the adverbs **ci**, **vi**, and **ne**) are used
with the gerund, they are added on to the end:

Conoscendo**lo**, non rinuncerà   Knowing **him**, he won't give up

However, when the gerund is used as part of the progressive
form, the pronoun is generally placed before **stare**:

Mi stavano seguendo   They were following **me**

See p. 67 for more information about the progressive form.

Reflexive pronouns with the gerund

When reflexive pronouns are used with the gerund, they are
added onto the end:

L'ho tagliato servendo**mi** di una lametta   I cut it using a razor
blade

However, when the gerund is used as part of the progressive
form, the pronoun is generally placed before **stare**:

Mi sto rendendo conto del suo valore   I'm becoming aware of its
value

I Impersonal pronouns

uno

Uno can be used as an indefinite pronoun corresponding to 'one' in English:

Uno può sempre sognare   *One can always dream*

si

Si can be used with a verb as a less formal alternative to the passive:

L'olio **si fa** con le olive   *Oil* **is made** *from olives*
Non si accettano carte di credito   *Credit cards* **are not accepted**

and to form impersonal constructions:

In campagna **si dorme** bene   **You sleep** *well in the country*
Si paga alla cassa   **You pay** *at the checkout*
Non si sa mai   *You never know*

It sometimes also replaces the first person plural ('we'):

Si prende un taxi?   **Shall we take** *a taxi?*

See p. 108 for more information about this use of **si**.

Verbs

What is a verb?

A verb is a word which indicates an action or a process:

The ladder **broke**

It can also tell us about a state of affairs:

The lift **is** out of order

The infinitive

The infinitive is the basic form of a verb, and has no indication of person or tense. In English it is often preceded by to: **to** talk, **to** live, **to** study. In Italian the infinitive ends in **-are**, **-ere**, **-ire**, or (less commonly) **-rre**. In dictionaries, verbs are listed under their infinitive form.

When an infinitive is immediately followed by another infinitive in Italian, very often the final **-e** of the first infinitive is dropped. This also happens in some fixed phrases and common expressions:

poter dormire   to be able to sleep
aver fame   to be hungry

The infinitive used to give instructions

The infinitive is often used in written Italian to give instructions, for example in recipes, signs, and instruction manuals:

Premere il pulsante   **Press** the button
Aggiungere due etti di zucchero   **Add** 200g of sugar

Constructions with the infinitive

The infinitive is used in a wide range of constructions. Verbs and adjectives in Italian can be followed by a range of different patterns, including the infinitive, the infinitive preceded by **a**, and the infinitive preceded by **di**. When you learn a new verb or adjective, you should also learn the particular construction that is used with it.

> **Note:** *See p. 134 and p. 144 for lists of the most important verb and adjective constructions.*

Verbs followed directly by an infinitive

A few verbs in Italian can be followed directly by an infinitive. These include **dovere**, **potere**, **preferire**, **sapere**, and **volere**:

Voglio partire presto   I *want* to leave early
Possiamo prendere un taxi   *We can* get a taxi
Ho dovuto dire di no   I *had* to say no

Verbs which require a preposition before the infinitive

With certain verbs, a preposition (usually **a** or **di**) must be inserted before the infinitive:

Comincia **a** piovere   It's starting **to** rain
Cerca **di** venire!   Try **to** come!

See p. 134 for a list of the most important verb constructions.

Adjectives followed by an infinitive

In impersonal constructions with **essere** + adjective, the infinitive follows on directly:

È facile sbagliare   It's easy to get it wrong
È inutile gridare   It's no use shouting
Era impossibile leggere i sottotitoli   It was impossible to read the subtitles

See p. 110 for information about impersonal verbs.

With some adjectives the infinitive is preceded by **a** or **di**:

Sei pronto **a** partire?   *Are you ready **to** go?*

È capace **di** farlo?   *Is she able **to** do it?*

See p. 144 for a list of the most important adjective constructions.

per + infinitive

When **per** is followed by an infinitive it means 'in order to':

Si è alzato in piedi **per** fare un discorso   *He stood up **to** make a speech*

Per is also used with **troppo** + adjective:

È troppo basso **per** arrivare all'interruttore   *He's **too** short **to** reach the switch*

da + infinitive

When **to do** means 'to be done', use **da**:

Ho un sacco di cose **da** fare   *I have loads of things **to** do*

The infinitive after verbs of perception

Italian uses the infinitive after verbs of perception like **vedere** and **sentire**:

Non ti ho sentito entrare   *I didn't hear you come in*

Abbiamo visto passare una macchina   *We saw a car go past*

If the action is more spread out in time, Italian tends to use the relative pronoun **che**:

Ho sentito i cani che abbaiavano   *I heard the dogs barking*

fare

Fare can be followed directly by an infinitive. The meaning can be of making somebody do something, or making something happen:

Mi **ha fatto** riempire un sacco di moduli   She **made** me fill in a whole load of forms

Mi **hai fatto** venire un colpo!   You gave me a shock!

or it can be of letting somebody do something, or letting something happen:

Fammi rispondere!   **Let me** answer!

Chi **ha fatto** uscire il gatto?   Who **let** the cat out?

If the infinitive has no direct object, the object of **fare** is a direct object:

Lo hanno fatto dormire   They let **him** sleep

If the infinitive has a direct object, the object of **fare** is an indirect object:

Gli hanno fatto guardare la tele   They let **him** watch TV

Note the word order when the object of **fare** is a noun rather than a pronoun:

Hanno fatto dormire **il bambino**   They let **the baby** sleep

Hanno fatto guardare la tele **a Matteo**   They let **Matteo** watch TV

Fare + infinitive can also have the meaning of 'having something done' or 'getting something done':

Ho fatto rilegare la mia tesi   I **had** my thesis **bound**

When the action is being carried out directly on the subject of the sentence, the reflexive form of **fare** is used:

Mi sono fatto tingere i capelli   I **had** my hair **coloured**

> **Note:** 'To have your hair cut' is simply **tagliarsi i capelli**, without **fare:**
> Mi sono tagliato i capelli   I had my hair cut

Farsi + infinitive can also express the idea of something happening whether you want it to or not:

Si è fatta mangiare da un coccodrillo   **She got eaten** by a crocodile

Tenses and conjugations

In order to talk about verbs in their different forms, it is necessary to divide them into groups which behave in similar ways. Verbs in Italian are classed as regular, in which case they follow one of three main patterns, or irregular, in which case some of their forms are not predictable.

The three main patterns of regular verbs are called *conjugations*, and can be recognized from their infinitive forms ending in **-are**, **-ere**, and **-ire** respectively:

first conjugation	*second conjugation*	*third conjugation*
parlare	vendere	finire

Within these groups there is a certain amount of variation due to Italian spelling rules, but it is a good idea to be familiar with all of the forms of these three conjugations: they are the models which allow you to form the vast majority of verbs.

Not all verbs ending in **-are**, **-ere**, or **-ire** fall into these three categories, however. Those which do not are *irregular verbs*. There are many of these, and it is a good idea to learn them gradually, starting with the most important ones. The list on *p. 233* gives the forms of all the irregular verbs which are commonly used in modern Italian.

Italian verbs have many different forms, far more than in English. This is because the ending of an Italian verb changes according to various factors, including the subject of the sentence and the tense of the verb.

Verbs in Italian are either first person, second person, or third person, and all can be singular or plural. The 'person' gives information about the subject of the verb. When giving the different forms of the verb for reference we give them in the form of a table consisting of six verb forms:

first person singular	(io) parl**o**	I speak
second person singular	(tu) parl**i**	you speak
third person singular	(lui/lei) parl**a**	he/she speaks
first person plural	(noi) parl**iamo**	we speak
second person plural	(voi) parl**ate**	you speak
third person plural	(loro) parl**ano**	they speak

Note that, whereas English always has an explicit subject (I, you, etc.), Italian can omit it. This is because the ending usually does the job of telling you what the subject is:

Parl**o** inglese   **I** speak English
Parl**ano** italiano   **They** speak Italian

The tense is the particular form of the verb that tells us approximately when the action of the verb takes place. Common tenses in Italian are the *present*, the *perfect*, the *future*, and the *imperfect*:

Sono bravo (present)   I'm good
Sono stato bravo (perfect)   I was good
Sarò bravo (future)   I'll be good
Ero bravo (imperfect)   I used to be good

To find the appropriate form of a verb, you should first try to find which verb to use as a model. If it is a regular verb (as the majority are) the model will be **parlare**, **vendere**, or **finire**. If it is an irregular verb it will be listed in the verb tables on *p. 233*.

The present tense

The present tense is the tense of a verb that refers to something that is happening now, or round about now:

I write, I am writing

How is the present tense formed?

To form the present tense, a set of endings is added to the verb. First of all the infinitive ending (-are, -ere, or -ire) is removed, then the present tense endings are added:

parlare	vendere	finire	sentire
parlo	vendo	finisco	sento
parli	vendi	finisci	senti
parla	vende	finisce	sente
parliamo	vendiamo	finiamo	sentiamo
parlate	vendete	finite	sentite
parlano	vendono	finiscono	sentono

Note that for verbs ending in **-ire** there are two possibilities. One group of verbs adds **-isc-** before the verb ending in the first, second, and third person singular, and in the third person plural. A smaller group of **-ire** verbs does not do this: they include **avvertire, bollire, cucire, divertire, dormire, fuggire, partire, seguire, sentire, servire, soffrire,** and **vestire.**

Spelling variations

For **-are** verbs, certain changes in spelling may be required in accordance with Italian spelling rules (*see p. 2* for more information about this). For verbs ending in **-care** or **-gare**, an *h* will need to be inserted to preserve the hard sound of the consonant in some forms of the verb:

giocare	*legare*
gioco	lego
giochi	leghi
gioca	lega
giochiamo	leghiamo
giocate	legate
giocano	legano

For verbs ending in **-ciare**, **-sciare**, or **-giare**, the *i* which is required to keep the consonant sound soft is dropped when the first letter of the ending is an *i*. Verbs ending in **-gliare** behave in a similar way:

cominciare	*lasciare*	*mangiare*	*sbadigliare*
comincio	lascio	mangio	sbadiglio
cominci	lasci	mangi	sbadigli
comincia	lascia	mangia	sbadiglia
cominciamo	lasciamo	mangiamo	sbadigliamo
cominciate	lasciate	mangiate	sbadigliate
cominciano	lasciano	mangiano	sbadigliano

For other verbs ending in **-iare** there are two options, depending on where the stress falls in the word. With **studiare**, the stress falls on the first syllable in the first and second person singular and in the third person singular and plural (**studio**, **studi**, etc.), and the *i* of the verb is dropped when the ending starts with an *i*. With **inviare** the stress is on the syllable preceding the ending in these forms (**invio**, **invii**, **invia**, **inviano**), and the *i* is retained in the second person singular:

studiare	*inviare*
studio	invio
studi	invii
studia	invia
studiamo	inviamo
studiate	inviate
studiano	inviano

How is the present tense used?

The basic use of the present tense is to talk about the present. This can include what is happening at this moment, or round about now:

I bambini **si divertono**   The children **are enjoying themselves**

Preparo un esame di chimica   **I'm studying for** a chemistry exam

It can also be used for actions which are habitual or occur with a stated frequency:

Mi alzo presto   **I get up** early

Ogni domenica **vado** a trovare i miei zii   **I go** to see my aunt and uncle every Sunday

The present tense in Italian can also be used to talk about plans and intentions for the near future:

Ci sposiamo il mese prossimo   **We're getting married** next month

Prendo la macedonia   **I'll have** fruit salad

The gerund

The gerund is the form of a verb that ends in **-ing**:
  rain**ing**

In Italian the gerund ends in **-ando** or **-endo**:
  nevic**ando**   *snowing*

Italian verbs ending in **-are** form the gerund with **-ando**. All other verbs form the gerund with **-endo**. The gerund is usually used in combination with another verb to show that the action happens at the same time as that verb:

  Torn**ando** a casa ho incontrato Sara   *Going home I met Sara*

The gerund is also used to give a reason for something:

  Ess**endo** più a nord, è molto più freddo   *Being further north, it's much colder*

or for expressing a way or method of doing something:

  Mi rilasso legg**endo**   *I relax by reading*
  Sbagli**ando** s'impara   *You learn by making mistakes*

The present progressive form

The present progressive is a form of the verb which is used to talk about what is happening at the moment of speaking:

What **are** you **thinking** about?

In Italian the present progressive is formed by combining the present tense of the verb **stare** with the gerund. The form of the gerund never changes, but the appropriate form of **stare** must be chosen:

parlare	*vendere*	*finire*
sto parlando	**sto** vendendo	**sto** finendo
stai parlando	**stai** vendendo	**stai** finendo
sta parlando	**sta** vendendo	**sta** finendo
stiamo parlando	**stiamo** vendendo	**stiamo** finendo
state parlando	**state** vendendo	**state** finendo
stanno parlando	**stanno** vendendo	**stanno** finendo

As in English, the present progressive is used to say what is happening at the moment of speaking:

Sta piovendo   It's raining

Che **stai facendo**?   What **are** you **doing**?

But this form is less common in Italian than in English, because it is perfectly normal to use the simple present tense to convey the same idea:

Piove   It's raining

Che fai?   What are you doing?

Unlike in English, the present progressive is never used to talk about future plans. Instead, use the simple present:

Quest'estate **vado** in Sardegna   **I'm going** to Sardinia this summer

The past participle

The past participle is a form of the verb which functions like an adjective. It conveys the idea that the action is completed. In English the past participle usually ends in **-ed** or **-en**:

a **broken** window

In Italian regular verbs form their past participles by removing the **-are**, **-ere**, or **-ire** ending and replacing it with **-ato**, **-uto**, or **–ito**:

parlare	parl**ato**
vendere	vend**uto**
finire	fin**ito**

Verbs which do not belong to these three groups form their past participles in irregular ways. See the verb tables on *p. 233* for more information.

Because the past participle is like an adjective, it agrees with the noun that it qualifies:

neve sciolt**a**   melted snow
sigarette acces**e**   lighted cigarettes

The perfect tense

What is the perfect tense?

The perfect tense is an Italian tense that refers to something that happened in the past. The perfect is generally used to talk about events in the fairly recent past, or that have had some kind of effect on the present. It looks similar to the English present perfect tense (I have written) because it is formed from an auxiliary and a past participle, but it is used much more widely:

Ha finito   He/she finished, he/she has finished

How is the perfect tense formed?

An *auxiliary verb* is a verb which is combined with another verb form to make a new tense, called a *compound tense*. In Italian auxiliary verbs are used along with the past participle to form the perfect tense. There are two auxiliary verbs in Italian, **avere** and **essere**, and each is used with a particular group of verbs. The majority of verbs form their perfect tense with **avere**. The form of the past participle does not usually change (*see p. 000* for an important exception), but the appropriate form of the present tense of **avere** must be used:

parlare	*vendere*	*finire*
ho parlato	**ho** venduto	**ho** finito
hai parlato	**hai** venduto	**hai** finito
ha parlato	**ha** venduto	**ha** finito
abbiamo parlato	**abbiamo** venduto	**abbiamo** finito
avete parlato	**avete** venduto	**avete** finito
hanno parlato	**hanno** venduto	**hanno** finito

Ho dormito bene   I slept well
Mi **hanno detto** la verità   They told me the truth

essere as an auxiliary

The auxiliary verb **essere** is less frequent, but must be used with certain verbs. It is used first of all to form the compound tenses of a group of verbs which are always intransitive (they never have a direct object), and are often verbs conveying movement or a change of state. Note that not all intransitive verbs take **essere** as their auxiliary. It is also used to form the compound tenses of all reflexive verbs (*see p. 116* for more information on reflexives).

Verbs which form their perfect tense with **essere** have an important peculiarity: the ending of the past participle changes to agree with the subject of the verb, masculine or feminine, singular or plural:

arrivare

sono arrivato/arrivata
sei arrivato/arrivata
è arrivato/arrivata
siamo arrivati/arrivate
siete arrivati/arrivate
sono arrivati/arrivate

These verbs of motion form their compound tenses with **essere**:

andare	to go
arrivare	to arrive
cadere/cascare	to fall
emigrare	to emigrate
entrare	to come in, to go in
fuggire	to flee
partire	to leave
salire	to go up, to come up
scappare	to run away
scivolare	to slip
scomparire	to disappear
sorgere	to rise
tornare	to return
uscire	to go out, to come out
venire	to come

Il pullman **è partito**   The bus has gone
La mamma **è uscita**   Mum's gone out

These verbs indicating a change of state form their compound tenses with **essere**:

ammattire	to go mad
apparire	to appear
arrossire	to go red
comparire	to appear
crescere	to grow
crollare	to collapse
dimagrire	to lose weight
diminuire	to go down
divenire/diventare	to become
esplodere	to explode
fallire	to fail
guarire	to get better
impazzire	to go mad
ingrassare	to get fat
invecchiare	to get old
morire	to die
nascere	to be born
scadere	to expire
scendere	to go down, to come down
scoppiare	to explode
sparire	to disappear
svenire	to faint

Quanto **sei cresciuta!**   You've grown so much!
Sono nato a Pavia   I was born in Pavia
È ingrassato molto   He's got really fat

These verbs indicating events form their compound tenses with
essere:

accadere	to happen
avvenire	to happen
capitare	to turn up, to happen
risultare	to result
riuscire	to succeed
succedere	to happen

È successo tante volte   It's happened so many times

These verbs indicating continuous states form their compound
tenses with **essere**:

bastare	to be enough
costare	to cost
dipendere	to depend
durare	to last
esistere	to exist
essere	to be
occorrere	to be necessary
parere	to seem
piacere	to please
restare	to stay
rimanere	to stay
sembrare	to seem
sopravvivere	to survive
valere	to be worth
volerci	to be necessary

C'è voluto un anno per finirlo   It took a year to finish it
Non **è valsa** la pena   It wasn't worth it

Verbs which take *avere* or *essere*

There is a group of verbs which can take either **essere** or **avere**. The verb **passare**, for example, uses **avere** when it has a direct object:

Abbiamo passato l'esame   **We *passed* the exam**

and **essere** when it has the idea of movement:

Siamo già **passati** di qua   **We've already *come* this way**

The following verbs use **avere** as an auxiliary when they have a direct object, and **essere** when they have no direct object:

affogare	to drown
affondare	to sink
annegare	to drown
aumentare	to increase
avanzare	to advance
calare	to lower, to fall
cambiare	to change
cessare	to cease
cominciare	to start
continuare	to continue
finire	to finish
importare	to import, to be important
iniziare	to start
mancare	to miss, to be missing
migliorare	to improve
montare	to assemble, to go up
passare	to pass
peggiorare	to worsen
risalire	to go back up
scattare	to click
seguire	to follow
servire	to serve, to be necessary
sfuggire	to escape
vivere	to experience, to live

Quanto **sei cambiata!**   How you've changed!
Abbiamo cambiato casa   We've moved house

> **!** Note: Mancare uses **avere** in the construction **mancare di**:
> **Ha mancato** di tatto   She was tactless

The following verbs use **avere** or **essere** as an auxiliary,
depending on the meaning:

correre   to run
gelare   to freeze
saltare   to jump
volare   to fly

Correre, **saltare**, and **volare** form their compound tenses with
essere when they have the meaning of 'going somewhere':
 Siamo corsi nel bosco   **We ran** into the woods
 È saltato dal letto   **He jumped** out of bed
 L'uccello **è volato** via   The bird **flew** away

Compare:
 Ho corso tutta la mattina   **I've been running about** all morning
 Ha saltato più in là dell'atleta australiano   **He jumped** further
   than the Australian athlete

Volare also uses **essere** when talking about time:
 Gli anni **sono volati**   The years **flew by**

Gelare uses **essere** when it means 'to freeze solid' and **avere** when
it refers to the the air temperature:
 L'acqua **è gelata** nel secchio   The water **froze** in the bucket
 Stanotte **ha gelato**   **There was a frost** last night

> **!** Note: The verbs **assomigliare** 'to resemble', **piovere** 'to rain', and **nevicare** 'to
> snow' can have either **avere** or **essere** as an auxiliary:
> **È piovuto/Ha piovuto** tutti i giorni   It rained every day

Agreement with the direct object

With the compound tenses where the verb is conjugated with
avere, it was stated above that the past participle does not usually
change its form:

Ho visto Angela   I *saw* Angela
Ho incontrato Renato e Andrea   I *met* Renato and Andrea
Ho perso le chiavi   I've *lost* the keys

However, when the object of the sentence is a third person
pronoun (**lo**, **la**, **li**, or **le**) placed before the verb, the ending of the
past participle changes according to the gender and number of the
object (for information about the endings of the past participle,
see p. 68):

Ho visto Angela   I saw Angela
becomes
  L'ho vista   I saw her

Ho incontrato Renato e Andrea   I met Renato and Andrea
becomes
  Li ho incontrati   I met them

Ho perso le chiavi   I've lost the keys
becomes
  Le ho perse   I've lost them

With the other direct object pronouns (**mi**, **ti**, **ci**, and **vi**),
agreement is optional:

La tigre **ci** ha sentiti/sentito   The tiger heard us

How is the perfect tense used?

The perfect is used to talk about events in the fairly recent past:

L'**ho ricevuto** ieri   I *received* it yesterday

Mi sono tuffato nell'acqua   I *dived* into the water

Ti sei divertita alla festa, Laura?   *Did you enjoy yourself* at the party, Laura?

It is also used to talk about events that have some connection with the present:

Ho trovato gli occhiali   I've *found* my glasses

Siamo arrivati   We've arrived

Ho già **visto** questo film   I've already *seen* this film

Compare the use of the past historic tense, which is described on p. 77.

The perfect of *dovere, potere,* and *volere*

When the verbs **dovere**, **potere**, and **volere** are used in the perfect tense, the auxiliary used may be **avere** or **essere**, depending on which auxiliary the verb which follows normally takes.

● When the verb which follows is normally conjugated with **avere**:

Non ho potuto dormire   I **wasn't able** to sleep

● When the verb which follows is normally conjugated with **essere**:

Non sono potuto uscire   I **wasn't able** to go out

● When no verb follows:

Non ho potuto   I wasn't able to

The past historic tense

What is the past historic tense?

The past historic is an Italian tense that refers to something that happened in the past. It is generally used to talk about events in the relatively distant past:

Pagò il conto e **se ne andò**   *He paid the bill and left*

How is the past historic tense formed?

The past historic tense in Italian is formed by adding a set of endings to the verb. Before adding the endings, the infinitive ending (**-are**, **-ere**, or **-ire**) is dropped. Here is the past historic of the three groups of regular verbs:

parlare	*vendere*	*finire*
parl**ai**	vend**ei** *or* vend**etti**	fin**ii**
parl**asti**	vend**esti**	fin**isti**
parl**ò**	vend**é** *or* vend**ette**	fin**ì**
parl**ammo**	vend**emmo**	fin**immo**
parl**aste**	vend**este**	fin**iste**
parl**arono**	vend**erono** *or* vend**ettero**	fin**irono**

For some **-ere** verbs there is a choice of endings for some forms. Both sets of endings are commonly used.

> ! **Note:** A large number of verbs form their past historic in irregular ways. For more information, see the verb tables on p. 233.

How is the past historic tense used?

The past historic is generally used for events which occurred in the relatively distant past. There is a considerable amount of variation in its use, however, across Italy. In the north of Italy it is rare in conversation, whereas in the centre and especially the south it is more common. As a general rule it should only be used for narrating events that took place more than a few days ago:

Poi ci **chiesero** di scendere dalla macchina   *Then they asked us to get out of the car*

The past historic is the tense used for narrating past events in fiction and other writing:

La città **fu fondata** nel 50 a.C.   *The city was founded in 50 BC*

The imperfect tense

What is the imperfect tense?

The imperfect is an Italian tense that refers to a continuous or habitual action in the past:

Fumavo   I was smoking, I used to smoke

How is the imperfect tense formed?

The imperfect tense in Italian is formed by adding a set of endings to the verb. Before adding the endings, the infinitive ending (**-are**, **-ere**, or **–ire**) is dropped. Here is the imperfect of the three groups of regular verbs:

parlare	*vendere*	*finire*
parl**avo**	vend**evo**	fin**ivo**
parl**avi**	vend**evi**	fin**ivi**
parl**ava**	vend**eva**	fin**iva**
parl**avamo**	vend**evamo**	fin**ivamo**
parl**avate**	vend**evate**	fin**ivate**
parl**avano**	vend**evano**	fin**ivano**

The following verbs do not follow this pattern, although the endings are exactly the same:

bere	bev**evo**, bev**evi**, bev**eva**, etc.
dire	dic**evo**, dic**evi**, dic**eva**, etc.
fare	fac**evo**, fac**evi**, fac**eva**, etc.
porre	pon**evo**, pon**evi**, pon**eva**, etc.
ridurre	riduc**evo**, riduc**evi**, riduc**eva**, etc.
trarre	tra**evo**, tra**evi**, tra**eva**, etc.

! **Note:** Verbs which are formed from the verbs above by adding or changing a prefix (e.g. **comporre**, **dedurre**, **contrarre**) form their imperfect tenses in the same way. See the verb tables on *p. 233* for more information.

The imperfect tense of **essere** is irregular:

ero
eri
era
eravamo
eravate
erano

How is the imperfect tense used?

The imperfect is used to say what was happening at a particular time in the past. It is often used for description:

Era alto, magro e brutto   *He was tall, thin, and ugly*
Il sole **splendeva**   *The sun was shining*

or to talk about an action which is interrupted:

Guardavo la televisione quando il telefono ha squillato   *I was watching TV when the phone rang*

The imperfect is also used to talk about past states or repeated events in the past:

A quell'epoca non **c'era** la televisione   *There was no TV in those days*
Andavo a scuola in bicicletta   *I used to go to school by bike*

The past progressive form

The past progressive is a form of the verb which is used to describe what was happening at a particular point in the past:

What **were** you **thinking** about when you said that?

In Italian the past progressive is formed by combining the imperfect tense of the verb **stare** with the gerund. The form of the gerund never changes, but the appropriate form of **stare** must be chosen:

parlare	*vendere*	*finire*
stavo parlando	**stavo** vendendo	**stavo** finendo
stavi parlando	**stavi** vendendo	**stavi** finendo
stava parlando	**stava** vendendo	**stava** finendo
stavamo parlando	**stavamo** vendendo	**stavamo** finendo
stavate parlando	**stavate** vendendo	**stavate** finendo
stavano parlando	**stavano** vendendo	**stavano** finendo

As in English, the past progressive is used to say what was happening at a particular point in the past:

Stava piovendo   It was raining
Che **stavi facendo**?   What were you doing?

But this form is less common in Italian than in English, because it is perfectly normal to use the imperfect tense to convey the same idea:

Pioveva   It was raining
Che **facevi**?   What were you doing?

The future tense

What is the future tense?

The basic function of the future tense is to talk about the future. In English the future tense can be recognized by the presence of **will** or **shall**:

There **will be** sunny spells and scattered showers

Note, however, that the use of the future in English and Italian do not always coincide. It is important to identify the function of what you want to say: are you making a prediction, talking about a plan, or making a promise? More information on uses and functions can be found on p. 190.

How is the future tense formed?

The future tense in Italian is formed by adding a set of endings to the infinitive of the verb. Before adding the endings, the final **-e** is dropped, and regular verbs ending in **-are** change the *a* to an *e*. Here is the future tense of the three groups of regular verbs:

parlare	*vendere*	*finire*
parler**ò**	vender**ò**	finir**ò**
parler**ai**	vender**ai**	finir**ai**
parler**à**	vender**à**	finir**à**
parler**emo**	vender**emo**	finir**emo**
parler**ete**	vender**ete**	finir**ete**
parler**anno**	vender**anno**	finir**anno**

The following verbs do not follow this pattern, although the endings are exactly the same:

andare	andrò, andrai, andrà, etc.
avere	avrò, avrai, avrà, etc.
bere	berrò, berrai, berrà, etc.
cadere	cadrò, cadrai, cadrà, etc.
dovere	dovrò, dovrai, dovrà, etc.
essere	sarò, sarai, sarà, etc.
parere	parrà, parranno
potere	potrò, potrai, potrà, etc.
rimanere	rimarrò, rimarrai, rimarrà, etc.
sapere	saprò, saprai, saprà, etc.
sedere	siederò, siederai, siederà, etc.
tenere	terrò, terrai, terrà, etc.
valere	varrò, varrai, varrà, etc.
vedere	vedrò, vedrai, vedrà, etc.
venire	verrò, verrai, verrà, etc.
vivere	vivrò, vivrai, vivrà, etc.
volere	vorrò, vorrai, vorrà, etc.

! **Note:** Verbs which are formed from the verbs above by adding prefixes (e.g. **contenere**, **prevalere**, **sopravvivere**) form their futures in the same way. See the verb tables on *p. 233* for more information.

Note that certain changes in spelling may be required in accordance with Italian spelling rules (*see p. 2* for more information):

giocare	giocherò, giocherai, giocherà, etc.
legare	legherò, legherai, legherà, etc.
cominciare	comincerò, comincerai, comincerà, etc.
mangiare	mangerò, mangerai, mangerà, etc.

Talking about the future

Although the future tense is commonly used in Italian, it is not actually the most common way of talking about future actions. To say what you plan to do or intend to do, the present tense is more normal:

Domani **vado** in città   **I'm going** into town tomorrow
Cosa **fai** giovedì?   What **are you doing** on Thursday?

But if more organization is involved, the future may be used:

Visiteremo Venezia, Verona e Vicenza   **We shall be visiting** Venice, Verona, and Vicenza

The present tense is also used to announce a decision:

Prendo la bistecca   **I'll have** the steak

But if the decision is rather vague or the action is still a long way off, the future may be used:

Ci **andremo** un altro giorno   **We'll go** another day
Ci **sposeremo** in chiesa   **We'll be getting married** in church

The future is used for promises:

Farò del mio meglio   **I'll do** my best
Prometto che lo **farò**   I promise **I'll do** it

and when making predictions about the future:

Arriveranno fra poco   **They'll be here** soon
Credo che **sarà** difficile   I think **it'll be** difficult
Pioverà?   Is it going to rain?

! **Note:** For other ways of talking about the future, *see p. 176.*
For the use of **se, quando**, etc. when referring to the future, *see p. 210.* **Will** and **shall** are also used in English to make requests, offers, and invitations. *See p. 178 and 190 for more information.*

The future perfect tense

What is the future perfect tense?

The future perfect tense is used to say what will have happened by a certain time in the future. In English it can be recognized by the presence of **will have** or **shall have**:

By this time next year I'll **have made** enough money to retire

How is the future perfect tense formed?

The future perfect is a compound tense formed with the future tense of **avere** (or **essere** if the verb forms its compound tenses with **essere**), followed by the past participle. If the verb uses **essere** as an auxiliary, the past participle agrees with the subject.

! **Note:** For information about which auxiliary to choose, **avere** or **essere**, *see p. 69.*

parlare	*vendere*	*finire*	*arrivare*
avrò parlato	**avrò** venduto	**avrò** finito	**sarò** arrivato/arrivata
avrai parlato	**avrai** venduto	**avrai** finito	**sarai** arrivato/arrivata
avrà parlato	**avrà** venduto	**avrà** finito	**sarà** arrivato/arrivata
avremo parlato	**avremo** venduto	**avremo** finito	**saremo** arrivati/arrivate
avrete parlato	**avrete** venduto	**avrete** finito	**sarete** arrivati/arrivate
avranno parlato	**avranno** venduto	**avranno** finito	**saranno** arrivati/arrivate

How is the future perfect tense used?

The future perfect is used, as in English, to talk about what will have happened:

Avremo già **finito** di mangiare quando voi arriverete   We'll already **have finished** eating by the time you get here

It is also used to look back on the past from a point in the future, usually with **quando, (non) appena**, etc. Note that English does not use a future perfect to translate it in this case:

Quando **avremo finito**, spegneremo le luci   When **we've finished** we'll put out the lights

Ti chiamerò non appena **sarò arrivato**   I'll call you as soon as I get there

The pluperfect tense

What is the pluperfect tense?

The pluperfect tense is used to talk about events that happened before the event that is the main focus of attention:

We **had spoken** about it many times before we decided to buy it

How is the pluperfect tense formed?

The pluperfect is a compound tense formed with the past tense of **avere** (or **essere** if the verb forms its compound tenses with **essere**), followed by the past participle. If the verb uses **essere** as an auxiliary, the past participle agrees with the subject.

> **!** **Note:** For information about which auxiliary to choose, **avere** or **essere**, *see p. 69.*

parlare	*vendere*	*finire*	*arrivare*
avevo parlato	**avevo** venduto	**avevo** finito	**ero** arrivato/arrivata
avevi parlato	**avevi** venduto	**avevi** finito	**eri** arrivato/arrivata
aveva parlato	**aveva** venduto	**aveva** finito	**era** arrivato/arrivata
avevamo parlato	**avevamo** venduto	**avevamo** finito	**eravamo** arrivati/arrivate
avevate parlato	**avevate** venduto	**avevate** finito	**eravate** arrivati/arrivate
avevano parlato	**avevano** venduto	**avevano** finito	**erano** arrivati/arrivate

How is the pluperfect tense used?

When the main focus of events is in the past (for example when telling a story set last year), it is sometimes necessary to make reference to events that took place before the main time focus. The pluperfect tense is used for this purpose in Italian:

Li **avevo conosciuti** l'estate prima   I **had met** them the summer before

Ci **eravamo** già **conosciuti**   We **had** already **met**

The subjunctive

What is the subjunctive?

The subjunctive is a special form of the verb that expresses doubt, unlikelihood, or desire. The subjunctive is not very common in modern English, and often forms with **let**, **should**, etc. do the same job:

Let there **be** light!

It's rare that this **should happen**

In Italian the subjunctive is very common, and is obligatory in certain circumstances. English often uses an infinitive instead:

Voglio che tu **venga**   I want you to come

There are four tenses of the subjunctive: present, past, perfect, and pluperfect.

The present subjunctive

The present subjunctive of regular verbs in Italian is formed by changing the endings of the present tense.

Here is the present subjunctive of the main groups of regular verbs:

parlare	*vendere*	*finire*	*sentire*
parl**i**	vend**a**	finisc**a**	sent**a**
parl**i**	vend**a**	finisc**a**	sent**a**
parl**i**	vend**a**	finisc**a**	sent**a**
parl**iamo**	vend**iamo**	fin**iamo**	sent**iamo**
parl**iate**	vend**iate**	fin**iate**	sent**iate**
parl**ino**	vend**ano**	finisc**ano**	sent**ano**

As in the present indicative, there are two possibilities for verbs ending in **-ire**. One group of verbs adds **-isc-** before the verb ending in the first, second, and third person singular, and in the third person plural. A smaller group of **-ire** verbs does not do this (*see p. 62* for more information).

For **-are** verbs, certain changes in spelling may be required in accordance with Italian spelling rules (*see p. 2*). For verbs ending in **-care** or **-gare**, an *h* will need to be inserted to preserve the hard sound of the consonant in all forms of the verb:

giocare	*legare*
gio**chi**	le**ghi**
gio**chi**	le**ghi**
gio**chi**	le**ghi**
gio**chi**amo	le**ghi**amo
gio**chi**ate	le**ghi**ate
gio**chi**no	le**ghi**no

For verbs ending in **-ciare**, **-sciare**, or **-giare**, the *i* which is required to keep the consonant sound soft is dropped, leaving only the *i* of the ending. Verbs ending in **-gliare** behave in a similar way:

cominciare	*lasciare*	*mangiare*	*sbadigliare*
cominc**i**	lasc**i**	mang**i**	sbadigl**i**
cominc**i**	lasc**i**	mang**i**	sbadigl**i**
cominc**i**	lasc**i**	mang**i**	sbadigl**i**
cominc**i**amo	lasc**i**amo	mang**i**amo	sbadigl**i**amo
cominc**i**ate	lasc**i**ate	mang**i**ate	sbadigl**i**ate
cominc**ino**	lasc**ino**	mang**ino**	sbadigl**ino**

For other verbs ending in **-iare** there are two options, depending on where the stress falls in the word. With **studiare**, the stress falls on the first syllable in the first and second person singular and in the third person singular and plural (**studi**, **studino**, etc.), and the *i* of the verb is dropped when the ending starts with an *i*. With **inviare** the stress is on the syllable preceding the ending in these forms (**invii**, **inviino**), and the *i* is retained in the first, second, and third person singular and in the third person plural:

studiare	*inviare*
studi	invii
studi	invii
studi	invii
studiamo	inviamo
studiate	inviate
studino	inviino

The past subjunctive

The past subjunctive of regular verbs in Italian is formed by removing the **-are**, **-ere**, or **-ire** endings of the infinitives and adding a set of endings. Here is the past subjunctive of the three groups of regular verbs:

parlare	*vendere*	*finire*
parl**assi**	vend**essi**	fin**issi**
parl**assi**	vend**essi**	fin**issi**
parl**asse**	vend**esse**	fin**isse**
parl**assimo**	vend**essimo**	fin**issimo**
parl**aste**	vend**este**	fin**iste**
parl**assero**	vend**essero**	fin**issero**

The perfect subjunctive

The perfect subjunctive is a compound tense formed with the present subjunctive of **avere** (or **essere** if the verb forms its compound tenses with **essere**), followed by the past participle. If the verb uses **essere** as an auxiliary, the past participle agrees with the subject.

! **Note:** For information about which auxiliary to choose, **avere** or **essere**, *see p. 69.*

parlare	*vendere*	*finire*	*arrivare*
abbia parlato	**abbia** venduto	**abbia** finito	**sia** arrivato/arrivata
abbia parlato	**abbia** venduto	**abbia** finito	**sia** arrivato/arrivata
abbia parlato	**abbia** venduto	**abbia** finito	**sia** arrivato/arrivata
abbiamo parlato	**abbiamo** venduto	**abbiamo** finito	**siamo** arrivati/arrivate
abbiate parlato	**abbiate** venduto	**abbiate** finito	**siate** arrivati/arrivate
abbiano parlato	**abbiano** venduto	**abbiano** finito	**siano** arrivati/arrivate

The pluperfect subjunctive

The pluperfect subjunctive is a compound tense formed with the
past subjunctive of **avere** (or **essere** if the verb forms its
compound tenses with **essere**), followed by the past participle. If
the verb uses **essere** as an auxiliary, the past participle agrees
with the subject.

> **!** **Note:** For information about which auxiliary to choose, **avere** or **essere**, *see* *p. 69.*

parlare	*vendere*	*finire*	*arrivare*
avessi parlato	**avessi** venduto	**avessi** finito	**fossi** arrivato/arrivata
avessi parlato	**avessi** venduto	**avessi** finito	**fossi** arrivato/arrivata
avesse parlato	**avesse** venduto	**avesse** finito	**fosse** arrivato/arrivata
avessimo parlato	**avessimo** venduto	**avessimo** finito	**fossimo** arrivati/arrivate
aveste parlato	**aveste** venduto	**aveste** finito	**foste** arrivati/arrivate
avessero parlato	**avessero** venduto	**avessero** finito	**fossero** arrivati/arrivate

How is the subjunctive used?

The subjunctive is commonly used to show that what is being said is not a concrete fact, for example after verbs of ordering, requiring, persuasion, and necessity. It contrasts with the *indicative*, the normal form of the verb, which always implies a greater degree of certainty. Normally there is not a free choice about which form to choose (although Italians often disregard the rules in speech and use the indicative in certain cases where the subjunctive would normally be preferred).

When the subjunctive is used after **che** or another conjunction, the tense chosen depends on the main verb in the sentence. When the main verb is in the present or future, the present or perfect subjunctive is used. When the main verb is in a past tense (for example the imperfect), the past or pluperfect subjunctive is used:

Voglio che tu mi **aiuti**   I want you to help me
Volevo che mi **aiutassi**   I wanted you to help me

● The subjunctive is used after expressions of emotion:

Sono contento che **abbiate vinto**   I'm pleased that **you won**
Mi dispiace che **sia andata** così   I'm sorry that **it happened** this way
Sono felice che Elisa **sia venuta**   I'm pleased Elisa**'s come**
Ero felice che Elisa **fosse venuta**   I was pleased Elisa **had come**

> **Note:** The indicative is often used in colloquial speech. This should be avoided in writing:
> Sono contento che **vieni** a trovarmi   I'm pleased **you're coming** to see me
> Mi dispiace che **non l'ho visto**   I'm sorry I **didn't see it**

● The subjunctive is used after expressions of hope, desire, permission, or prevention:

Vuole che **faccia** tutto io   He wants me to do everything
Preferisco che tu ci **sia**   I'd prefer you to be there
Spero che questo problema **si risolva**   I hope this problem **is solved**
Mi auguro che **vada** tutto bene   I hope it all **goes** well
Il tubo fa sì che l'aria **entri**   The pipe allows the air in
La crema impedisce che la pelle **si disidrati**   The cream prevents the skin from drying out

Other structures are possible with some of these verbs:

Spero **di rivederti** presto   I hope **to see you again** soon

Mia moglie non mi permette **di fumare** in casa   My wife won't let me **smoke** in the house

Qualcosa mi impedisce **di parlare**   Something prevents me **from talking**

● The subjunctive is used after verbs and expressions indicating doubt or unconfirmed belief:

Credo che tu **abbia** ragione   I think you**'re** right

Mi sembrava che **fosse** solo una fase   I thought **it was** just a phase

Si aspettavano che **vincessimo** noi   They expected us to win

Dubito che **sia** facile   I doubt if **it'll be** easy

Mi ha chiesto se **sapessi** nuotare   He asked me if I **could** swim

Mi domando che cosa mi **voglia** dire   I wonder what he **wants** to tell me

> **!** Note: Other structures are possible with some of these verbs: Non credo che
> **verrà**   I don't think **he'll come**
> Credo **di aver** ragione   I think I'm right
> Mi ha chiesto se **sapevo** nuotare   He asked me if I **could** swim

● The subjunctive is used after impersonal verbs:

È importante che **non dimentichiate**   It's important that you **don't forget**

Era strano che non **avesse chiamato**   It was strange that he **hadn't called**

È inutile che **pianga**   It's no use your crying

È impossibile che **sia scappata**   It's impossible that she's escaped

Bisogna che tu **legga** tutto   It's necessary for you to read it all

Basta che **ci sia** l'ascensore...   As long as **there's** a lift...

Sembra che **ci sia stato** un errore   It seems **there's been** a mistake

See p. 110 for information about impersonal verbs.

> **!** Note: The indicative is also common after **basta che**:
> Basta che mi **avvisate** prima...   As long as you **let** me **know** beforehand...

● The subjunctive is used after certain conjunctions (*see p. 201* for more information):

Continuiamo domani, **a meno che tu non sia** occupato Let's carry on tomorrow, **unless you're** busy

Andiamo a casa **prima che si faccia** buio Let's go home **before it gets** dark

It is used after the indefinite expressions **chiunque**, **qualunque**, **qualsiasi**, and **qualunque/qualsiasi cosa**:

chiunque **chieda**... whoever **asks**...

qualunque lingua **parlino**... whatever language **they speak**...

qualunque/qualsiasi cosa **succeda**... whatever **happens**...

● It is used with comparatives and superlatives. **Non** is sometimes added to the verb, but this has no effect on the meaning, despite its appearance. The forms without **non** are more common in spoken Italian:

Era più interessante di quanto (non) **mi aspettassi** It was more interesting than I **thought**

Era l'emozione più forte che io (non) **avessi** mai **provato** It was the strongest emotion I'd ever **felt**

The conditional

What is the conditional?

The basic function of the conditional is to talk about a hypothetical action. In English the conditional can be recognized by the presence of **would** or **should** (often shortened to **'d**):

  I'd try

How is the conditional formed?

The conditional in Italian is formed by adding a set of endings to the infinitive of the verb. Before adding the endings, the final **-e** is dropped and regular verbs ending in **-are** change the *a* to an *e*. Here is the conditional of the three groups of regular verbs:

parlare	*vendere*	*finire*
parler**ei**	vender**ei**	finir**ei**
parler**esti**	vender**esti**	finir**esti**
parler**ebbe**	vender**ebbe**	finir**ebbe**
parler**emmo**	vender**emmo**	finir**emmo**
parler**este**	vender**este**	finir**este**
parler**ebbero**	vender**ebbero**	finir**ebbero**

The following verbs do not follow this pattern, although the endings are exactly the same:

andare	andr**ei**, andr**esti**, andr**ebbe**, etc.
avere	avr**ei**, avr**esti**, avr**ebbe**, etc.
bere	berr**ei**, berr**esti**, berr**ebbe**, etc.
cadere	cadr**ei**, cadr**esti**, cadr**ebbe**, etc.
dovere	dovr**ei**, dovr**esti**, dovr**ebbe**, etc.
essere	sar**ei**, sar**esti**, sar**ebbe**, etc.
parere	parr**ebbe**, parr**ebbero**
potere	potr**ei**, potr**esti**, potr**ebbe**, etc.
rimanere	rimarr**ei**, rimarr**esti**, rimarr**ebbe**, etc.
sapere	sapr**ei**, sapr**esti**, sapr**ebbe**, etc.
sedere	sieder**ei**, sieder**esti**, sieder**ebbe**, etc.
tenere	terr**ei**, terr**esti**, terr**ebbe**, etc.
valere	varr**ei**, varr**esti**, varr**ebbe**, etc.
vedere	vedr**ei**, vedr**esti**, vedr**ebbe**, etc.
venire	verr**ei**, verr**esti**, verr**ebbe**, etc.
vivere	vivr**ei**, vivr**esti**, vivr**ebbe**, etc.
volere	vorr**ei**, vorr**esti**, vorr**ebbe**, etc.

Verbs which are formed from the verbs above by adding prefixes (e.g. **contenere**, **prevalere**, **sopravvivere**) form their conditionals in the same way. See the verb tables on *p. 233* for more information.

Note that certain changes in spelling may be required in accordance with Italian spelling rules (*see p. 2*):

giocare	giocher**ei**, giocher**esti**, giocher**ebbe**, etc.
legare	legher**ei**, legher**esti**, legher**ebbe**, etc.
cominciare	comincer**ei**, comincer**esti**, comincer**ebbe**, etc.
mangiare	manger**ei**, manger**esti**, manger**ebbe**, etc.

The conditional used to express politeness

The conditional is often used instead of the present because it gives a more polite, less aggressive impression. In particular, the conditional of **volere** and **potere** are used to make polite requests:

Vorrei un gelato alla fragola   **I'd like** a strawberry ice cream

Vorremmo noleggiare una barca   **We'd like** to hire a boat

Potrei fare una proposta?   **Could I** make a suggestion?

Potrebbe ripetere?   **Could you** repeat, please?

The imperfect can produce a similar effect:

Volevo farle qualche domanda   **I'd like** to ask you a few questions

The conditional can also be used to tone down the force of a statement:

Io **sarei** contro questa proposta   **I'm** against this proposal

The conditional for advice

The conditional of the verb **dovere** has a special use. It is used to talk about what should be done, and to give advice:

Dovrei andare a letto presto   **I should** go to bed early

Dovresti stare zitto   **You ought** to be quiet

Non dovrebbe far male   **It shouldn't** hurt

! Note: *See p. 210* for the use of the conditional in conditional sentences.

The past conditional

What is the past conditional?

The past conditional is used to say what would have happened under certain conditions:

I **would have done** the same thing

How is the past conditional formed?

The past conditional is a compound tense formed with the conditional of **avere** (or **essere** if the verb forms its compound tenses with **essere**), followed by the past participle. If the verb uses **essere** as an auxiliary, the past participle agrees with the subject:

parlare	*vendere*	*finire*	*arrivare*
avrei parlato	**avrei** venduto	**avrei** finito	**sarei** arrivato/arrivata
avresti parlato	**avresti** venduto	**avresti** finito	**saresti** arrivato/arrivata
avrebbe parlato	**avrebbe** venduto	**avrebbe** finito	**sarebbe** arrivato/arrivata
avremmo parlato	**avremmo** venduto	**avremmo** finito	**saremmo** arrivati/arrivate
avreste parlato	**avreste** venduto	**avreste** finito	**sareste** arrivati/arrivate
avrebbero parlato	**avrebbero** venduto	**avrebbero** finito	**sarebbero** arrivati/arrivate

! **Note:** *See p. 210* for the use of the past conditional in conditional sentences.

| Negatives

non

English uses **not** to form negative statements. Italian uses **non**:

Non sono stanco   I'm **not** tired

> **!** **Note:** Note that English often uses the auxiliary **do** as well as **not** (*don't*, *doesn't*, *didn't*) to form negative statements. Italian has no equivalent for this, always adding **non** to the verb:
> **Non** mi ricordo   I *don't* remember

When the sentence contains an auxiliary, **non** is placed before it:

Non ho sentito il telefono   I did**n't** hear the phone
Non saranno puniti   They will **not** be punished

Double negatives

In English double negatives are usually considered ungrammatical:

I did**n't** tell **nobody**

but in Italian double negatives are an essential feature of the grammar.

Note these common double negative expressions:

non... mai	never
non... nessun/nessuna	no
non... nessuno	no one
non... alcun/alcuna	no
non... niente, non... nulla	nothing
non... più	no longer

Non dire **niente**!   Don't say **anything**!
Non parlare con **nessuno**!   Don't speak to **anybody**!
Non sei **più** un bambino   You're **not** a baby **any more**
Non piange **mai**   She **never** cries

When **nessuno** means 'no one' it never changes in form. **Nessun/nessuna**, meaning 'no', is used before a singular noun, and its endings change according to the gender and first letter of the noun. The endings are the same as those for **un/una** (*see p. 19*):

Non c'è **nessun** problema   There's **no** problem

When the negative word comes first in the sentence, **non** is omitted:

Nessuno verrà   *No **one** will come*
Nulla può succedere   ***Nothing** can happen*

but it is more common to express the same thing by placing the negative word at the end and using **non** at the beginning:

Non verrà **nessuno**   *No **one** will come*
Non può succedere **nulla**   ***Nothing** can happen*

Negative words can also be combined in the same sentence:

Luca **non** aiuta **mai nessuno**   *Luca **never** helps **anyone***
In questa città **non** succede **mai niente**   ***Nothing ever** happens in this town*

Non... mica   (or **mica** on its own at the beginning of the sentence) is also common in spoken Italian. It has a more emphatic meaning than the simple negative:

Non è **mica** brutto   *He's **not** bad-looking, actually*
Non è **mica** un gruppo di cinquanta persone!   *It's **not** a group of fifty people, you know!*
Mica si può vivere così!   *You **can't** live like that!*

I Questions

English uses **do** to form questions and other constructions; Italian has no equivalent for this. Usually the form of a question is the same as a statement, and the only clue to the fact that it is a question is a rise in pitch in speech or the presence of a question mark in writing:

Ci vieni spesso?   *Do you come here often?*

Negative questions are also possible:

Non ti piace?   *Don't you like it?*

For more information on question words like **who...?**, **what...?**, etc., *see p. 116.*

I The imperative

What is the imperative?

The imperative is the form of the verb that expresses a command:
  Go away!

There is also a form of the imperative which is used to influence the behaviour of the group you are part of. In English this is shown by using **let's** before the verb:
  Let's *go home!*

How is the imperative formed?

Italian has two forms of the imperative, depending on whether the informal **tu** form or the more formal **lei** form is being used. There is also a **voi** form of the imperative, used when speaking to more than one person:
  Stai zitto!   *Be quiet!* (informal)
  Venga!   *Come in!* (formal)
  State zitti!   *Be quiet!* (speaking to more than one person)

The **tu** form of the imperative is the same as the **tu** form of the present tense, except for the imperative of verbs ending in **-are**, where the **-i** changes to an **-a**:
  Vendi la macchina!   *Sell your car!*
  Compra una moto!   *Buy a motorbike!*

The **voi** form of the imperative is the same as the **voi** form of the present tense:
  Andate a casa!   *Go home!*

The **lei** form of the imperative is the same as the present subjunctive of the third person singular. In general the **lei** imperative of **-are** verbs ends in **-i** and that of **-ere** verbs ends in **-a**:
  Si accomodi!   *Sit down!*
  Faccia come se fosse a casa sua!   *Make yourself at home!*

! **Note:** There are many exceptions: *see p. 86* and the verb tables for more
  information on the forms of the subjunctive.

Irregular imperatives

These verbs have irregular forms for the **tu** and **voi** imperatives:

	tu	*voi*
essere	sia!	siate!
avere	abbi!	abbiate!
sapere	sappia!	sappiate!

These verbs have special imperatives for the **tu** form:

andare	va'!
dare	da'!
dire	di'!
fare	fa'!
stare	sta'!

Sta' zitto!   Be quiet!
Di' qualcosa!   *Say something!*

! Note: The forms **vai!**, **dai!**, **fai!**, and **stai!** are also commonly used:
Vai via!   *Go away!*

Suggestions

The form of the imperative used for making suggestions, which is usually translated by 'let's' in English, has forms which are identical to the first person plural of the present tense:

Andiamo a casa   **Let's go** home
Facciamo un gioco   **Let's play** a game

Negative imperatives

For the negative form of the imperative, **non** is used:

Non parlate! **Don't speak**!

Non apra la finestra! **Don't open** the window!

The **tu** form of the negative imperative is obtained simply by putting the infinitive after **non**:

Non fare così! **Don't do** that!

The imperative with pronouns

When a pronoun object (direct or indirect) is used with the imperative, it is attached to the end of the verb:

Port**alo**! Bring **it**!

Aiutate**mi**! Help **me**!

but this does not happen with the **lei** form of the imperative:

Lo porti! Bring **it**!

Mi dica! Tell **me**!

When **mi**, **lo/la**, **ci**, **li/le**, or **ne** is added to the imperative of **andare**, **dare**, **dire**, **fare**, and **stare**, the first letter of the pronoun is doubled:

Di**llo**! Say **it**!

Fa**mmi** un piacere! Do **me** a favour!

Da**nne** di più a Rachele! Give some more (**of it**) to Rachele!

Sta**mmi** bene! Look after yourself! (literally Stay well for me!)

Note that there are two possible forms of the negative imperative with pronouns:

Non far**lo**!/Non **lo** fare! Don't do it!

! Note: *See p. 52* for more information about pronouns with imperatives.

| Reflexive verbs

What is a reflexive verb?

Reflexive verbs are verbs where the object is the same person or thing as the subject. In English they can be recognized by the presence of **myself**, **yourself**, **himself**, etc. Sometimes these verbs give an idea of the person performing the action on himself or herself:

She **wrapped herself** *in a blanket*

but very often this meaning is not apparent:

We really **enjoyed ourselves**

Reflexive verbs in Italian also fall into the same categories, where someone performs an action on himself or herself:

Mi sono tagliato   *I cut myself*

or where this meaning is not present:

La porta **si è aperta**   *The door* **opened**

> **!** **Note:** A reflexive verb in Italian may not correspond to a reflexive in English, so 'myself', etc. is not always used in the translation.

Reflexive verbs are often used in Italian to talk about a change in state:

I chiodi **si sono arrugginiti**   *The nails* **have gone rusty**

How are reflexive verbs formed?

The reflexive pronouns in Italian are **mi** 'myself', **ti** 'yourself', **si** 'oneself', 'himself', 'herself', 'yourself', 'themselves', **ci** 'ourselves', **vi** 'yourselves'. The reflexive pronoun comes before the verb:

present

mi alzo
ti alzi
si alza
ci alziamo
vi alzate
si alzano

The infinitive of reflexive verbs

When a reflexive verb is used in the infinitive, the reflexive pronoun is attached to the end of the verb (the **-e** of the infinitive is dropped first):

alzarsi   *to get up*

Note that the pronoun changes according to the subject of the verb, even when the verb is used in the infinitive:

devo alzar**mi**   *I have to get up*

devi alzar**ti**   *you have to get up*

deve alzar**si**   *he has to get up/she has to get up/you have to get up*

dobbiamo alzar**ci**   *we have to get up*

dovete alzar**vi**   *you have to get up*

devono alzar**si**   *they have to get up*

> **!** **Note:** Spoken Italian often puts the reflexive pronoun before the auxiliary verbs
> dovere, potere, and volere, instead of attaching it to the infinitive:
> **Mi** devo alzare   *I have to get up*

The imperative of reflexive verbs

The reflexive pronoun is attached to the imperative:

Alza**ti**/Alza**tevi**!   *Get up!*

> **!** **Note:** These are the imperative forms of the reflexives **farsi** and **darsi**:
> **Fatti** vedere da un medico!   *Get yourself seen by a doctor!*
> **Datti** una mossa!   *Get a move on!*

With the imperative of the **lei** form, the pronoun always comes first:

Si alzi!   *Get up!*

Compound tenses of reflexive verbs

The compound tenses (perfect, pluperfect, etc.) are always formed with the auxiliary **essere**. The ending of the past participle changes to agree with the subject:

perfect	*pluperfect*
mi **sono** alzato/alzata	mi **ero** alzato/alzata
ti **sei** alzato/alzata	ti **eri** alzato/alzata
si **è** alzato/alzata	si **era** alzato/alzata
ci **siamo** alzati/alzate	ci **eravamo** alzati/alzate
vi **siete** alzati/alzate	vi **eravate** alzati/alzate
si **sono** alzati/alzate	si **erano** alzati/alzate

Reflexive verbs followed by a direct object

In all of the examples above, the reflexive pronoun is the direct object of the verb. Often, however, the reflexive pronoun is an indirect object and the verb is then followed by a direct object:

Mi sono fatto un bel caffè   I **made myself** a nice coffee

Reciprocal verbs

Reciprocal verbs are verbs in which two or more people perform an action on each other. In English they can be recognized by the presence of **each other** or **one another**:

We love each other very much

In Italian the form of reciprocal verbs is the same as reflexive verbs. Only verbs in the plural can be reciprocal:

Ci vogliamo bene   We love each other
Si sono guardati   They looked at each other

Sometimes the meaning is reinforced by the expressions **a vicenda** and **l'un l'altro**:

Si aiutano **a vicenda**   They help each other
Si sono guardati **l'un l'altro**   They looked at each other

Reciprocal verbs can also take a direct object:

Si scrivono lettere appassionate   They **write** passionate letters
to each other

I The passive

What is the passive?

The passive is a form of the verb in which the subject of the sentence undergoes an action, rather than performing it:

The plants **are treated** with weedkiller

How is the passive formed?

Essere together with the past participle is used to form the passive in Italian. The appropriate tense of **essere** should be chosen, and the endings of the past participle agree with the subject of the sentence. The table shows the most common tenses, but all other tenses are also possible in the passive:

present	*perfect*
sono colpito/colpita	sono stato colpito/sono stata colpita
sei colpito/colpita	sei stato colpito/sei stata colpita
è colpito/colpita	è stato colpito/è stata colpita
siamo colpiti/colpite	siamo stati colpiti/siamo state colpite
siete colpiti/colpite	siete stati colpiti/siete state colpite
sono colpiti/colpite	sono stati colpiti/sono state colpite

future	*imperfect*
sarò colpito/colpita	ero colpito/colpita
sarai colpito colpita	eri colpito/colpita
sarà colpito/colpita	era colpito/colpita
saremo colpiti/colpite	eravamo colpiti/colpite
sarete colpiti/colpite	eravate colpiti/colpite
saranno colpiti/colpite	erano colpiti/colpite

I motori **sono fabbricati** in Germania   The engines are made in Germany

Tutti gli alberi **sono stati tagliati**   All the trees **have been cut down**

Da can be used to indicate the person or thing that performs the action:

Sono stato punto **da** una vespa   I was stung by a wasp

> **!** **Note:** There is no progressive form in the passive. Italian often uses an active
> verb where English uses a progressive form in the passive:
> **Stanno riparando** la macchina   My car is being repaired

Venire can also be used to form the passive in the present and imperfect tenses, but this is usually confined to the spoken language:

I fiori **vengono mangiati** dalle lumache   The flowers **get eaten** by slugs

Avoiding the passive

The passive is less common in Italian than it is in English, and can sound quite formal. Italians often avoid it by using the active form of the verb instead:

Mi **ha colpito** il fatto che c'erano pochi bambini   I *was struck by the fact that there weren't many children*

When the subject of the sentence is a vague external force, such as people in general, or the powers that be, Italian often uses a third person plural verb:

Vogliono introdurre una nuova tassa   **They want** *to introduce a new tax*

Uses of *si*

Another alternative to the passive which is very common is to use a reflexive verb:

Il vino **si fa** con l'uva   *Wine* **is made** *from grapes*
Le olive **si raccolgono** a novembre   The olives **are picked** in November

! Note: The verb is plural if its grammatical subject is plural (**le olive** in the second example).

This structure is very common in spoken Italian, where it can be used to make impersonal statements ('you' or 'one') and as a replacement for the first person plural form of the verb (the we form):

Non **si sa** mai   *You never* **know**
Come **si dice** in italiano?   *How* **do you say it** *in Italian?*
Domani **si va** al mare   *Tomorrow* **we're going** *to the seaside*
Si vedrà   *We'll see*

! Note: When the reflexive is used in this way in speech, the verb remains in the singular even when the grammatical subject (**ciliege** in this example) is plural:
Si mangiava ciliege   **We were eating** cherries

The reflexive can even replace the first person plural verb of a reflexive verb:

Ci si alza sempre presto   *We always* **get up** *early*
Là **ci si diverte** sempre   *We always* **have a good time** *there*

A common use of this structure is to make suggestions:

Si prende un taxi?   **Shall we take** *a taxi?*
Ci si rivede?   *Shall we see each other again?*

I *mi piace*, etc.

A group of verbs in Italian, including **piacere**, **dispiacere**, and
mancare, behave differently from their English equivalents 'like',
'dislike', and 'miss'. What is the subject in English is an indirect
object in Italian, and what is the direct object in English is the
subject in Italian. It may help to think of **piacere** as meaning 'to
please'. So **io piaccio a te** means 'you like me' ('I please you'),
and not 'I like you'. **Piacere** is mostly used in the third person
singular and plural, and the subject is very often put at the end of
the sentence. Remember that if the thing which is liked is
singular, the verb must be singular (**piace** in the present tense);
and if the thing which is liked is plural, the verb must be plural
(**piacciono** in the present tense):

mi piace/piacciono...	I like...
ti piace/piacciono...	you like...
gli piace/piacciono...	he likes...
le piace/piacciono...	she likes..., you like...
ci piace/piacciono...	we like...
vi piace/piacciono...	you like...
a loro piace/ piacciono..., gli piace/piacciono...	they like...

Mi piace la pizza   **I like** pizza
Mi piacciono i tuoi orecchini   **I like** your earrings
Ci piaceva passeggiare in campagna   **We used to like** walking in the country
Ti è piaciuta Venezia?   **Did you like** Venice?
Non mi dispiace questa giacca   **I quite like** this jacket
Mi manca la mia famiglia   **I miss** my family
Le mancano gli amici   **She misses** her friends

Impersonal verbs

Impersonal verbs in English have **it** as their subject, where it does not refer to anything that has been mentioned:

It's nice to be here

In Italian these verbs have no subject, and can only be used in the third person singular.

Some refer to the weather:

Pioveva forte   **It was raining** hard
Fa freddo   **It's** cold

Essere is used as an impersonal verb with adjectives. The adjective can be followed by an infinitive or **che** + verb, usually in the subjunctive:

È bello **essere** qua   It's nice **to be** here
Non è facile **essere** madre   It's not easy **being** a mother
È importante che **arriviate** presto   It's important that **you arrive** early

Note these common impersonal verbs:

basta	it is enough
bisogna	it is necessary
occorre	it is necessary
pare/sembra	it seems
si tratta di	it's a matter of

Basta!   That's enough!
Basta chiedere   All you have to do is ask
Sembra che se ne siano dimenticati   It seems they've forgotten
Bisogna annaffiare le piante   We need to water the plants
Bisogna che sia chiaro   It has to be clear
Di che cosa **si tratta**?   What's it about?

Adverbs

I What is an adverb?

An adverb is used to add extra information to a verb, an adjective, or another adverb. In English adverbs often end in -*ly*:

to walk **quickly, extremely** important

but they may have other forms:

to walk **fast, very** important

Phrases can also function as adverbs. These are called *adverbial phrases*:

to walk **at a fast pace**, important **beyond belief**

I Adverbs of manner

In Italian adverbs which describe actions (adverbs of manner) often end in **-mente**. With adjectives which end in **-o/-a**, this ending is added to the feminine form of the adjective:

lento + mente: lentamente

With adjectives which end in **-e**, simply add **-mente**:

corrente + mente: correntemente

With adjectives which end in **-ale**, **-ile**, or **-are**, the **-e** is removed before adding **-mente**:

gentile + mente: gentilmente

camminare **lentamente** to walk **slowly**
parlare **correntemente** to speak **fluently**
chiedere **gentilmente** to ask **politely**

These common adverbs do not follow the above rule:

violento + mente: violentemente
leggero + mente: leggermente

I Irregular adverbs

Some adverbs have forms which are quite different from the related adjective:

buono: bene
cattivo: male

Suona **bene** il pianoforte   He plays the piano **well**
Non cucina **male**   She's not a bad cook

Some adverbs have forms which are not related to adjectives at all:

È **spesso** malata   She's **often** ill

Sometimes the adjective is used in place of the adverb. When the adjective is used like this, it never changes its form, and the masculine ending is used exclusively:

correre **veloce**   to run fast
parlare **piano**   to speak quietly

I Position of adverbs

Adverbs can come between the main verb and the object, unlike in English:

Dipinge **accuratamente** ogni vaso   She **painstakingly** paints every pot
Mi piace **tanto** la musica   I **really** like music

| Adverbial phrases

Often phrases are used to do the same job as an adverb. In English you can say with affection or affectionately, in a helpful way or helpfully.

Italian uses many idiomatic adverbial phrases formed from a preposition and a noun:

L'avevano tagliato **senza cura**   They had cut it **carelessly**
Lo puoi leggere **con calma**   You can read it **at your leisure**
L'avrà fatto **di proposito**?   Do you think he did it **on purpose**?
Non mi trattengo **a lungo**   I won't stay **long**

and many other adverbial phrases with prepositions are possible:

Ho pagato **con la carta di credito**   I paid **by credit card**
L'ho letto **da cima a fondo**   I read it **from beginning to end**

Italian also forms adverbial phrases using in (un) modo... or in (una) maniera...:

Parlava **in un modo strano**   He was speaking **strangely**
Hanno agito **in maniera professionale**   They acted **professionally**

In Italian there are many phrases where the noun which follows the preposition is used without an article:

Devo fare un salto **in banca**   I have to pop **into the bank**
Non è **in casa**   He's not in

! **Note:** For information about adverbs and adverbial phrases referring to time and place, *see p. 170.*

Comparative and superlative

The comparative of adverbs

The comparative of the adverb is similar to the comparative of the adjective (*see p. 30*).

In English the comparative is formed by putting **more** before the appropriate adverb. Some shorter English adverbs have a special comparative ending in *–er* (for example **faster**):

You should drive **more slowly/faster**

The Italian equivalent of **more** is **più**, which is placed before the adverb:

Bisogna leggerlo **più attentamente**   You need to read it **more carefully**

Note that 'than' is expressed in Italian by **di**. This is used before nouns, pronouns, and adverbs:

Tu parli l'italiano più correntemente **di** me   You speak Italian more fluently **than** me

Lo vedo più raramente **di** prima   I see him more rarely **than** before

But before prepositions, or if the comparison is between two adjectives, two adverbs, or two verbs, **che** is used:

Vanno più forte in Inghilterra **che** in Italia   They're more popular in England **than** in Italy

L'ha detto più scherzosamente **che** seriamente   He said it more jokingly **than** seriously

meglio tardi **che** mai   better late **than** never

The superlative of adverbs

The superlative of the adverb is rarely used in Italian, and the idea of 'the most' is expressed in other ways, for example by using the comparative:

Ha parlato **più a lungo** degli altri   He spoke **for the longest**

Tra tutti i miei studenti, Tina è quella che s'impegna di più   Tina works the hardest of all my students

The true superlative forms with **il più** are mainly used before **possibile** or phrases like **che posso**:

Sono partito **il più presto possibile**   I left *as early as possible*
L'ho scritto **il più chiaramente che potevo**   I wrote it *as clearly as I could*

Irregular comparatives and superlatives

In English a few adverbs have an irregular comparative and superlative form: **well** (comparative **better**, superlative **best**), **badly** (comparative **worse**, superlative **worst**). In Italian there are two common adverbs which have an irregular comparative form: **bene** and **male**.

	comparative	*superlative*
bene	meglio	il meglio
male	peggio	il peggio

Tu sai meglio **di** me   *You know better* **than** *me*
Canta meglio **di** prima   *She sings better* **than** *before*
Chi balla **meglio**?   *Who dances* **the best**?
Cerca di farlo **il meglio possibile**   *Try to do it* **as well as you can**

The absolute superlative

The absolute superlative of the adverb is similar to the absolute superlative of the adjective (*see p. 33*). It intensifies the meaning of an adverb. To form the absolute superlative, the final vowel of the adjective is replaced with the ending **-issimamente**, which never changes:

Guidava **lentissimamente**   *He drove* **extremely slowly**
Ci vediamo **pochissimo**   *We see* **very little** *of each other*

Interrogatives

When asking a question in Italian, the word order is the same as that of a normal statement:

Mauro abita qua   Mauro lives here
Mauro abita qua?   Does Mauro live here?

What changes is the intonation: the pitch of the question is higher at the end than the pitch of the statement. Note that there is no equivalent of **do** in the Italian question.

Italian does not use short 'tag' answers as in English:
'Ti piace?' 'Sì.'   'Do you like it?' 'Yes, I do.'

Asking about things: 'what?'

There are three ways of saying 'what...?' in Italian which are more or less interchangeable: **che cosa...?**, **che...?**, and **cosa...?**. Of the three, **cosa...?** is the most informal:

Che cosa fai?/Che fai?/Cosa fai?   **What** are you doing?

Cosa is shortened to **cos'** before forms of **essere** and **avere** beginning with a vowel sound:

Che cos'è?   **What** is it?
Cos'hai detto?   **What** did you say?

A preposition can never be put at the end of a question, as in English:

Con che cosa l'hai tagliato?   What did you cut it **with**?

Che can also be used before a noun:

Che numero porta?   **What** shoe size do you take?
Di **che** colore è?   **What** colour is it?
Che tipo di lavoro fa?   **What** kind of work do you do?

Asking about people: 'who?'

To ask a question about a person's identity, use **chi...?**:

Pronto, **chi** parla?   Hello, **who**'s speaking?

Chi ha spostato la macchina?   **Who** moved the car?

Chi hanno scelto?   **Who** did they choose?

To ask who something belongs to, use **di chi...?**:

Questi soldi **di chi** sono?   **Whose** money is this?

A preposition can never be put at the end of a question, as in English:

Con chi vuoi ballare?   Who do you want to dance **with**?

Per chi è questa lettera?   Who is this letter **for**?

Specification: 'which?'

Quale...? (plural **quali...?**) is used before a noun to mean 'which':

Quale cavallo ha vinto?   **Which** horse won?

Quali colori preferisci?   **Which** colours do you prefer?

> **!** Note: **Quale** is shortened to **qual** before forms of **essere** beginning with a vowel. Note that there is no apostrophe:
> **Qual** è il tuo posto?   **Which** is your place?

Quale...? also corresponds to 'what...?' in English:

Qual è il tuo quadro preferito?   **What** is your favourite painting?

A preposition can never be put at the end of a question, as in English:

Con quali salse si abbina?   Which sauces does it go **with**?

Quale is also used as a pronoun meaning 'which one...?':

Quale hai scelto?   **Which one** did you choose?

Reason: 'why?'

To ask the reason for something, use **perché...?**:
  Perché ridi? **Why** are you laughing?

Come mai...? is an alternative to **perché...?**. It expresses a greater degree of surprise or curiosity:
  Come mai sei vestito così? **Why ever** are you dressed like that?

Manner: 'how?'

To ask a question about the manner in which something is done, Italian uses **come...?**:
  Come funziona? **How** does it work?

The verb **fare** is sometimes used in addition to **come**. It is followed by the preposition **a**:
  Come hai fatto ad uscirne? **How did you** get out?
  Come si fa a lavorare così? **How can you** work like that?

Come is also used to ask what something is like:
  Come sono le scarpe nuove? **What** are your new shoes **like**?

Come is shortened to **com'** before forms of **essere** beginning with a vowel:
  Com'era il tempo? **What** was the weather **like**?

Place: 'where?'

To ask where something is or where someone is going, use **dove...?**:
  Dove sei? **Where** are you?
  Dove vai? **Where** are you going?

Dove is shortened to **dov'** before forms of **essere** beginning with a vowel:
  Dov'è l'entrata? **Where**'s the entrance?

Time: 'when?'

To ask about the time of an action, use **quando...?**:
Quando vuoi venire? **When** *do you want to come?*
Quando è successo questo? **When** did this happen?

Quantity and number: 'how much?', 'how many?'

To ask about a quantity, use **quanto...?** (feminine **quanta...?**):
Quanto vino hanno bevuto? **How much** *wine did they drink?*
Quanta birra hanno bevuto? **How much** *beer did they drink?*

To ask about a number, use **quanti...?** (feminine **quante...?**):
Quanti anni ci vogliono? **How many** years does it take?
Quante volte hai provato? **How many** times did you try?

Quanto...? and **quanti...?** can also be used without a noun. It may be necessary to use **ne** (*see p. 46* for more information):
Quanto prendono? **How much** *do they charge?*
Quanti hanno detto di sì? **How many people** said yes?
Quanto ne vuoi? **How much** (of it) do you want?
Quante ne hai scritte? **How many** (of them) have you written?

Quanto can be shortened to **quant'** before forms of **essere** beginning with a vowel:
Quant'è? **How much** is it?

Quanto is often used to ask how long a period of time is:
Quanto dura? **How long** does it last?

Quanto is also used with adjectives. It never changes its form:
Quanto è lungo? **How long** is it?
Quanto sei alta? **How tall** are you?

Prepositions

I What is a preposition?

A preposition is a word that stands in front of a noun (or a phrase including a noun) or a pronoun, relating it to the rest of the sentence. Many prepositions are connected with place:

I was born **in** the north-east of Scotland

or time:

Come **after** six o'clock

but many other uses are possible:

Do you want to play **with** me?

I did it **for** you

Often prepositions have a purely grammatical function in the sentence:

I'm tired **of** waiting

Prepositions in Italian

Prepositions in Italian may be followed by a noun (or a phrase including a noun):

È **sotto la sedia**   It's **underneath the chair**

and most prepositions can be followed by a pronoun:

Vuoi giocare **con me**?   Do you want to play **with me**?
L'ho fatto **per te**   I did it **for you**

Certain prepositions must insert **di** between the preposition and the pronoun, however. These are **contro, dentro, dietro, dopo, presso, senza, sopra, sotto, su,** and **verso**:

senza di te   without you
dentro di me   inside me
verso di noi   towards us

With **fra** (and **tra**, which means the same thing), **di** is optional:

Litigavano **fra (di) loro**   They were quarrelling among themselves

Di is never used when the meaning is 'between one person and another':

Resta **fra me e te**   It'll stay between me and you

Articulated forms

When some Italian prepositions are followed by a definite article
(**il/la**, etc.) they combine with the article to form a word. The
prepositions which are affected are **a**, **con**, **da**, **di**, **in**, and **su**:

a		*con*		*da*	
a + il:	al	con + il:	col	da + il:	dal
a + lo:	allo	con + lo:	(collo)	da + lo:	dallo
a + la:	alla	con + la:	(colla)	da + la:	dalla
a + l':	all'	con + l':	(coll')	da + l':	dall'
a + i:	ai	con + i:	coi	da + i:	dai
a + gli:	agli	con + gli:	(cogli)	da + gli:	dagli
a + le:	alle	con + le:	(colle)	da + le:	dalle

di		*in*		*su*	
di + il:	del	in + il:	nel	su + il:	sul
di + lo:	dello	in + lo:	nello	su + lo:	sullo
di + la:	della	in + la:	nella	su + la:	sulla
di + l':	dell'	in + l':	nell'	su + l':	sull'
di + i:	dei	in + i:	nei	su + i:	sui
di + gli:	degli	in + gli:	negli	su + gli:	sugli
di + le:	delle	in + le:	nelle	su + le:	sulle

le ruote **della** macchina   *the wheels **of the** car*
nella scatola   *in the box*
un programma **sugli** inca   *a programme **about the** Incas*
bruciato **dal** sole   *burnt **by the** sun*

! **Note:** Of the forms with **con**, only **col** and **coi** are used extensively in modern
standard Italian (and even they can be replaced by **con il** and **con i**). The other
forms always remain as separate words (**con lo**, **con la**, **con l'**, **con gli**, and **con
le**):
con le forbici   *with the scissors*
con il/col bastone   *with the stick*

Prepositions followed directly by a noun

Whilst the above combinations of prepostion and article are very common, Italian also has a certain number of phrases where the preposition is followed directly by a noun, with no article:

Si può parcheggiare **in centro**? Can you park **in the centre** of town?

Mi piacerebbe vivere **in campagna** I'd like to live **in the country**

Nonna è **in cucina** Granny's **in the kitchen**

Mettilo **in frigo** Put it **in the fridge**

Ci siamo fermati **per strada** We stopped **on the way**

Prepositional phrases

Some common prepositional phrases are formed from an adverb followed by a preposition:

È **vicino a** Genova It's **near** Genova

Mettiti **accanto a** me! Sit **next to** me!

C'è un parcheggio **davanti alla** stazione There's a car park **opposite the** station

Cantate **insieme a** noi! Sing along **with** us!

Sono arrivati **prima di** mezzanotte They arrived **before** midnight

Ci vado domani **invece di** martedì I'm going tomorrow **instead of** Tuesday

Note these prepositional phrases with **in** and **di**:

È **in cima alle** scale It's **at the top of the** stairs

C'era una ragazza **di fronte a** me There was a girl **opposite** me

È **in fondo al** corridoio It's **at the end of the** corridor

Aspettavano **in mezzo alla** piazza They were waiting **in the middle of the** square

Prepositions followed by an infinitive

Certain verbs which are followed by an infinitive need a preposition before the infinitive. The main prepositions used in this way are **di** and **a**. There are a large number of these, and you should learn the appropriate preposition to use whenever you learn a new verb.

Verbs followed by **di** + infinitive:

Ho cercato **di** fermarli   I tried **to** stop them
Mi hanno chiesto **di** smettere   They asked me **to** stop

Verbs followed by **a** + infinitive:

Mi aiuti **a** scendere?   Can you help me **to** get down?
Voglio imparare **a** guidare   I want to learn **to** drive

Some adjectives can also be followed by **di** or **a** + infinitive:

Sono pronto **ad** offrirgli mille   I'm prepared **to** offer him a
    thousand
Non è capace **di** capire   He's not capable **of** understanding

> **!** **Note:** *See p. 134 and p. 144* for lists of the most important verb and adjective constructions.

Prepositional objects

Some verbs in English require a preposition when followed by a noun or pronoun:

Listen **to** me!

The same happens in Italian:

Credo **nella sua** innocenza   I believe **in his** innocence

It is rarely the case, however, that the preposition in English corresponds to the preposition in Italian:

pensare **a** qualcosa   to think **about** something
dipendere **da** qualcosa   to depend **on** something
sposarsi **con** qualcuno   to get married **to** someone

There may be a preposition present in one language but not in the other.

● Preposition in Italian:

accorgersi di qualcosa **to notice** something
fidarsi di qualcuno **to trust** someone
ricordarsi di qualcosa **to remember** something
resistere a qualcosa **to resist** something
rispondere a qualcuno **to answer** someone
telefonare a qualcuno **to telephone** someone
ubbidire a qualcuno **to obey** someone

● No preposition in Italian:

ascoltare qualcuno **to listen to** someone
aspettare qualcuno **to wait for** someone
cercare qualcosa **to look for** something
chiedere/domandare qualcosa **to ask for** something
guardare qualcosa **to look at** something
operare qualcuno **to operate on** someone
pagare qualcosa **to pay for** something

> **! Note:** There are a large number of these differences between English and Italian, and you should learn the appropriate preposition to use whenever you learn a new verb. *See p. 134* and *p. 144* for lists of the most important verb and adjective constructions.

Prepositional phrases replaced by pronouns

Verbs which normally take prepositions can be used with pronouns.

Verbs which are followed by **a** use the indirect object pronouns (*see p. 42*). 'It' is expressed by **ci**:

Telefona**tegli** appena arrivate *Phone **him** as soon as you arrive*
Non **ci** resisto *I can't resist **it***

Verbs which are followed by **di** keep the **di** and use the strong pronoun (*see p. 44*) after it. The exception is 'it', which is expressed by **ne**:

Non mi fido **di lui** *I don't trust **him***
Non me **n'**ero accorto *I hadn't noticed **it***

Some uses of prepositions

di

! **Note:** Uses of **di** following certain verbs and adjectives are treated above.

Possession

The basic function of **di** is to show possession or a 'belonging to' relationship:

La macchina **di** Vittorio   *Vittorio's car*

le gambe **della** sedia   *the legs of the chair*

Quantity

It is also used in expressions of quantity:

due etti **di** burro   *200g of butter*

un piatto **di** spaghetti   *a plate of spaghetti*

Origins

It is used to say one's place of origin:

Sono **di** Lucca   *I'm from Lucca*

Specifying

It is used to specify what one is talking about:

il problema **dell'**inquinamento   *the problem of pollution*

la città **di** Roma   *the city of Rome*

Material

It is used to talk about the material something is made of:

È **di** legno   *It's made of wood*

una casa **di** mattoni   *a brick house*

Age

It is also used to talk about age:

un ragazzo **di** tredici anni   *a thirteen-year-old boy*

di in comparatives

Di is also used in comparatives to mean 'than' (*see p. 30* for more information):

Nessuno cucina meglio **di** me   *No one cooks better **than** me*

'covered with', 'equipped with'

Di can convey the meaning 'covered with' or 'equipped with' after certain verbs and adjectives:

un fazzoletto macchiato **di** sangue   *a bloodstained handkerchief*
un giovane armato **di** pistola   *a youth armed **with** a gun*

Time phrases

It is used in time phrases (*see p. 170* for more information):

Odio guidare **di** notte   *I hate driving **at** night*
D'estate vado al mare   *I go to the seaside **in** summer*

> **!** **Note:** The preposition **di** may be shortened to **d'** before a vowel in certain common combinations:
> una bottiglia **d'**acqua   *a bottle of water*

a

> **!** **Note:** Uses of **a** following certain verbs and adjectives are treated above.

Position and destination

A is used to show the position of something:

Sono **alla** stazione   *I'm **at the** station*
Abbiamo passato tre notti **a** Verona   *We spent three nights **in** Verona*

or destination:

Vanno **a** scuola con l'autobus   *They go **to** school by bus*
Vorrei andare **a** Pompei   *I'd like to go **to** Pompeii*

> **!** **Note:** See p. 186 for more information about position and destination.

Recipient

It is used to show the recipient of something:

L'ho dato **a** Flavio   *I gave it **to** Flavio*

> **!** **Note:** With certain verbs, **a** can convey the idea of 'from someone':
> Ho levato i fiammiferi **ai** bambini   *I took the matches **from the** children*
> Hanno tolto la patente **al** mio nonno   *They took away my grandfather's licence*

Distance

It is used to show distance (**a** is not translated in English):

Abito **a** quindici chilometri da Catania   *I live fifteen kilometres from Catania*

Time phrases

It is used in time phrases (*see p. 170* for more information):

alle undici   *at eleven o'clock*
a Natale   *at Christmas*

Frequency, speed, distribution, and price

A is used to talk about frequency:

due volte **al** mese   *twice **a** month*

speed:

duecento chilometri **all'**ora   *200 kph*

distribution:

un litro **a** testa   *one litre each*

and how much something costs for a certain quantity:

nove euro **al** chilo   *nine euros **a** kilo*

Manner

A shows the way something is done:

lenzuola ricamate **a** mano   *sheets embroidered **by** hand*
baccalà **alla** livornese   *Livornese-style salt cod*
un panino **al** formaggio   *a cheese roll*
Chiudila **a** chiave!   *Lock it!*

> **!** **Note:** The preposition **a** also has the form **ad**, which can be used before vowels, especially in writing:
> Vivono **ad** Ancona   *They live in Ancona*

in

Position and destination

In is used to show the position of something:

Le camicie sono **nell'**armadio   *The shirts are **in the** wardrobe*

Sono nato **in** Brasile   *I was born **in** Brazil*

or destination:

Voglio andare **in** città   *I want to go **into** town*

Quest'anno vogliamo andare **in** Grecia   *We want to go **to** Greece this year*

> **!** **Note:** *See p. 186 for more information about position and destination.*

Time phrases

It is used in time phrases (*see p. 170 for more information*):

in autunno   **in** *autumn*

nel 1901   **in** *1901*

Transport

In is often used to show a means of transport:

Vanno a scuola **in** autobus   *They go to school **by** bus*

Ci vado **in** bicicletta   *I'll go **by** bike*

Siamo venuti **in** macchina   *We came **by** car*

Vado in Sardegna **in** aereo   *I'm flying to Sardinia*

The preposition **con** + definite article is used when speaking about specific journeys, but not when speaking about travel in general:

Siamo venuti **con la** macchina   *We came **in our** car*

> **!** **Note:** There is an exception:
> Sono venuta **a piedi**   *I came **on foot***

da

Origin

The basic function of **da** is to show the origin or starting point of something:

Vengono **da** Lecce   They come **from** Lecce

da Parigi a Venezia   **from** Paris to Venice

dalle nove alle diciassette   **from** 9 a.m. till 5 p.m.

Position and destination

It can also means 'to' or 'at' someone's house, and is used for shops and business premises:

Perché non vieni **da** me?   Why don't you come back **to** my place?

Passiamo il Natale **dalla** nonna   We're spending Christmas **at** Granny's

Devo andare **dal** dentista   I have to go **to the** dentist's

! Note: *See p. 186 for more information about position and destination.*

Value

Da can be used to show the value of something:

un anello **da** un milione di dollari   a million-dollar ring

un biglietto **da** cento euro   a one hundred euro note

Function

It can show the function of something:

una sala **da** pranzo   a dining room

pantaloni **da** uomo   men's trousers

un cane **da** caccia   a hunting dog

un cucchiaino **da** caffè   a coffee spoon

! Note: Compare the last example with:
un cucchiaino **di** caffè   *a teaspoon of coffee*

Describing

Da can also mean 'as' or 'like'. In this meaning there is no indefinite article (**un, una**, etc.) after **da**:

Da bambino ero biondo   **As a baby** I was fair

Era vestito **da** suora   He was dressed **as a nun**
Cosa farai **da grande**?   What are you going to do **when you grow up?**

It is used when describing people:

un uomo **dai** capelli bianchi   a man **with** white hair

da with passive verbs

It is used with passive verbs to mean 'by':

La città è stata distrutta **dai** Goti   The city was destroyed **by the** Goths

da with the infinitive

Da followed by the infinitive gives the idea of something 'to be done':

C'è ancora tanto **da fare**   There's still a lot **to be done**
Ho quattro camicie **da** stirare   I've got four shirts **to** iron
Era **da ridere!**   It was **ridiculous!**

and is used after words like **qualcosa**, **niente**, etc.:

Vuole qualcosa **da** bere?   Do you want something **to** drink?
Non c'era niente **da fare**   There was nothing **to be done** about it

Duration

Da means 'for' or 'since' when talking about duration:

Ci conosciamo **da** anni   We've known each other **for** years
Aspetto **da** gennaio   I've been waiting **since** January

> **!** Note: See p. 182 for more information about this use of **da**.

per

Recipient

Per is used to talk about the intended recipient of something:

C'è una lettera **per** te   There's a letter **for** you

Destination

or the intended destination of something:

il treno **per** Parigi   the train **for** Paris

Time phrases

It is used in time phrases (*see p. 170* for more information):

Ci siamo rimasti bloccati **per** due ore   We were stuck there **for** two hours

Deve essere pronto **per** le dieci   It must be ready **by** ten

per with the infinitive

Per followed by an infinitive means 'in order to':

Cantavamo **per** tenerci su   We sang **to** keep our spirits up

It is also used with an infinitive after **troppo**:

È **troppo** piccolo **per** capire   He's **too** young **to** understand

con

Con usually corresponds to 'with' in English:

Vieni **con** me!   *Come **with** me!*

Giocavano **con** la palla   *They were playing **with** the ball*

fragole **con** limone   *strawberries **with** lemon*

Treatment

It is also used with certain adjectives when talking about the way someone is treated:

Sono sempre stati molto gentili **con** me   *They've always been very kind **to** me*

su

Position and destination

Su usually corresponds to 'on' or 'onto':

I tuoi occhiali sono **sul** tavolo   *Your glasses are **on the** table*

Subject

It can also mean 'about':

un programma **sugli** etruschi   *a programme **about the** Etruscans*

Ages and numbers

It is used to express approximate ages and numbers:

È **sulla** quarantina   *He's about forty*

Dovrebbe durare **sui** dieci, quindici minuti   *It should last about ten, fifteen minutes*

Marks and statistics

Su with numbers can express a mark in an exam:

Ho preso nove **su** dieci   *I got nine **out of** ten*

or a statistic:

un uomo **su** dieci   *one man **in** ten*

Verb and adjective constructions

Verb constructions

Verbs in Italian can be followed by a range of grammatical patterns, for example a noun, a verb in the infinitive, or a noun plus a verb in the infinitive. This section lists the most important verbs in Italian which are followed by such constructions.

Verbs with the infinitive (no preposition)

Verb + infinitive

dover fare qualcosa	to have to do something
osare fare qualcosa	to dare to do something
poter fare qualcosa	to be able to do something
preferire fare qualcosa	to prefer to do something
saper fare qualcosa	to know how to do something
sembrare fare qualcosa	to seem to do something
voler fare qualcosa	to want to do something

Non devi gridare   You mustn't shout

Note these impersonal verbs which are followed by the infinitive:

basta fare qualcosa	it's enough to do something
bisogna fare qualcosa	it's necessary to do something
(mi, ti, etc.) conviene fare qualcosa	it's better (for me, you, etc.) to do something
mi, ti, etc. dispiace fare qualcosa	I am, you are, etc. sorry to do something
non importa fare qualcosa	it's not important to do something
occorre fare qualcosa	it's necessary to do something

mi, ti, etc. piace fare qualcosa   I, you, etc. like doing something
mi, ti, etc. tocca fare qualcosa   I, you, etc. have to do something

> Basta darmi un colpo di telefono   All you have to do is give me a call

Verb + noun + infinitive

lasciare qualcuno fare qualcosato let someone do something

> Lasciami parlare!   Let me speak!

> **!** Note: **Fare** is also followed by a noun plus an infinitive. *See p. 58* for more information.

Verbs with *a*

Verb + *a* + noun

accennare a qualcosa	to mention something
addattarsi a qualcosa	to adapt to something
aderire a qualcosa	to stick to something
appartenere a qualcuno	to belong to someone
assomigliare a qualcosa/qualcuno	to look like something/someone
credere a qualcuno/qualcosa	to believe someone/something
dispiacere a qualcuno	to be sorry
giocare a qualcosa	to play something
importare a qualcuno	to matter to someone
mancare a qualcuno	to miss
obbedire a qualcuno	to obey someone
opporsi a qualcosa	to oppose something
partecipare a qualcosa	to take part in something
pensare a qualcosa	to think about something
perdonare a qualcuno	to forgive someone
piacere a qualcuno	to like
resistere a qualcosa	to resist something
riferirsi a qualcuno/qualcosa	to refer to someone/something
rispondere a qualcuno/qualcosa	to answer someone/something

servire a qualcuno   to be useful to someone
sparare a qualcuno   to shoot someone
telefonare a qualcuno   to phone someone
toccare a qualcuno   to be someone's turn
ubbidire a qualcuno   to obey someone

Pensavo **alle** vacanze   I was thinking **about the** holidays

> **Note:** When **pensare** is used to talk about opinions, **di** is used:
> Che ne pensi **dei** risultati?   What do you think **of the** results?
> See p. 109 for more information about **piacere**, **dispiacere**, and **mancare**.

Verb + *a* + infinitive or noun

abituarsi a (fare) qualcosa   to get used to (doing) something
consentire a (fare) qualcosa   to consent to (do) something
contribuire a (fare) qualcosa   to contribute to (doing) something
rinunciare a (fare) qualcosa   to give up (doing) something
servire a (fare) qualcosa   to be useful for (doing) something

Ha rinunciato **al** titolo   He gave up the title
Ha rinunciato **a** difendere la sua posizione   He's given up trying
  to defend his position

Verb + noun + *a* + noun

chiedere qualcosa a qualcuno   to ask someone for something
concedere qualcosa a qualcuno   to allow someone something
dare qualcosa a qualcuno   to give someone something
dire qualcosa a qualcuno   to tell someone something
domandare qualcosa a qualcuno   to ask someone for something
insegnare qualcosa a qualcuno   to teach someone something
levare qualcosa a qualcuno   to take something from someone
nascondere qualcosa a qualcuno   to hide something from someone
portare via qualcosa a qualcuno   to take something away from someone
prendere qualcosa a qualcuno   to take something from someone
regalare qualcosa a qualcuno   to give someone something
ricordare qualcosa a qualcuno   to remind someone of something
rubare qualcosa a qualcuno   to steal something from someone
sconsigliare qualcosa a qualcuno   to advise someone against something
spiegare qualcosa a qualcuno   to explain something to someone
togliere qualcosa a qualcuno   to take something from someone

Ho chiesto il conto **al** cameriere   I asked the waiter for the bill

Verb + *a* + infinitive

andare a fare qualcosa	to go to do something
arrivare a fare qualcosa	to manage to do something
cominciare a fare qualcosa	to start doing something
continuare a fare qualcosa	to continue doing something
divertirsi a fare qualcosa	to enjoy doing something
esercitarsi a fare qualcosa	to practise doing something
esitare a fare qualcosa	to hesitate to do something
farcela a fare qualcosa	to manage to do something
imparare a fare qualcosa	to learn (how) to do something
impegnarsi a fare qualcosa	to commit yourself to doing something
insistere a fare qualcosa	to insist on doing something, to persist in doing something
mettersi a fare qualcosa	to start doing something
prepararsi a fare qualcosa	to prepare to do something
provare a fare qualcosa	to try doing something
riuscire a fare qualcosa	to manage to do something
tenerci a fare qualcosa	to be keen to do something
venire a fare qualcosa	to come to do something
vergognarsi a fare qualcosa	to be ashamed to do something

Cominciano **a** preoccuparsi   They're starting **to** get worried
Ha continuato **a** leggere   He continued **to** read
Sei riuscito **a** trovarla?   Did you manage **to** find her?

! Note: It is also possible to say **vergognarsi *di* fare qualcosa**.

Verb + noun + *a* + infinitive

aiutare qualcuno a fare qualcosa	to help someone to do something
convincere qualcuno a fare qualcosa	to persuade someone to do something
costringere qualcuno a fare qualcosa	to force someone to do something
incoraggiare qualcuno a fare qualcosa	to encourage someone to do something
invitare qualcuno a fare qualcosa	to invite someone to do something
obbligare qualcuno a fare qualcosa	to force someone to do something
persuadere qualcuno a fare qualcosa	to persuade someone to do something

Aiutava la mamma **a** fare da mangiare   She helped her mother **to** do the cooking

Verb + *a* + noun + *a* + infinitive

insegnare a qualcuno a fare qualcosa   to teach someone to do something

Ho insegnato a mio figlio **a** guidare   I taught my son **to** drive

Verbs with *di*

Verb + *di* + noun

aver bisogno di qualcosa	to need something
accorgersi di qualcosa	to notice something
chiedere di qualcuno	to ask about someone
dimenticarsi di qualcosa	to forget about something
dubitare di qualcosa	to doubt something
fidarsi di qualcuno	to trust someone
innamorarsi di qualcuno	to fall in love with someone
intendersi di qualcosa	to know about something
lamentarsi di/per qualcosa	to complain about something
mancare di qualcosa	to lack something
meravigliarsi di qualcosa	to be amazed at something
morire di qualcosa	to die of something
occuparsi di qualcuno/ qualcosa	to look after someone/something
preoccuparsi di/per qualcosa	to worry about something
ridere di qualcuno/qualcosa	to laugh at someone/something
scusarsi di qualcosa	to apologize for something
servirsi di qualcosa	to use something
sospettare di qualcuno	to suspect someone
vivere di qualcosa	to live on something

Si è scusato **del** ritardo   He apologized **for** being late
Non si sono accorti **dell'**errore   They didn't notice the mistake

Verb + noun + *di* + noun

convincere qualcuno di qualcosa	to convince someone of something
coprire qualcosa di qualcosa	to cover something with something
riempire qualcosa di qualcosa	to fill something with something

Nessuno mi convincerà **della sua** innocenza   No one will convince me **of his** innocence

Verb + *di* + infinitive

accettare di fare qualcosa	to agree to do something
aspettarsi di fare qualcosa	to expect to do something
badare di fare qualcosa	to be careful to do something
cercare di fare qualcosa	to try to do something
cessare di fare qualcosa	to stop doing something
decidere di fare qualcosa	to decide to do something
dimenticare di fare qualcosa	to forget to do something
evitare di fare qualcosa	to avoid doing something
fingere/far finta di fare qualcosa	to pretend to something
finire di fare qualcosa	to finish doing something
mancare di fare qualcosa	to fail to do something
meritare di fare qualcosa	to deserve to do something
offrirsi di fare qualcosa	to offer to do something
pensare di fare qualcosa	to intend doing something
pretendere di fare qualcosa	to expect to do something
proporre di fare qualcosa	to suggest doing something
rifiutarsi di fare qualcosa	to refuse to do something
scegliere di fare qualcosa	to choose to do something
sforzarsi di fare qualcosa	to make an effort to do something
smettere di fare qualcosa	to stop doing something
sognare di fare qualcosa	to dream of doing something
sopportare di fare qualcosa	to tolerate doing something
sperare di fare qualcosa	to hope to do something
tentare di fare qualcosa	to try to do something

Sto cercando **di** capire   I'm trying **to** understand

Abbiamo deciso **di** vendere la casa   We've decided **to** sell the house

Hai dimenticato **di** spegnere le luci   You forgot **to** switch off the lights

Verb + *di* + infinitive or noun

contentarsi di (fare) qualcosa	to be happy to do something, to be happy with something
interessarsi di (fare) qualcosa	to be interested in (doing) something
parlare di (fare) qualcosa	to speak about (doing) something
ricordarsi di (fare) qualcosa	to remember (to do) something
stufarsi di (fare) qualcosa	to get fed up with (doing) something

> **!** **Note:** The impersonal verb **si tratta di** can also be followed by a noun or a verb:
> Si tratta **di** oro a ventidue carati   We're talking twenty-two carat gold here
> Si trattava **di** trovare una soluzione   We had to find a solution

Verb + *di* + past infinitive or noun

pentirsi di (aver fatto) qualcosa	to regret (doing) something
vergognarsi di (aver fatto) qualcosa	to be ashamed of yourself for doing something, to be ashamed of something

Mi pento **di** averlo detto   I regret saying it

Verb + noun + *di* + infinitive

pregare/supplicare qualcuno di fare qualcosa	to beg someone to do something

Ti prego **di** aiutarmi   I beg you **to** help me

Verb + *a* + noun + *di* + infinitive

chiedere a qualcuno di fare qualcosa	to ask someone to do something
consigliare a qualcuno di fare qualcosa	to advise someone to do something
dire a qualcuno di fare qualcosa	to tell someone to do something
domandare a qualcuno di fare qualcosa	to ask someone to do something
impedire a qualcuno di fare qualcosa	to prevent someone from doing something
ordinare a qualcuno di fare qualcosa	to order someone to do something
proibire a qualcuno di fare qualcosa	to forbid someone to do something

raccomandare a qualcuno di fare qualcosa	*to advise someone to do something*
vietare a qualcuno di fare qualcosa	*to forbid someone to do something*

With the following verbs, it is possible to omit the reference to a person:

consentire (a qualcuno) di fare qualcosa	*to allow someone to do something, to make it possible to do sth*
dire (a qualcuno) di fare qualcosa	*to tell someone to do something, to say to do something*
suggerire (a qualcuno) di fare qualcosa	*to suggest that someone should do something, to suggest doing something*
permettere (a qualcuno) di fare qualcosa	*to allow someone to do something, to make it possible to do something*
promettere (a qualcuno) di fare qualcosa	*to promise someone that you will do something, to promise to do something*

Questi occhiali permettono **di** vedere al buio   *These glasses make it possible **to** see in the dark*

L'esposizione permette al pubblico **di** riscoprire l'arte del Settecento   *The exhibition allows the public **to** rediscover the art of the 18th century*

Verb + object + *di* + past infinitive or noun

accusare qualcuno di (aver fatto) qualcosa	*to accuse someone of (doing) something*
ricordarsi di (aver fatto) qualcosa	*to remember (doing) something*
sospettare qualcuno di (aver fatto) qualcosa	*to suspect someone of (doing) something*

Hanno accusato la polizia **di** aver reagito in modo esagerato   *They accused the police **of** overreacting*

Sono accusati **di** genocidio   *They are accused **of** genocide*

Verbs with other constructions

avere da fare qualcosa	to have to do something
basarsi su qualcosa	to be based on something
concentrarsi su qualcosa	to concentrate on something
credere in qualcosa	to believe in something
dipendere da qualcosa	to depend on something
entrare in qualcosa	to enter something
parlare con qualcuno	to speak to someone
ringraziare qualcuno per (aver fatto) qualcosa	to thank someone for (doing) something
scusarsi per (aver fatto) qualcosa	to apologize for (doing) something
sperare in qualcosa	to hope for something

Hai **da** firmare qua   You have to sign here
Dipende **da** te   It's up to you

! Note: It is also possible to say **ringraziare qualcuno *di* qualcosa**.

A large number of verbs can be followed by **che**. With some verbs the subjunctive must be used (*see p. 86*):

Si è accorta che stavo male   She realized I wasn't well
Crede che io guidi male   He thinks I drive badly

Some of these verbs, mostly connected with 'thinking' and 'saying', can also be followed by **di** + infinitive. This is possible when the implied subject of the infinitive is the same as the subject of the main verb:

Si è accorta **di** essere l'unica rimasta   She realized she was the only one left
Crede **di** saper guidare meglio di me   He thinks he can drive better than me
Afferma **di** essere innocente   She claims she is innocent

Note also **mi sembra/mi pare di**:

Mi è sembrato **di** sentire qualcosa   I thought I heard something
Gli sembrava **di** volare   He felt as if he were flying

I Adjective constructions

Some adjectives in Italian can be followed by an infinitive, often with a preposition. This section lists the most important adjective constructions in Italian.

Impersonal constructions with the infinitive

Many adjectives are used in impersonal constructions with **essere**. The adjective is followed by the infinitive without any preposition:

È bello dormire fino a tardi   It's nice to sleep till late

Era difficile capirla   It was difficult to understand her

È inutile piangere   It's no use crying

Sarà facile trovare un lavoro   It will be easy to find a job

! **Note:** *See p. 110 for information about impersonal verbs.*

Adjectives with *a*

Adjective + *a* + noun

adatto a qualcosa	suitable for something
affezionato a qualcuno	fond of someone
allergico a qualcosa	allergic to something
antipatico a qualcuno	not on the same wavelength as someone
contrario a qualcosa	against something
favorevole a qualcosa	in favour of something
fedele a qualcuno	faithful to someone
grato a qualcuno per qualcosa	grateful to someone for something
identico a qualcosa	identical to something
simile a qualcosa	similar to something
simpatico a qualcuno	on the same wavelength as someone
uguale a qualcosa	the same as something
vicino a qualcuno/qualcosa	close to someone/something

È uguale **a** quello vecchio   It's the same **as** the old one
Ai mei genitori è simpatica   My parents like her

Adjective + *a* + verb

abituato a fare qualcosa	used to doing something
bravo a fare qualcosa	good at doing something
deciso a fare qualcosa	determined to do something
disposto a fare qualcosa	willing to do something
occupato a fare qualcosa	busy doing something
pronto a fare qualcosa	ready to do something
tenuto a fare qualcosa	obliged to do something

Sei disposta **ad** aiutarmi?   Are you willing **to** help me?
Sono abituato **ad** alzarmi presto   I'm used **to** getting up early

! **Note:** It is also possible to use **abituato a** with a noun:
Ormai siamo abituati **alle** critiche   We're used **to** criticism now

Adjectives with *di*

Adjective + *di* + noun

carico di qualcosa	loaded with something
colpevole di qualcosa	guilty of something
consapevole di qualcosa	aware of something
convinto di qualcosa	convinced of something
coperto di qualcosa	covered with something
degno di qualcuno/qualcosa	worthy of someone/something
entusiasta di qualcosa	enthusiastic about something
fiero di qualcuno/qualcosa	proud of someone/something
geloso di qualcuno/qualcosa	jealous of someone/something
orgoglioso di qualcuno/qualcosa	proud of someone/something
pazzo di/per qualcuno/qualcosa	crazy about someone/something
pieno di qualcosa	full of something
pratico di qualcosa	good with something
privo di qualcosa	without something
responsabile di qualcosa	in charge of something
ricco di qualcosa	rich in something
soddisfatto di qualcosa	satisfied with something
tipico di qualcuno	typical of someone

L'isola è ricca **di** minerali   The island is rich **in** minerals
È tipico **di** lei   It's typical of her

Note the following construction with **convinto**:

Era convinto **di essere** un genio   He was convinced he was a genius

Adjective + *di* + verb or noun

ansioso di (fare) qualcosa	*anxious to do something, anxious for something*
capace di (fare) qualcosa	*capable of (doing) something*
certo di (fare) qualcosa	*sure of (doing) something*
contento di (fare) qualcosa	*pleased to do something, pleased with something*
curioso di (fare) qualcosa	*curious to do something, curious about something*
felice di (fare) qualcosa	*happy to do something, happy with something*
incapace di (fare) qualcosa	*incapable of (doing) something*
libero di fare qualcosa	*free to do something*
lieto di (fare) qualcosa	*happy to do something, happy with something*
sicuro di (fare) qualcosa	*sure of (doing) something*
stanco di (fare) qualcosa	*tired of (doing) something*
stufo di (fare) qualcosa	*fed up with (doing) something*

Erano sicuri **di** vincere   *They were sure **of** winning*
Sono stanco **delle tue** domande   *I'm tired **of your** questions*

Adjectives with other prepositions

bravo in qualcosa	*good at something*
differente/diverso da qualcuno/ qualcosa	*different from someone/something*
fissato con qualcosa	*obsessed with something*
lontano da qualcuno/qualcosa	*far from someone/something*
negato per qualcosa	*hopeless at something*
portato per qualcosa	*good at something*
preoccupato per qualcuno/qualcosa	*worried about someone/something*
sposato con qualcuno	*married to someone*

È bravo **in** matematica   *He's good **at** maths*
È diversa **dalle** solite canzoni   *It's different **from the** usual songs*

Possessives

di chi...?

To ask who something belongs to, **di chi...?** is used:
  Di chi è questa macchina?   *Whose car is this?*
  Di chi sono queste scarpe?   *Whose shoes are these?*

The verb **appartenere** can also be used:
  A chi **appartiene** questa casa?   *Who does this house belong to?*

To say that something belongs to somebody, the most common way is to use **di**:
  Questi occhiali sono **di** Vittorio   *These glasses are Vittorio's*
  Dov'è la casa **di** Ugo?   *Where is Ugo's house?*

The verb **appartenere** can also be used:
  l'Alaska **appartiene agli** Stati Uniti   *Alaska belongs to the US*

Di is used for things as well as people:
  le gambe **della** sedia   *the legs of the chair*
  le chiavi **della** macchina   *the car keys*

Possessive adjectives

Possessive adjectives are used to say who something belongs to when the person is not mentioned by name. In English the possessive adjectives are **my**, **your**, **his**, etc. Italian possessive adjectives agree in number and gender with the noun they go with, and they are usually preceded by the definite article:

masculine singular	feminine singular	masculine plural	feminine plural	
il mio	la mia	i miei	le mie	my
il tuo	la tua	i tuoi	le tue	your (familiar)
il suo	la sua	i suoi	le sue	his/her/its, your (formal)
il nostro	la nostra	i nostri	le nostre	our
il vostro	la vostra	i vostri	le vostre	your (plural)
il loro	la loro	i loro	le loro	their

In Italian there is no distinction between **his** and **her**. **Il suo** changes its form to agree with the thing which is owned, but gives no information about the gender of the owner:

Francesca ha pagato **il suo** biglietto   Francesca paid for **her** ticket

Davide mi ha dato **la sua** risposta   Davide gave me **his** answer

Il suo is also used to mean 'your' when addressing someone using the **lei** form:

Questa è **la sua** giacca, signore?   Is this **your** jacket, sir?

! Note: Loro does not change in form in the feminine or the plural:
le loro opinioni   *their opinions*

The possessive adjectives are also used without the definite article after the verb **essere**:

Queste lettere sono **mie**   These letters are **mine**
È **tua** questa valigia?   Is this suitcase **yours**?

They are also used without the article when they follow the noun. This happens only in certain fixed expressions:

Vieni a **casa mia**!   Come to **my house**!
È **colpa tua**!   It's **your fault**!

proprio

Proprio means 'one's own'. It is used with the definite article but without the possessive adjective:

È importante avere **la propria** camera   It's important to have **your own** room

un mio amico

The possessive adjective is used with the indefinite article with
the meaning 'one of my', 'one of your', etc.:

un **mio** amico   a friend **of mine**
un **tuo** amico   a friend **of yours**

Possessive adjectives with family members

Possessive adjectives are also used to show relationships between
people. When they are used with **madre**, **padre**, **fratello**, **sorella**,
moglie, and **marito**, the article is omitted:

Mia madre li conosce bene   My mother knows them well
gli amici di **mia** sorella   my sister's friends

But if these words are used in the plural, the article must be used.
It is also used with other words for relatives (including **mamma**,
papà, and **babbo**):

I miei fratelli sono tutti più grandi di me   **My** brothers are all
   older than me
Il mio nonno era di Verona   **My** grandfather was from Verona

Avoiding possessive adjectives

Italian tends to use possessive adjectives less than English. Where
it is obvious who the owner is, it is often preferable to use the
definite article on its own:

Ho perso **gli** occhiali   I've lost **my** glasses
Voglio vendere **la** macchina   I want to sell **my** car

We assume that this person wants to sell his or her own car, and
not someone else's.

Possessive adjectives are rarely used with parts of the body,
because it is usually clear from the context who the body part
belongs to:

Ha alzato **la** mano   He raised **his** hand
Chiudi **gli** occhi!   Close **your** eyes!

Instead of a possessive, a phrase with **a** or an indirect object
pronoun (**mi**, **ti**, **gli**, etc.) is often used:

Ho cambiato il pannolino **ai bimbi**   I changed the babies' nappies
Mi ha tirato i capelli   He pulled my hair
Ci ha rovinato la vacanza   It ruined our holiday
Mi fa male la pancia   My stomach hurts

When the person referred to by the subject of the sentence performs an action on himself or herself, Italian often uses a reflexive pronoun rather than a possessive adjective:

Mi sono messo le scarpe   I put on my shoes

Si è rotta la gamba   She's broken her leg

Si lavava le mani   He was washing his hands

Possessive pronouns

The possessives can also be used without a noun following if it is clear from the context what is being referred to. These forms are called *possessive pronouns*, and are identical to possessive adjectives:

Se non hai l'ombrello, prendi **il mio**   If you *don't* have an umbrella, take **my one**

Il suo appartamento è bello ma preferisco **il mio**   Her flat is nice, but I prefer **mine**

I miei, **i tuoi**, etc. means 'my family', 'your family', etc.:

Come stanno **i tuoi**?   How's **your family**?

Demonstratives

Demonstratives are words which are used to identify exactly which person, thing, etc. you are talking about. Demonstratives in English include **this** and **that**.

| Demonstrative adjectives

questo

Questo is used before nouns to mean 'this'. **Questo** has the following forms:

- **quest'** before a singular noun (masculine or feminine) beginning with a vowel:
  quest'appartamento   this flat
  quest'azienda   this firm

- **questo** before a masculine singular noun beginning with a consonant:
  questo camion   this lorry

- **questa** before a feminine singular noun beginning with a consonant:
  questa chiesa   this church

- **questi** before a masculine plural noun:
  questi fiori   these flowers

- **queste** before a feminine plural noun:
  queste montagne   these mountains

Questo can be reinforced by using **qui** or **qua** after the noun:
  questa casa **qui**   **this** house
  questi ragazzi **qua**   **these** kids

quello

Quello is used before nouns to mean 'that'. **Quello** has the following forms:

- **quell'** before a singular noun (masculine or feminine) beginning with a vowel:

  quell'appartamento   *that flat*

  quell'azienda   *that firm*

- **quello** before a masculine singular noun beginning with *z*, *ps*, *gn*, or *s* + another consonant:

  quello scherzo   *that joke*

- **quel** before a masculine singular noun beginning with any other consonant:

  quel film   *that film*

- **quella** before a feminine singular noun beginning with any consonant:

  quella zona   *that area*

- **quegli** before a masculine plural noun beginning with a vowel or *z*, *ps*, *gn*, or *s* + another consonant:

  quegli occhi   *those eyes*

- **quei** before a masculine plural noun beginning with any other consonant:

  quei ragazzi   *those boys*

- **quelle** before any feminine plural noun:

  quelle ragazze   *those girls*

Quello can be reinforced by using **lì** or **là** after the noun:

  quelle cartoline **là**   *those* postcards

| Demonstrative pronouns

questo/questa, quello/quella

Questo and **quello** can also take the place of a noun. They take the gender and number of the noun they are replacing.

These are the pronoun forms of **questo** and **quello**:

masculine singular	questo	quello
feminine singular	questa	quella
masculine plural	questi	quelli
feminine plural	queste	quelle

Questi sono più buoni di **quelli**   **These ones** are tastier than **those**

Qui, qua, lì, and **là** can be used after **questo** and **quello**:

Voglio **quello là**   I want **that one**

Mi piacciono **questi qua**   I like **these ones**

When used to refer to people, they can have a pejorative effect:

Chi è **quella là**?   Who's **she**?

Quello can be followed by an adjective:

La casa nuova è più grande di **quella vecchia**   Our new house is bigger than **the old one**

Preferisco **quelli rossi**   I prefer **the red ones**

It can be followed by **di**:

Preferisco l'acconciatura di Giulia a **quella di Simonetta**   I prefer Giulia's hairstyle to **Simonetta's**

I miei risultati sono migliori di **quelli dei miei amici**   My results are better than **my friends'**

It can also be followed by **che**:

Ho comprato una bicicletta nuova per sostituire **quella che è stata rubata**   I bought a new bicycle to replace **the one which** was stolen

questo, quello, ciò

Questo and **quello**, used in the masculine singular, can have a
neutral meaning. They are translated by 'this' and 'that':

Cos'è **quello**?   What's **that**?

Questo succede spesso   **This** often happens

Questo and **quello** can be replaced by **ciò**:

Non siamo sicuri di **ciò**   We're not sure of **that**

Ciò che, **quel che**, and **quello che** all mean 'that which' or 'what':

Ciò che dici è vero   **What** you say is true

Non puoi avere **tutto quello che** vuoi   You can't have **everything**
you want

Counting and measuring

Cardinal numbers

Cardinal numbers are the numbers used when counting. In English they are **one**, **two**, **three**, etc. These are the Italian cardinal numbers:

1	uno
2	due
3	tre
4	quattro
5	cinque
6	sei
7	sette
8	otto
9	nove
10	dieci
11	undici
12	dodici
13	tredici
14	quattordici
15	quindici
16	sedici
17	diciassette
18	diciotto
19	diciannove
20	venti
21	ventuno
22	ventidue
23	ventitré
24	ventiquattro
25	venticinque
26	ventisei

27	ventisette
28	ventotto
29	ventinove
30	trenta
40	quaranta
50	cinquanta
60	sessanta
70	settanta
80	ottanta
90	novanta
100	cento
101	centouno
102	centodue
103	centotré
108	centootto
200	duecento
300	trecento
1000	mille
2000	duemila
3000	tremila
10 000	diecimila
100 000	centomila
1 000 000	un milione
2 000 000	due milioni
1 000 000 000	un miliardo

In numbers, the plural of **mille** is **–mila**. It is only used in combination with other numbers.

> **Note:** When writing large numbers in figures, Italian uses a full stop (or a space), never a comma:
> 30.000   *30 000*
> 25.000.000   *25 000 000*

Counting things

The cardinal numbers are used to count things:

Ci sono rimaste **quattro** bottiglie di rosso e **due** di bianco
*There are **four** bottles of red wine and **two** bottles of white left over*

Ho **due** maschi e **una** femmina *I've got **two** boys and **one** girl*

One of something

One is **uno** when counting in a sequence. Before a noun, however, **un** is used in the masculine (**uno** before *z, ps, gn,* or *s* + another consonant) and **una** in the feminine (usually **un'** before a vowel):

un anno *one year*
una copia *one copy*
uno studente *one student*
un'unità *one unit*

Large numbers

When **un milione**, **un miliardo**, and multiples of these numbers are followed by a noun, **di** is used:

cinque **milioni di** euro *five **million** euros*

Approximate numbers

Italian uses the ending **–ina** with some numbers to show that they are approximate. Only certain numbers take this ending. The forms which are used are **una decina**, **una ventina**, **una trentina**, **una quarantina**, **una cinquantina**, **una sessantina**, **una settantina**, **un'ottantina**, and **una novantina**:

una quarantina di clienti *about forty customers*
una cinquantina di chilometri *about fifty kilometres*

Ne hanno comprato **una ventina** *They bought **about twenty** (of them)*

Cento and **mille** have their own forms **centinaio** and **migliaio**:
 un centinaio di metri quadrati *about a hundred square metres*

Centinaio and **migliaio** can be used in the plural (note their irregular plural forms **centinaia** and **migliaia**). **Milioni** and **miliardi** are also used in the same way:
 centinaia di lettere *hundreds of letters*
 migliaia di stelle *thousands of stars*
 miliardi di anni fa *billions of years ago*

ne with numbers

The pronoun **ne** ('of it' or 'of them') must be used when talking about numbers in cases where the objects that are being counted are not expressed. Compare these examples:
 Abbiamo trenta camere *We have thirty rooms*
 Ne abbiamo trenta *We have thirty (**of them**)*

! **Note:** For more information about **ne**, *see p. 46.*

Telephone numbers

Telephone numbers are said in a different way from English. The digits are grouped together in twos or threes:
 cinquantuno ventuno ottantuno *512181*
 trecentoquarantacinque sessantotto ventinove *345 6829*

0 in telephone numbers is always **zero**:
 zero zero trentanove *0039*

| Ordinal numbers

Ordinal numbers are used to talk about the order of things, for example in time or on a list. In English the ordinal numbers are **first**, **second**, **third**, etc. These are the Italian ordinal numbers:

1st	primo / prima
2nd	secondo / seconda
3rd	terzo / terza
4th	quarto / quarta
5th	quinto / quinta
6th	sesto / sesta
7th	settimo / settima
8th	ottavo / ottava
9th	nono / nona
10th	decimo / decima
11th	undicesimo / undicesima
12th	dodicesimo / dodicesima
13th	tredicesimo / tredicesima
14th	quattordicesimo / quattordicesima
15th	quindicesimo / quindicesima
16th	sedicesimo / sedicesima
17th	diciassettesimo / diciassettesima
18th	diciottesimo / diciottesima
19th	diciannovesimo / diciannovesima
20th	ventesimo / ventesima
21st	ventunesimo / ventunesima
22nd	ventiduesimo / ventiduesima
23rd	ventitreesimo / ventitreesima
24th	ventiquattresimo / ventiquattresima
25th	venticinquesimo / venticinquesima
26th	ventiseiesimo / ventiseiesima
27th	ventisettesimo / ventisettesima
28th	ventottesimo / ventottesima
29th	ventinovesimo / ventinovesima
30th	trentesimo / trentesima
40th	quarantesimo / quarantesima
50th	cinquantesimo / cinquantesima
60th	sessantesimo / sessantesima
70th	settantesimo / settantesima
80th	ottantesimo / ottantesima
90th	novantesimo / novantesima

100th	centesimo/centesima
101st	centunesimo/centunesima
102nd	centoduesimo/centoduesima
200th	duecentesimo/duecentesima
300th	trecentesimo/trecentesima
1000th	millesimo/millesima
2000th	duemillesimo/duemillesima
3000th	tremillesimo/tremillesima
10 000th	decimillesimo/decimillesima
100 000th	centomillesimo/centomillesima
1 000 000th	milionesimo/milionesima
2 000 000th	duemilionesimo/duemilionesima
1 000 000 000th	miliardesimo/miliardesima

| Fractions, decimals, and percentages

Fractions are formed by taking the masculine form of the ordinal number. The only exception is **a half**:

un mezzo   *a half*
un terzo   *a third*
due terzi   *two thirds*
un quarto   *a quarter*
tre quarti   *three quarters*
un centesimo   *a hundredth*

Italian also has another word for 'half', **metà**. It is used when talking about half of a quantity or half of a number, and is usually used with the definite article **la**:

Ha venduto **la metà** delle sue azioni   *She sold **half** of her shares*
Mi dia **la metà** di quello   *Give me **half** of that*
È **metà** inglese, **metà** italiana   *She's **half** English, **half** Italian*

In decimal fractions, the decimal point is replaced by the comma:
2,5 (say due virgola cinque)   *2·5*

Percentages are expressed by using **per cento**. This is used with the definite article **il**:

nel cinquanta per cento dei casi   *in **50%** of cases*

The partitive article

The partitive article in Italian is a small word which is placed before nouns to express an indefinite number or quantity. It can be expressed in English by 'some', but sometimes it is not translated at all:

Compra **del** miele   Buy **some** honey
Ci sono **delle** differenze fra i due quadri   *There are differences between the two paintings*

The form of the partitive article depends on the gender and the first letter of the noun which follows:

● **dello** followed by a masculine singular beginning with *z*, *ps*, *gn*, or *s* + another consonant:

dello zucchero   *some sugar*

● **del** followed by a masculine singular beginning with any other consonant:

del dentifricio   *some toothpaste*

● **della** followed by a feminine singular beginning with a consonant:

della tinta   *some paint*

● **dell'** followed by a masculine or feminine singular beginning with a vowel:

dell'olio   *some oil*
dell'acqua   *some water*

● **degli** followed by a masculine plural beginning with a vowel or with *z*, *ps*, *gn*, or *s* + another consonant:

degli avanzi   *some leftovers*
degli zucchini   *some courgettes*

● **dei** followed by a masculine plural beginning with any other consonant:

dei gamberetti   *some shrimps*

● **delle** followed by a feminine plural:

delle acciughe   *some anchovies*

! **Note:** If another word comes between the article and the noun, the form of the article depends on the first letter of the word which follows the article:
Ha fatto **degli** ottimi lavori   *He's done **some** excellent jobs*

The partitive article is frequently omitted in speech:

Abbiamo mangiato gamberi, calamari e cozze   We had prawns, squid, and mussels

and can sometimes be replaced by the definite article:

Vado a comprare il pane   I'm going to buy bread

It is never used after **di**:

l'odore di pesce   the smell of fish

and is not normally used after any preposition:

Ha fatto un dolce con fichi e yogurt   He made a dessert with figs and yoghurt

I Expressions of quantity

How much?

To ask how much of something, use **quanto...?** The feminine form **quanta** is used with feminine nouns:

Quanto tempo abbiamo?   **How much** time have we got?

Quanta margarina ci vuole?   **How much** margarine do you need?

Indefinite quantities

There are some common words and expressions which are used to refer to indefinite quantities. They are all used with a singular noun (for plural uses, see below):

poco/poca	little, not much
molto/molta	much, a lot of
parecchio/parecchia	quite a lot of
tanto/tanta	much, a lot of
troppo/troppa	too much

Mettici **poco** sale   Don't put **much** salt in

C'era **parecchio** traffico in città   There was **quite a lot of** traffic in town

C'è rimasta **molta** colla   There's **a lot of** glue left over

Mangi **troppa** cioccolata   You eat **too much** chocolate

Here are some useful ways of talking about indefinite quantities using common phrases:

un po' di sale   **a little** salt

un sacco di tempo   **loads of** time

| Expressions of number

How many?

To ask how many of something, use **quanti...?** The feminine form **quante** is used with feminine nouns:

Quanti figli avete?   **How many** children have you got?

Quante sigarette fuma al giorno?   **How many** cigarettes do you smoke a day?

Quanti ce ne sono?   **How many** (of them) are there?

Indefinite numbers

There are some common words which are used to refer to indefinite numbers. The following group are used in the plural:

parecchi/parecchie   several
pochi/poche   few, not many
alcuni/alcune   some
molti/molte   many
tanti/tante   a lot of
troppi/troppe   too many

They can all be followed directly by a plural noun:

Parecchi studenti sono rimasti a casa   **Several** students stayed at home

Mancano **pochi** giorni al mio compleanno   There are **not many** days until my birthday

Ha letto **alcuni** brani del suo nuovo libro   He read **some** passages from his new book

È successo **molti** anni fa   It happened **many** years ago

Abbiamo avuto **tanti** problemi   We had **lots of** problems

Devo prendere **troppe** decisioni   I have to make **too many** decisions

Molti and **tanti** have absolute superlative forms, which are more emphatic:

Ho fatto **moltissime** telefonate   I made **loads of** telephone calls

Ci sono **tantissimi** italiani in Australia   There are **loads of** Italians in Australia

All of these words can also be used as pronouns. They can be used on their own, with **di**, or with **ne**:

Alcuni di noi vorrebbero smettere *Some of us would like to stop*
Molti hanno avuto la stessa impressione **Many** *had the same impression*
Ne ho visti **tanti** *I've seen **so many** (of them)*

qualche, ogni, ciascun/ciascuna

The following words have a plural meaning, but are singular in form. They must be followed by a singular noun:

qualche	*a few*
ogni	*every*
ciascun/ciascuna	*each*

! Note: Ciascun/ciascuna has the same endings as **un/una** when used before a noun (*see p. 19*).

Hanno avuto **qualche** contrattempo *They had **a few** hiccups*
Ogni anno diventa più difficile trovarli *It gets harder to find them **every year***
ciascuna lingua dell'Unione europea **each** *language of the European Union*

They have these forms when they are used as pronouns (they are all singular). They can be used on their own, with **di**, or with **ne**:

qualcuno/qualcuna	*a few*
ognuno/ognuna	*every one*
ciascuno/ciascuna	*each one*

Ne ho mangiato **qualcuno** *I've eaten **a few** (of them)*
Qualcuno la pensa così **Some people** *think that way*
Ognuno di loro ha dato la sua opinione **Every one** *of them gave their opinion*
C'erano due regali per **ciascuno** *There were two presents for **each one***

Qualcuno, **ognuno**, and **ciascuno** also have special meanings.
Qualcuno means 'somebody':

C'è **qualcuno** alla porta   There's *somone* at the door

and both **ognuno** and **ciascuno** mean 'everybody':

Ognuno deve fare come meglio crede   *Everybody* must do as he
or she thinks best

Se **ciascuno** di noi avesse la macchina, sarebbe un guaio   If
everybody had a car it would be a problem

Here are some useful ways of talking about indefinite numbers
using common phrases:

un sacco di problemi   **loads of** problems
una barca di gente   **masses of** people

| *ne* with indefinite quantities

The pronoun **ne** ('of it' or 'of them') must be used when talking about quantities in cases where the thing that is being measured is not expressed. Compare these examples:

Abbiamo due etti di salame   *We have 200g of salami*

Ne abbiamo due etti   *We have 200g (**of it**)*

For more information about **ne**, *see p. 167.*

| *tutto*

Tutto, like **all** in English, is followed by a definite article. It is never followed by **di**, however:

Hanno mangiato **tutto** il salame   *They ate **all (of)** the salami*

Tutto is also used with the meaning of 'everything':

Hanno mangiato **tutto**   *They ate **everything***

| *tutti/tutte*

In the plural, **tutti/tutte** is used with a plural noun (or pronoun) or on its own. Like **all** in English, **tutti** can be followed by a definite article. It is never followed by **di**, however:

Tutte le sedie sono sparite   *All (**of**) the chairs have disappeared*

Tutti noi abbiamo vissuto quest'esperienza   *All **of** us have had that experience*

It can also be used after a verb:

Sono **tutti** ladri!   *They're **all** thieves!*

Tutti is also used with the meaning of 'everybody'. Unlike **everybody** in English, it is plural, and adjectives and verbs which are used with it must agree with it:

Tutti sono d'accordo   ***Everybody** agrees*

Ha pagato da bere a **tutti**   *He stood **everybody** a drink*

| Measurements

To ask about the size or weight of somebody or something,
quanto is used. When giving a measurement, the adjective is
placed before the number.

● Length:

'Quanto è lunga la corda?' 'È lunga cinque metri.'   'How long is
the rope?' 'It's five metres long.'

● Height:

'Quanto sei alto?' 'Sono alto un metro e ottanta.'   'How tall are
you?' 'I'm six feet tall.'

● Distance:

Quanto dista Vicenza da Verona?   How far is it from Vicenza to
Verona?

Abitiamo a quindici chilometri da Brighton   We live fifteen
kilometres from Brighton

● Width:

'Quanto è largo il fiume?' 'È largo quindici metri.'   'How wide is
the river?' 'It's fifteen metres wide.'

● Depth:

'Quanto è profondo il lago?' 'È profondo quattro metri.'   'How
deep is the lake?' 'It's four metres deep.'

● Weight:

'Quanto pesa?' 'Pesa quattro chili.'   'How much does it weigh?'
'It weighs four kilos.'

| Prices

Names of currencies are used in the plural where appropriate:

un dollaro   *one dollar*

trecentomila sterline   *£300 000*

Note that **euro** does not change in the plural:

cinquanta euro   *50 euros*

The currency symbol is written before the figure, as in English:

€249

To ask the price of something, say **quanto viene...?** or **quanto costa...?**

'Quanto **vengono** le cartoline?' '**Vengono** 50 centesimi.'   *'How much **are** the postcards?' 'They're 50 cents.'*

To ask what the total is, use **Quant'è?**:

Quant'è in totale?   *How much is it altogether?*

To talk about the price of a certain quantity of something, use the preposition **a**:

Quanto costa **al** litro?   *How much is it **a** litre?*

Costa cinque dollari **al** litro   *It costs five dollars **a** litre*

Soldi is the most common word for 'money'. Note that it is plural (a **soldo** is a coin), so adjectives and verbs which go with it must agree:

Quanti soldi hai?   *How much money have you got?*

Abbiamo pochi soldi   *We haven't got much money*

I soldi **sono** finiti   *The money **is** finished*

Talking about time

Days, months, and dates

The days of the week

All the days of the week are masculine except **domenica**. Note that Italian uses small letters, not capitals, for the names of the days:

lunedì	Monday
martedì	Tuesday
mercoledì	Wednesday
giovedì	Thursday
venerdì	Friday
sabato	Saturday
domenica	Sunday

To say that something happens on a particular day, when this is a one-off occurrence, Italian simply uses the name of the day without any preposition:

Ci vediamo lunedì   *See you on Monday*

If it is a regular occurrence, Italian uses the definite article:

Il lunedì gioco a bridge   *I play bridge on Mondays*
Mi alzo sempre tardi **la** domenica   *I always get up late on Sundays*

Ogni can also be used:

ogni lunedì   *every Monday*

Note the following common phrases used with days of the week:

lunedì sera   *on Monday evening*
martedì **scorso**   *last Tuesday*
domenica **prossima**   *next Sunday*
giovedì **sul presto**   *early on Thursday*

Note these ways of talking about parts of the day:

il mattino/**la** mattina   **in the** morning
nel pomeriggio   **in the** afternoon
la sera   **in the** evening
di notte   **at** night

The months of the year

As with the days of the week, do not use capitals to spell the names of the months in Italian. All the months are masculine:

gennaio	January
febbraio	February
marzo	March
aprile	April
maggio	May
giugno	June
luglio	July
agosto	August
settembre	September
ottobre	October
novembre	November
dicembre	December

Note the following common phrases used with the months:

a maggio   **in** May
ad aprile   **in** April
verso la metà di maggio   around the middle of May
a fine giugno   at the end of June

Seasons

These are the names of the seasons in Italian. Note that **estate** is feminine:

la primavera   spring
l'estate   summer
l'autunno   autumn
l'inverno   winter

To say 'in spring', 'in summer', etc., the following forms are used:

a primavera   in spring
in estate/d'estate   in summer
in autunno   in autumn
in inverno/d'inverno   in winter

The preposition **a** is used with other periods of the year such as Christmas and Easter:

a Natale   at Christmas
a Pasqua   at Easter

Dates

To ask the date:

Quanti ne abbiamo oggi?   What's today's date?

Italian uses the cardinal numbers, not the ordinal numbers, when giving dates (*see p. 156*):

È il **tredici** febbraio   It's the **thirteenth** of February

The exception is the first of the month, when **primo** is used:

il **primo** maggio   the **first** of May

'On' is not translated when giving dates:

il primo maggio   on May 1
il due maggio   on May 2
l'otto maggio   on May 8

Years

Years in Italian are pronounced as if they were normal numbers:
  1968 (say millenovecentosessantotto)
  2005 (say duemilacinque)

The article is used when talking about years:
  Il 1995 è stato un anno incredibile   *1995 was an incredible year*

Shortened forms of some years are possible:
  l'ottantacinque   *'85*

When giving the date in full, **il** is not used before the year:
  l'undici settembre millenovecentocinquantotto   *11 September 1958*

To say 'in' a particular year, use **nel**:
  È nata **nel** 2001   *She was born in 2001*

Centuries

There are two ways to refer to centuries in Italian. The first is as in English **the 20th century**. The second is similar to the English **the 1900s** and can be used only for the centuries from the 13th to the 20th. It is used especially when talking about history or art:
  il ventunesimo secolo   *the 21st century*
  nel Quattrocento   *in the 15th century*

Decades

To specify a decade, Italian uses **gli anni...**:
  gli anni novanta   *the 90s*

Telling the time

Saying what time it is

To ask what time it is, use:
  Che ore sono? *What time is it?*

The answer is usually **sono le...**:
  Sono le tre *It's three o'clock*

If it is one o'clock, or a time like midnight or noon, **è** is used:
  È l'una *It's one o'clock*
  È mezzanotte *It's midnight*
  È mezzogiorno *It's noon*

To express minutes after the hour, use **e**:
  Sono le otto **e** cinque *It's five past eight*
  Sono le otto **e** dieci *It's ten past eight*
  Sono le otto **e** un quarto *It's quarter past eight*
  Sono le otto **e** venti *It's twenty past eight*
  Sono le otto **e** venticinque *It's twenty-five past eight*
  Sono le otto **e** mezzo *It's half past eight*

The same system can be used for times between half past and the hour:
  Sono le otto **e** trentacinque *It's eight thirty-five*
  Sono le otto **e** quarantacinque *It's eight forty-five*

Alternatively, **meno** can be used to say how many minutes there are to go before the hour:
  Sono le nove **meno** dieci *It's ten to nine*
  Sono le nove **meno** un quarto *It's quarter to nine*

Another way uses the verb **mancare**. It is always used in the singular:
  Manca un quarto alle nove *It's a quarter to nine*
  Mancava venti alle nove *It was twenty to nine*

Saying what time something happens

To ask what time something happens, use **a che ora...?**:

   A che ora ti sei alzato? *What time did you get up?*

The answer is usually **alle...**:

   alle nove *at nine o'clock*

   alle quattro e mezzo *at half past four*

   alle nove meno dieci *at ten to nine*

'At one o'clock' is **all'una**:

   all'una e mezzo *at half past one*

For 'at midnight' and 'at noon' **a** is used:

   a mezzanotte *at midnight*

   a mezzogiorno *at noon*

   a mezzogiorno e mezzo *at half past twelve*

The 24-hour clock is used more in Italian than in English, for example when making appointments:

   L'appuntamento è alle 15.30 (say quindici e trenta) *The appointment is at 3.30 pm*

To talk about approximate times, use **verso**:

   Mi sono alzato **verso** le undici *I got up **at about** eleven*

and **in punto** for precise times:

   Sono le quattro **in punto** *It's **exactly** four o'clock*

Italian always uses the preposition **a** (or another preposition like **verso** or **dopo**) even where it is often omitted in English:

   A che ora è successo? ***What time** did it happen?*

   Arriveranno **verso le cinque** *They'll be arriving **about five***

Past time

To specify how long ago something happened, use **fa**:

Quanto tempo fa è successo?   **How long ago** did it happen?
Ci siamo conosciuti tre anni **fa**   We met three years **ago**
una settimana **fa**   a week **ago**
poco tempo **fa**   not long **ago**

The following expressions are useful for talking about the past:

la settimana **scorsa**   **last** week
martedì **scorso**   **last** Tuesday
ieri mattina/sera   yesterday morning/evening

Future time

To specify how far in the future an action is, use **fra** or **tra**. **Fra** and **tra** are usually interchangeable, but it is best to avoid combinations that are difficult to say, like **tra trentatré anni**:

fra tre giorni   **in** three days' **time**
Lo farò **tra** cinque minuti   I'll do it in five minutes
Ce ne andiamo **fra** una settimana   We're leaving **in** a week
Arrivo **fra poco**   I'm coming **soon**

Note these useful ways of talking about plans and intentions for the future, **avere intenzione di** + infinitive and **pensare di** + infinitive:

Ho intenzione di smettere di fumare   **I intend to** stop smoking
Penso di andarci   I think I'll go

Italian uses the expression **stare per** + infinitive to give the idea of an imminent action:

Sto per partire   I'm just about to leave
Sta per cadere!   It's going to fall!

The following expressions are useful for talking about the future:

l'anno **prossimo**/la settimana **prossima**   **next** year/week
a partire da domani   **starting from** tomorrow
entro sabato   **by** Saturday
d'ora in poi   from now on

| Age

'how old...?'

Italian uses the verb **avere** to talk about ages. To ask someone's age, use **quanti anni...?**:

Quanti anni hai? *How old are you?*

The word **anni** is always used in the answer:

Ha quarantadue **anni** *He's forty-two (years old)*

Before the word **anni**, the numbers 18, 20, 30, 40, etc. up to a hundred replace their final vowel with an apostrophe:

La casa ha cent'anni *The house is a hundred years old*

To say 'twenty-year-old', 'thirty-year-old', etc. Italian uses the ending –**enne** added to the number. Note that this system is not used for numbers below 11:

una ragazza **diciottenne** *an eighteen-year-old girl*
i tredicenni *thirteen-year-olds*

An alternative which always works is to use the preposition **di**:

una ragazza **di diciott'anni** *an eighteen-year-old girl*
ragazzi **di tredici anni** *thirteen-year-olds*

Comparing ages

Note these ways of comparing ages:

Elisa ha tre anni di meno *Elisa's three years younger*
Gabriele ha cinque anni più di Andrea *Gabriele's five years older than Andrea*

Approximate ages

Note these expressions for talking about approximate ages:

È sulla cinquantina *He's about fifty*
Ha appena superato i sessanta *She's just over sixty*

Sequence

The following conjunctions are used to show the specific order in which events happen. Note that Italian usually uses a future tense with these conjunctions when referring to future actions, where English uses the present tense. Similarly, where Italian uses the future perfect, English uses the present perfect. Examples are given below.

quando

Quando is used to specify the time that something happens. It can imply that two actions happen more or less at the same time:

Quando si arrabbia, diventa rosso in faccia   *His face goes red* **when** *he gets angry*

Quando cambieremo casa, faremo una festa   **When** *we move house we'll have a party*

or it can imply that one action happens before the other:

Quando ha finito di parlare, ha buttato giù il telefono   **When** *she finished talking, she slammed the phone down*

Quando sarà grande farà il calciatore   *He'll be a footballer* **when** *he grows up*

Quando avremo finito di rifare la casa, costruiremo una piscina   **When** *we've finished renovating the house we'll build a swimming pool*

> **Note:** The future or the future perfect is used after **quando** when referring to a future action.

Note the use of **una volta**. It is usually followed by a past participle:

Una volta sposati cambieremo casa   *We'll move* **once** *we're married*

dopo

Dopo can be an adverb:

Lo farò **dopo**   *I'll do it* **afterwards**

or a preposition, followed by a noun:

Lo farò **dopo** pranzo   *I'll do it* **after** *lunch*

It can also be used with **che** with a verb:

Dopo che ha spiegato la situazione, tutti si sono calmati
After he explained the situation, everyone calmed down

Dopo che avrai messo in ordine la camera, potrai uscire   **After**
you've tidied your room, you can go out

> **!** Note: The future or the future perfect is used after **dopo che** when referring to
> a future action.

When the subject in both parts of the sentence is the same, it is
possible to use the past infinitive after **dopo**. The past infinitive
consists of **avere** (usually shortened to **aver**) or **essere** followed by
the past participle:

dopo aver lavorato tutto il giorno   **after** working all day

Dopo averci pensato un po', abbiamo detto di no   **After**
thinking about it for a bit we said no

Dopo can also be followed directly by the past participle:

dopo mangiato   **after** eating

appena

Appena is used to say that an action has just happened:

Ci siamo **appena** alzati   We've **just** got up

It also means 'as soon as'. In more formal Italian it is preceded by
non, but this does not affect the meaning:

Non appena saremo in possesso dei documenti, spediremo la
merce   **As soon as** we are in possession of the documents we
will dispatch the goods

Non appena avranno finito di cantare, cominceranno i fuochi
d'artificio   **As soon as** they've finished singing, the fireworks
will start

> **!** Note: The future or the future perfect is used after **appena** when referring to a
> future action.

Appena can also be followed directly by the past participle:

Chiamami **appena** arrivata   Call me **as soon as you arrive**

prima

Prima is an adverb:

Dovevi pensarci **prima**! *You should have thought about it before!*

It is used with **di** followed by a noun or a pronoun:

Mi sono svegliato **prima di** te *I woke up before you*
prima delle otto *before eight o'clock*

Prima di can also be used before an infinitive:

prima di andare a letto *before going to bed*

Prima che is used with a verb. The verb is usually in the present subjunctive when referring to the future, and the past subjunctive when referring to the past:

Devo lavare i piatti **prima che** tornino *I've got to wash up before they come back*
prima che ci fossero i computer *before computers existed*

mentre

Mentre indicates that two actions are going on at the same time:

Tu taglia le verdure **mentre** io metto l'acqua *You cut the vegetables while I put the water on*

! **Note:** *See p. 204 for another use of* **mentre**.

Note the expression **nel frattempo**:

Nel frattempo avevano pulito tutta la casa *In the meantime they had cleaned the whole house*

finché

Finché means 'for as long as':

Divertiti **finché** dura il bel tempo   Enjoy yourself **for as long as** the good weather lasts

When it is used with a negative verb it means 'until'. Note that although the verb is negative in Italian, it is translated by an affirmative verb in English:

Canta **finché non** si addormenta   Sing **until** he falls asleep

> **!** **Note:** The future or the future perfect is used after **finché** when referring to a
> future action:
> **Finché non** arriveranno non possiamo fare nulla   We can't do anything **until** they get here
> **Finché non** avrai lavato i piatti, non puoi guardare la tele   You can't watch TV **until** you've done the washing-up

The **non** is sometimes omitted in informal conversation:

Aspettiamo qua **finché** smette di piovere   Let's wait here **until** it stops raining

Duration

Duration of a past or future action

Per is used to show the duration of an action:

Abbiamo ballato **per** ore   We danced **for** hours

but it can very often be omitted:

Abbiamo aspettato un'ora   We waited **for** an hour

To ask the question 'how long...?', use **quanto tempo** or simply **quanto**:

Quanto (tempo) ci vuoi stare?   **How long** do you want to stay?

Duration of a continuing action

When the action is still continuing in the present, Italian differs from English. The present tense is used with the preposition **da**:

Vivo in Italia **da** sette anni   I've lived in Italy **for** seven years (i.e. and I still live there now)

Compare:

Sono vissuto in Italia **per** sette anni   I lived in Italy **for** seven years (i.e. but I don't live there now)

To ask the question 'how long...?', use **quant'è che...?** with the present tense:

Quant'è che studi l'italiano?   **How long have you been studying** Italian?

Some more examples:

Li conosco **da** tre mesi   I've known them **for** three months

Lavoro qui **da** anni   I've been working here **for** years

The same structure is used to specify the *starting point* of an action that is still continuing in the present:

Vive in questa casa **dal** 1943   She's been living in this house **since** 1943

Siamo in piedi **dalle** sei   We've been up **since** 6 o'clock

If the focus is on a point of time in the past rather than on the present, the imperfect tense is used:

Vivevo in Italia da sette anni   **I'd been living** in Italy for seven years

Viveva in questa casa dal 1943   **She'd been living** in this house since 1943

Time taken

To say how long something takes, Italian uses **ci vuole** (**ci vogliono** in the plural):

Quanto tempo **ci vuole**?   How long *does it take*?

Ci vogliono cinque minuti   *It takes* five minutes

To say how long somebody takes to do something, **mettere** + **ci** is used:

Quanto tempo **ci hai messo**?   How long *did you take*?

Ci ho messo un'ora   *I took* an hour

Note these ways of specifying duration:

'Quanto **dura**?' '**Dura** due ore.'   'How long *does it last*?' '*It lasts* two hours.'

L'ho fatto **in** cinque minuti   *I did it in* five minutes

Frequency

Specifying frequency

To ask 'how often...?', Italian uses the following construction
with the preposition **a** with the definite article **il/la**, etc.:

Quante volte **alla** settimana?   *How many times a week?*
Quante volte **al** giorno?   *How many times a day?*

> **Note:** It is also possible to say **ogni quanto...?** or **quanto spesso...?**:
> **Ogni quanto/Quanto spesso** vengono?   *How often do they come?*

To specify the frequency, **a** is used in the answer:

due volte **alla** settimana   *twice a week*
una volta **al** giorno   *once a day*

Other constructions are possible:

Vengono **tutte le settimane**   *They come every week*
Lo faccio **ogni anno**   *I do it every year*
Lo pulisco **ogni tre mesi**   *I clean it every three months*
Mi chiama **ogni tanto**   *He calls me every so often*

Adverbs of frequency

Adverbs such as **mai, spesso, sempre**, etc. can also be used to talk
about frequency. They are usually placed after the main verb, or
between the auxiliary and the past participle in compound tenses:

Succede **spesso**   *It often happens*
Non esco **mai** la domenica   *I never go out on Sundays*
Devo **sempre** comprargli il giornale   *I always have to buy a paper for him*
Ho **sempre** detto la verità   *I've always told the truth*

Di solito usually comes at the beginning of the sentence:

Di solito parla poco   *She doesn't usually say much*

I How much an hour, a day, etc.

When talking about speed, rates of pay, etc. the preposition **a** is used:

Quanto guadagni **all'**ora?   How much do you earn **an** hour?

tremila euro **al** mese   three thousand euros **a** month

duecento chilometri **all'**ora   two hundred kilometres **an** hour

Talking about places

Countries, regions, and continents

The names of countries are usually used with the definite article:

L'Italia fa parte dell'Unione europea   *Italy is a member of the European Union*

The exception is with the preposition **in**:

in Inghilterra   *in England*

'in' and 'to' a country

In is used in Italian for both 'in' and 'to' in English. When 'in' is used, the article is generally omitted:

Vivono **in** Italia   *They live in Italy*

Sono andati **in** Cina   *They went **to** China*

È nata **in** Messico   *She was born in Mexico*

Siamo andati **in** Brasile   *We went **to** Brazil*

An exception to this is when the name of the country is plural:

Vivo **negli** Stati Uniti   *I live **in the** United States*

or if it includes a word which indicates the type of state it is, for example **Repubblica** or **Unione**:

Vive **nella** Repubblica Ceca   *She lives **in the** Czech Republic*

Sono andati **nell'**ex Unione Sovietica   *They went **to the** former Soviet Union*

Regions

Italian regions (including the islands of Sicily, **Sicilia**, and Sardinia, **Sardegna**) are treated in the same way as countries, whether they are masculine or feminine:

È nato **in** Sicilia   *He was born **in** Sicily*

Andiamo **in** Veneto   *We're going **to** Veneto*

Lazio is an exception:

Ho passato un mese **nel** Lazio   *I spent a month **in** Lazio*

Regions of other countries (including states of the USA and counties of Britain) which are feminine are also treated in the same way as countries:

Vive **in** California   *She lives **in** California*
Vado **in** Cornovaglia   *I'm going **to** Cornwall*

If the name of the region is masculine, however, **nel** may be used instead of **in**. With masculine names of counties, **nel** is always used:

Sono andati **nel/in** Texas   *They went **to** Texas*
Vivevamo **nel** Kent   *We lived **in** Kent*

I Towns and cities

Names of towns and cities are almost always feminine. They are always used without the definite article, with the exception of a few which have the article as part of their name:

C'è un treno per la Spezia   *There's a train for La Spezia*

With **di**, **a**, **da**, and **su**, the pronoun combines with the definite article:

Vanno **alla** Spezia   *They're going **to La** Spezia*
Arrivano **dal** Cairo   *They're arriving **from** Cairo*

'in' and 'to' a town or city

A (or **ad** before a vowel) is used in Italian for both 'in' and 'to' in English:

Vivono **a** Parma   *They live **in** Parma*
Sono andati **ad** Assisi   *They went **to** Assisi*

Origins

Nationality

To say where something comes from, the verb **venire** + **da** is used:

I pomodori **vengono dalla** Spagna   *The tomatoes* **come from** *Spain*

But when talking about people, it is more common to use the adjective derived from the name of the country. Note that the adjective does not have a capital letter:

Sono **irlandese**   *I'm* **Irish**
Sono **scozzesi**   *They're* **from Scotland**

Exactly the same forms are used for the inhabitants of the country:

gli scozzesi   *the Scots*
due irlandesi   *two Irishmen*
una tedesca   *a German woman*

> **! Note:** The Italian word for 'British' is **britannico**, although **inglese** is more widely used. Note that there is no word in Italian for 'the British': **gli inglesi** is the only alternative.

It is also possible to use the preposition **di** to say where somebody or something comes from:

una nave **della** Croazia   *a Croatian ship*

Towns and cities

To specify the town or city that someone comes from, it is possible to use the verb **essere** + **di**:

Sono **di** Napoli   *I'm* **from** *Naples*
Siamo **di** Edimburgo   *We're* **from** *Edinburgh*

It is also possible to use the adjective derived from the name of the town. Note that there is no capital letter:

Sono tutti **fiorentini**   *They're all* **from Florence**

Exactly the same forms are used for the inhabitants of the town:

un pisano   *a Pisan*
i dublinesi   *Dubliners*

I Directions

These are the points of the compass in Italian. They are all masculine:

il nord   north
l'est   east
il sud   south
l'ovest   west
il **sud** della Francia   the **south** of France
i paesi dell'**est** europeo   **East** European countries

Intermediate points are formed as in English:

È nel **nordest** della Scozia   It's in the **north-east** of Scotland

To specify a direction, the preposition **a** is used:

Si dirigevano **ad** ovest   They were heading west

A is also used with **destra** and **sinistra**:

Gira **a** destra al semaforo   Turn right at the traffic lights

Italian often uses the adjectives **settentrionale**, **orientale**, **meridionale**, and **occidentale** instead of the names of the points of the compass:

l'Italia settentrionale   northern Italy
la Germania orientale   eastern Germany
l'Italia meridionale   southern Italy
la Germania occidentale   western Germany

Functional language

The functions of a language are the things that it is used for, such as asking for things and talking about possibility. The other chapters in this book have dealt with the *forms* of the language: tenses, plurals, and so on. This chapter looks at the problem from a different angle and examines how to achieve certain aims and express certain concepts using the grammatical forms that have been covered. As well as looking at the grammatical ways of performing certain functions, we also suggest alternative ways, using common words and phrases to achieve the same aims.

Interacting with people

In order to to carry out certain interactions with other people, very little grammar is necessary. When asking for something, for example, you can just say the name of it:

un gelato al limone!   *a lemon ice cream!*

But Italian has a variety of ways of performing functions such as asking for things and making offers and invitations, and many of these ways use grammar as a powerful tool.

Asking for things

volere

Volere is used to make requests. It can be followed by a direct object or the infinitive:

Voglio un gelato   **I want** *an ice cream*
Vogliamo dormire   **We want** *to sleep*

These requests are not particularly polite. To form polite requests, **volere** is used in the conditional (*see p. 94* for more information about the forms of **volere** in the conditional):

Vorrei un caffè   **I'd like** *a coffee*
Vorremmo prenotare due posti   **We'd like** *to book two seats*

dare

The verb **dare** is also used to ask for things:

Mi dà cinque panini? *Can you give me five rolls, please?*

It can also be used in the imperative. It is less abrupt in Italian than its form might suggest to an English speaker:

Mi dia cinque panini! *Five rolls, please!*

Getting people to do things

The imperative

To ask someone to do something, the most direct way is to use the imperative (*see p. 100*):

Passami lo zucchero! *Pass me the sugar!*

The present tense

The present tense can also be used, which sounds less abrupt:

Mi **passi** lo zucchero? *Can you pass me the sugar?*

Ci **porta** il conto? *Can you bring us the bill?*

potere

Potere is used for greater politeness:

Può chiamarci un taxi, per favore? *Can you call us a taxi, please?*

dispiacere

Another polite form is **ti dispiace...?** (informal) or **le dispiace...?** (formal). It is followed by the infinitive:

Ti dispiace chiudere la finestra? *Would you mind closing the window?*

Le dispiace cambiarmi cento euro? *Would you mind changing a hundred euros for me?*

volere

Volere che... is a very direct way of telling someone to do something:

Voglio che tu mi dica la verità   *I want you to tell me the truth*

! Note: The subjunctive is used after **volere che**.

The conditional form of **volere** is slightly less direct. The imperfect subjunctive must be used:

Vorrei che cambiasse l'olio   *I'd like you to change the oil*

Suggestions

dovere

Dovere is used in the conditional to express the idea of 'ought to' or 'should' (*see p. 94* for more information about the forms of **dovere** in the conditional):

Dovresti accettare la loro offerta   **You should** *accept their offer*

The imperative

Using the imperative is a way of making a stronger suggestion:

Accetta la loro offerta!   **Accept** *their offer!*

To make suggestions when you are part of a group, the first person plural imperative can be used:

Andiamo a casa!   **Let's go** *home!*

! Note: The following expressions are also used to make suggestions:
Si va a casa?   **Shall** *we go home?*
Perché non si va a casa?   *Why* **don't** *we go home?*
Che ne dici di andare a casa?   **How about** *going home?*

Offers

dovere

Dovere is used to make polite offers:
  Ti **devo** sbucciare le patate?   **Shall I** peel the potatoes for you?

The present tense

It is also possible simply to use the present tense:
  Ti **sbuccio** le patate?   **Shall I peel** the potatoes for you?

potere

Note the use of **potere** in these expressions:
  Posso fare qualcosa?   **Can I** do something?
  Possiamo essere di aiuto?   **Can we** be of any help?

volere

Volere can be used to offer things, as well as to offer to do
something:
  Vuoi qualcosa da bere?   **Would you like** a drink?
  Vuoi che sbucci le patate?   Would you like me to peel the
  potatoes?

  ! Note: The subjunctive is used after **volere che**.

The conditional of **volere** has a more polite effect:
  Che colore **vorrebbe**?   What colour **would you like**?

Invitations

volere

Volere is commonly used to make invitations:

Volete venire a cena sabato? *Do you want to come for dinner on Saturday?*

The conditional of **volere**, as usual, is more polite:

Vorreste venire a cena sabato? *Would you like to come for dinner on Saturday?*

> **Note: Prego** is used with the imperative to make invitations:
> Si accomodi, **prego!** *Sit down, please!*

ti va di...?

Note the expression **ti va di...?**:

Ti va di andare al cinema? *Do you fancy going to the cinema?*

Permission

potere

To ask permission to do something, **potere** is used:

Posso venire con te? *Can I come with you?*

Si può entrare? *Can we come in?*

The conditional of **potere** expresses a higher degree of politeness (*see p. 94* for more information about the forms of **potere** in the conditional):

Potrei fare un suggerimento? *Might I make a suggestion?*

Potere is also used in granting permission:

Puoi prendere tutto, se vuoi *You can take it all if you want*

> **Note:** To show that you are granting permission, it is possible to use **pure** with the imperative:
> Venga **pure!** *Do come in!*

dispiacere

Another polite way to ask for permission is to use **ti dispiace se...** (informal) or **le dispiace se...** (formal):

Ti dispiace se vengo con te? *Do you mind if I come with you?*

Le dispiace se fumo? *Do you mind if I smoke?*

Prohibition

dovere

The negative of **dovere** can be used to express the idea of prohibition:

Non devi parlare così!   You mustn't speak like that!
Non si deve correre   You mustn't run
Non dovevi dirglielo   You weren't supposed to tell him

potere

The negative of **potere** can also be used:

Non si può fumare qua   You can't smoke here

Note the expression **vietato** + infinitive, which is often seen on signs:

Vietato fumare   No smoking

I Expressing basic concepts

There are some basic concepts, often connected with expressing the speaker's attitude towards a particular situation as opposed to a simple statement of facts, which can be expressed by verbs and other expressions. Here are some of the most important.

Ability and success

sapere

To talk about an ability that is learned, use **sapere**:
   Non so nuotare   I *can't* swim

potere

Potere expresses a physical ability:
   Non posso camminare più   I *can't* walk any more

farcela

A similar idea can be expressed using **fare** + **ci** + **la**:
   Non ce la faccio più a camminare   I *can't* walk any more
   Spero di **farcela**   I hope to **make it**

riuscire

Riuscire + **a** expresses success:
   Sono riuscito a rintracciarla   I **managed to** contact her

Riuscire can also be used with an impersonal construction. No preposition is used with this construction:
   Non mi è riuscito rintracciarla   I **didn't manage** to contact her

essere in grado, essere capace

When talking about intellectual abilities, Italian uses **essere in grado di** + infinitive:
   Non ero in grado di rispondere   I **wan't able to** answer

or **essere capace di** + infinitive:
   Non sono capaci di far fronte alla situazione   They're **unable to**
   cope with the situation

Probability

è probabile che

È probabile che... is used to express a strong probability:
  È probabile che vincano   They're likely to win

ci sta che

Ci sta che... expresses a slightly less strong probability:
  Ci sta che vincano   They might well win

! Note: Both **è probabile che...** and **ci sta che...** are followed by the subjunctive.

Possibility

forse, può darsi

To express a possibility, Italian uses **forse**:
  Forse verranno   **Perhaps** they'll come
  Forse si è dimenticato   **Perhaps** he's forgotten

or **può darsi che** + subjunctive:
  Può darsi che vengano   Perhaps they'll come
  Può darsi che abbia dimenticato   Perhaps he's forgotten

Può darsi can also be used on its own:
  'Vieni?' '**Può darsi.**'   'Are you coming?' '**Maybe.**'

potere

Potere is also used to express possibility:
  Può nevicare anche a maggio   It **can** snow even in May
  Può essere stato un incidente   It **may** have been an accident

Used in the conditional, it expresses a more remote possibility:
  Potrebbe essere utile   It **might** be useful

To refer to a possibility in the past, use the past conditional of **potere**:
  Avresti potuto avvisarmi!   You **could have** told me!

The imperfect tense is a common alternative to the past conditional in spoken Italian:
  Potevi avvisarmi!   You **could have** told me!

Deductions and assumptions

dovere

Dovere is used when making a logical deduction:
  Ci **deve** essere una perdita There **must** be a leak
  Dev'essere stato il vento It **must** have been the wind

It is also used in the negative where English uses **can't**:
  Non **dev**'essere facile It **can't** be easy

The future tense

It is possible to use the future tense for assumptions:
  Sarà il postino **That must be** the postman
  Sarai stanca **You must be** tired
  Chi **sarà**? Who **can that be**?

Obligation

dovere

Dovere is used to talk about obligation and necessity:
  Devo andare I **have to** go
  Dobbiamo agire subito **We must** do something at once
  Abbiamo dovuto prendere un taxi We **had to** get a taxi

If there is no obligation, **dovere** is used in the negative:
  Oggi **non devo** lavorare I **don't have to** work today

bisogna

Bisogna is an impersonal verb. It can be followed by the infinitive, or by **che** + subjunctive:
  Bisogna chiudere a chiave la porta **We have to** lock the door
  Bisogna che lo veda prima I have to see it first

va fatto

Andare + past participle expresses a passive idea:
  L'erba **va tagliata** The grass **needs cutting**
  Va fatto subito **It has to be done** immediately

non c'è bisogno

Non c'è bisogno expresses an absence of necessity:
  Non c'è bisogno di gridare **There's no need to** shout
  Non c'è bisogno che tu mi aiuti You **don't have to** help me

Need

aver bisogno

To express the idea of 'need' **aver bisogno di** is commonly used:

Ho bisogno di tempo   I *need* time

Ho bisogno di rifletterci   I *need to* think about it

volerci

Volere can also be used with **ci** to form **ci vuole, ci vogliono**, etc.
Volerci behaves like **piacere**, as the subject in Italian corresponds
to the object in English (*see p. 109* for more information):

Ci vuole pazienza   You *need* patience

C'è voluto un po' di tempo   It *took* some time

Aver bisogno and **ci vuole** can also be used to ask for things:

Ho bisogno di un tuo consiglio   I *need* some advice from you

Mi ci vogliono delle olive   I *need* some olives

Desirability

dovere

Dovere is used in the conditional to express the idea of 'ought to'
or 'should' (*see p. 94* for more information about the forms of
dovere in the conditional):

Dovrei andare   I *ought to* go

This form can also express what is desirable or expected:

Non dovrebbe fare quel rumore   It *shouldn't* make that noise

Dovrebbero arrivare alle undici   They *should* arrive at eleven

To refer to the past, use the past conditional of **dovere**:

Avresti dovuto avvisarmi!   You *should have* told me!

The imperfect tense is a common alternative to the past
conditional in spoken Italian:

Dovevi avvisarmi!   You *should have* told me!

> ! **Note:** These expressions express desirability: **è meglio che** + subjunctive and
> **conviene** + infinitive:
> **È meglio che** me ne vada   It's best if I leave
> **Mi conviene** stare zitto   It's best for me not to say anything

Wishes and regrets

volere

The conditional of **volere** is used to express wishes and regrets. It can be followed by the infinitive:

Vorrei essere con te   I *wish* I were with you

When the person who is supposed to perform the action is different from the person who is making the wish, use the conditional of **volere** + **che**:

Vorrei che tu mi chiamassi più spesso   I *wish* you would call me more often

Vorrei che tu fossi qui   I *wish* you were here

! **Note:** The imperfect subjunctive is used after **vorrei che...**

When expressing regrets about the past, Italian uses the past infinitive (**avere** + past participle), or the pluperfect subjunctive after **che**:

Vorrei avergli detto tutto   I *wish* I had told them everything

Vorrei che mi avessero detto tutto   I *wish* they had told me everything

magari

Magari is commonly used in spoken Italian to express wishes. It can be used on its own, or with the imperfect or the pluperfect subjunctive:

'Hai finito?' '**Magari!**'   'Have you finished?' '*I wish!*'

Magari potessi venire anch'io!   I *wish* I could come too!

! **Note:** **Magari** used with the indicative expresses possibility:
! **Magari** domani avremo qualche notizia   *Perhaps* we'll hear some news tomorrow

se soltanto

Se soltanto means 'if only'. It is followed by the subjunctive:

Se soltanto fosse qui Antonella   If only Antonella were here

Organizing your message

| Linking words and sentences

Spoken Italian, like spoken English, often simply runs sentences together, leaving the listener to interpret the connections between them:

Vado a letto. Sono stanca.   *I'm going to bed. I'm tired.*

It would also be possible to be more explicit and say:

Vado a letto **perché** sono stanca   *I'm going to bed **because** I'm tired*

In writing, it is usually necessary to be more explicit in this way, using words to link the two parts. A *conjunction* is a word used to join words or sentences together:

James **and** Thomas   *I think it was him, **but** I'm not sure*

As well as conjunctions, other classes of word such as adverbs can be used to make links between sentences:

The train was late. **Consequently**, we missed our connection.

This section looks at the methods Italian has of linking words and sentences in different ways.

Adding information

e

To add extra information, the simplest way is to use **e**:

Rachele **e** Rebecca sono gemelle   *Rachele **and** Rebecca are twins*

Mi è piaciuta **e** l'ho comprata   *I liked it **and** bought it*

! **Note: E** has the optional alternative form **ed**, which can be used before vowels: i genitori **ed** i figli   *the parents **and** the children*

anche, pure

Anche or **pure** can be used to add information:

i genitori e **anche** i figli   *the parents and the children **too***
i genitori e i figli **pure**   *the parents and the children **too***

Anche must be placed immediately before the word or phrase that it refers to:

Anche Luca vorrebbe provare   *Luca would like to try **too***

> **Note: Anche** is shortened to **anch'** before a pronoun beginning with a vowel: Voglio venire **anch'io**!   *I want to come **too**!*

Anch'io, **anche tu**, etc. can be used on their own in response to a previous comment:

'Ho fame.' '**Anch'io**.'   *'I'm hungry.' 'So am I.'*
'Io uso uno shampoo antiforfora .' '**Anch'io**.'   *'I use an anti-dandruff shampoo.' 'So do I.'*

Anche is commonly used with the meaning of 'even':

Anche un bambino lo sa   ***Even** a child would know that*
Si può **anche** provare...   *Well, we can try...*

sia... che...

The idea of 'both... and...' is conveyed by **sia... sia...** or **sia... che...**:

Parla **sia** inglese **che/sia** italiano   *She speaks **both** English **and** Italian*

neanche, neppure, nemmeno

Neanche, **neppure**, or **nemmeno** can be used to show that both parts of a sentence are negative. It is often placed at the end:

Il primo appartamento non andava bene e il secondo **neanche/ neppure/nemmeno**   *The first flat wasn't right, and **nor** was the second*

Neanch'io, **nemmeno tu**, etc. can be used on their own in response to a previous comment:

'Non ho fame.' '**Nemmeno** io.'   *'I'm not hungry.' '**Neither** am I.'*
'A lui non piace l'idea.' '**Neppure** a lei.'   *'He doesn't like the idea.' '**Nor** does she.'*

Neanche, **nemmeno**, etc. are commonly used with the meaning of 'not even':

Non ci avevo **neanche** pensato   *I hadn't **even** thought about it*

né... né...

The idea of 'neither... nor...' is conveyed by **né... né...**. Note that Italian uses a plural verb:

Né Marina **né** Chiara mangiano la carne   **Neither** Marina **nor** Chiara eats meat

Giving alternatives

o, oppure

To talk about an alternative, use **o** or **oppure**:

Preferisci carne **o** pesce?   Would you prefer meat **or** fish?

Vuoi bere il vino, **oppure** preferisci l'acqua?   Do you want some wine, **or** would you prefer water?

o... o...

When putting forward two alternatives, it is possible to use **o... o...**:

Voglio andare **o** in Spagna **o** in Grecia   I want to go **either** to Spain **or** to Greece

Contrasting information

ma

Ma implies a contrast:

È incredibile **ma** vero   It's incredible **but** true

Dice che l'ha fatto da sé, **ma** non è vero   He says he did it himself, **but** it's not true

però, tuttavia

Però and **tuttavia** have a similar meaning, but they can also be placed at the end of the sentence:

Dice che l'ha fatto da sé. Non è vero, **però**.   He says he did it himself, **but** it's not true.

Mio marito crede che sia possibile. Io **tuttavia** non sono d'accordo.   My husband thinks it's possible, **but** I don't agree.

mentre, invece

Mentre and **invece** can be used to contrast information:

Carlo vive in città, **mentre** Simone vive in campagna   Carlo
lives in town, **whereas** Simone lives in the country

Carlo vive in città. Simone **invece** vive in campagna.   Carlo
lives in town. Simone, **on the other hand**, lives in the country.

anzi

Anzi is used to say 'not one thing, but another':

Non mi dispiace. **Anzi**, mi piace molto.   I don't dislike it. **On the
contrary**, I like it a lot.

It is also used to correct what you have just said:

L'ho visto mercoledì, **anzi** giovedì   I saw him on Wednesday, **no**,
Thursday

sì, no

Sì and **no** can be used to stand for a whole sentence in Italian:

'Avete mangiato?' 'Io **sì**, gli altri **no**.'   'Have you eaten?' 'I have,
the others haven't.'

Gli altri non parlano portoghese ma io **sì**   The others don't
speak Portuguese, but I do

'Vuoi venire oggi?' 'Oggi **no**.'   'Do you want to come today?' 'No,
not today.'

una settimana **sì**, una settimana **no**   every other week

Credo di **sì**/di **no**   I think so/I don't think so

Giving reasons and drawing conclusions

perché

Perché is used to give the reason for something:

Vado a letto **perché** sono stanca   I'm going to bed **because** I'm tired

siccome, poiché

Perché is never used at the beginning of the sentence. When explaining the reason *before* giving the result, use **siccome** or **poiché**. **Poiché** is more formal than **siccome**:

Siccome/Poiché ero malato sono rimasto a casa   **As** I was ill, I stayed at home

sicché

Sicché is used when giving the reason in second place in the sentence:

Ero malato, **sicché** sono rimasto a casa   I was ill, **so** I stayed at home

dunque, quindi, perciò, allora

All of these words are used to draw or ask for conclusions:

Sono studenti, **allora** pagano meno   They're students, **so** it costs them less

Il motore è più piccolo e **quindi** consuma meno benzina   The engine is smaller, and **therefore** it uses less petrol

È tre metri per quattro, **perciò** sono dodici metri quadri   It's three metres by four metres, **so** that's twelve square metres

E **allora**?   So what?

They are also used to attract people's attention, to check that the other person has understood, and to move the conversation on:

Allora rimaniamo così   **Right**, let's leave it at that

Dunque... cosa stavo dicendo?   OK... what was I saying?

Explaining, rephrasing, and confirming

cioè

Cioè is used to explain or rephrase a previous statement:

Anna e Filippo, **cioè** gli sposi   Anna and Filippo, **that is**, the bride and groom

Non la conosco, **cioè** non l'ho mai incontrata di persona   I don't know her, **I mean** I've never met her

'Gli scriverò un giorno o l'altro' '**Cioè** mai.'   I'll write to him sometime.' '**You mean** never.'

infatti

Infatti is used to confirm what has just been said:

Ci avevano avvertito dei pericoli, e **infatti** avevano ragione   They'd warned us of the dangers, and **indeed** they were right

Result

così... che

Così... che is used to describe the result or outcome of a certain state:

Ero **così** stanco **che** mi sono addormentato subito   I was **so** tired (**that**) I fell asleep immediately

troppo... per

Troppo... per is used when the state mentioned makes something impossible:

L'acqua era **troppo** fredda **per** nuotare   The water was **too** cold **to** swim

Purpose

per

The most common way of expressing purpose is to use the preposition **per** 'in order to':

Si è alzato **per** abbassare il volume   *He got up **to** turn the music down*

affinché, perché

It is also possible to use the conjunctions **affinché** or **perché** 'in order that'. Both are followed by the subjunctive:

Parla piano **affinché** la gente possa capire   *Speak slowly **so that** people can understand*

Concessions

nonostante

Nonostante 'despite', 'in spite of' is followed by a noun:

Voleva continuare **nonostante** i rischi   *He wanted to carry on **despite** the risks*

When followed by the subjunctive it means 'although'. **Che** is optional:

Nonostante (che) sia inglese parla italiano benissimo   ***Although** she's English, she speaks Italian very well*

sebbene, benché, anche se

These conjunctions are also used to express the same idea. **Anche se**, when it means 'although', is followed by the indicative, whereas **sebbene** and **benché** (which are more formal) are followed by the subjunctive:

Anche se era stanco, ha voluto continuare   ***Although** he was tired, he wanted to carry on*

Sebbene/Benché fosse stanco, ha voluto continuare   ***Although** he was tired, he wanted to carry on*

Relative pronouns

che

Che is a relative pronoun which corresponds to 'who', 'whom', 'which', and 'that' in English. Sometimes it is not translated at all:

il tizio **che** guidava   the guy **who** was driving

la ragazza **che** abbiamo conosciuto   the girl (**that**) we met

il programma **che** è stato trasmesso   the programme **which** was broadcast

la macchina **che** abbiamo comprato   the car (**which**) we bought

cui

The relative pronoun **che** is never used after a preposition. Instead, **cui** is used:

il film **di cui** ti ho parlato   the film (**which**) I told you **about**

il ragazzo **con cui** parlavi   the boy (**that**) you were speaking **to**

il motivo **per cui** se ne sono andati   the reason (**why**) they left

In cui is used with time phrases:

l'anno **in cui** ci siamo conosciuti   the year we met

In spoken Italian **in cui** is often replaced by **che**:

l'anno **che** ci siamo conosciuti   the year we met

il quale

Che and **cui** can be replaced by **il quale/la quale** (**i quali/le quali** in the plural). It is more formal than **che**:

Dovevo venire con Giorgio, **il quale** però ha cambiato idea   I was supposed to come with Giorgio, **who** changed his mind, though

È una cosa **senza la quale** sarebbe impossibile vivere   It is a thing **which** it would be impossible to live **without**

il cui

Il cui/la cui (plural **i cui/le cui**) corresponds to 'whose' in English. The definite article agrees in number and gender with the noun that follows:

una cantante **la cui voce** è inconfondibile   a singer **whose voice** is unmistakeable

un libro **il cui significato** è stato molto discusso   a book **whose meaning** has been much talked about

il che

Il che is used when referring to a whole idea which has just been mentioned, rather than to an individual word:

Vogliono partire presto, **il che** mi sembra una buona idea   They want to leave early, **which** seems like a good idea to me

chi

Chi, as well as being used in questions, can also mean 'anyone who...':

Chi vuole andare a casa alzi la mano   **Anyone who** wants to go home, put up their hand

Chi rompe paga   If you break anything, you have to pay for it

Note the indefinite expressions **chiunque**, **qualunque**, **qualsiasi**, and **qualunque/qualsiasi cosa**:

chiunque chieda...   **whoever** asks...

qualunque/qualsiasi lingua parlino...   **whatever** language they speak...

qualunque/qualsiasi cosa succeda...   **whatever** happens...

Conditional sentences

Conditional sentences are ones which tell you what would happen under certain specified conditions. In English they usually contain **if**; the Italian equivalent is **se**. There are two parts to a conditional sentence: one which specifies the condition (**If I were a millionaire...**) and another which tells you the outcome (**... I would buy a big house**). The tenses used in Italian conditional sentences can be quite different from those used in English ones.

Real conditions

When there is a real possibility of the condition coming true, Italian uses the tenses which are appropriate for the time referred to, which will usually correspond to the tenses used in English:

Se **apri** la finestra, **entra** il fumo   If you **open** the window, the smoke **comes in**

Se **non ti sbrighi**, **perderai** il treno   If you **don't hurry up**, you'll **miss** the train

But if both actions referred to are future actions, the future tense is used for both verbs. Here Italian differs from English, where the future is not used after **if**:

Se domani **farà** bel tempo, **faremo** un picnic   If it's nice weather tomorrow we'll **have** a picnic

In spoken Italian it also common to use the present tense for both parts of the sentence:

Se domani **fa** bel tempo, **facciamo** un picnic   If it's nice weather tomorrow we'll **have** a picnic

Note that in both cases the tense is the same for both parts of the sentence, which is not the case in English.

Hypothetical conditions

Hypothetical conditions refer to a possibility which is quite
remote, or even impossible. Here Italian uses the past subjunctive
to specify the condition and the conditional tense to state what
the outcome would be:

> Se **sapessi** la risposta, te la **direi**   If I **knew** the answer, I **would
> tell** you
>
> Se **fossi in te**, non direi nulla   If I **were you**, I wouldn't say
> anything

The past subjunctive of **dovere** is sometimes used to indicate a
remote possibility:

> Se **dovessi seguire** i tuoi consigli, starei fresco   If I **were to
> follow** your advice, I'd be in trouble

Another type of hypothetical condition refers to what *would have
happened* under certain conditions. Here there is no possibility of
the condition coming true because it refers to a time which is past.
Italian uses the pluperfect subjunctive to specify the condition
and the past conditional to state what the hypothetical outcome
would have been:

> Se Paolo non **avesse perso** i biglietti, **saremmo arrivati** in orario
> If Paolo **hadn't lost** the tickets, we **would have arrived** on time

This implies that Paolo *did* lose the tickets, and that we *did not*
arrive on time.

Reporting speech

When reporting another speaker's words, the tense is sometimes affected by the main verb of the sentence.

Reporting statements

If the main verb is in the present, there is no effect on the tense of the reported words:

Sono cari   They're expensive
Dice che sono cari   He says they're expensive
Sono già partiti   They've already left
Dice che sono già partiti   She says they've already left
Ci aiuteranno   They'll help us
Dicono che ci aiuteranno   They say they'll help us

But if the verb of reporting is in the past, the tense of the reported speech moves a step further back into the past.

● Present becomes past:

Sono cari   They're expensive
Ha detto che erano cari   He said they were expensive

● Perfect becomes pluperfect:

Sono già **partiti**   They've already left
Ha detto che **erano** già **partiti**   She said **they had** already **left**

● Future becomes past conditional (*not* conditional, as in English):

Ci **aiuteranno**   **They'll help** us
Hanno detto che ci **avrebbero aiutato**   They said they **would help** us

Reporting questions

The rules for the tenses of reported questions are similar to those for reported statements:

Quanti anni hai? *How old are you?*

Dimmi quanti anni hai *Tell me how old you are*

Come stai? *How are you?*

Mi ha chiesto come stavo *He asked me how I was*

Questions which require the answer yes or no use **se** when they are reported:

Mi hanno chiesto **se** sapevo guidare *They asked me **whether** I could drive*

In more formal Italian, the subjunctive can be used in reported questions:

Mi hanno chiesto se **sapessi** guidare *They asked me whether I **could** drive*

I Exclamations

Greeting and taking leave

The choice of greeting depends on whether the **tu** form or the **lei** form is being used between the people involved. **Ciao** is only used in informal situations, and is used to say both hello and goodbye:

Ciao, ragazzi!   *Hi/Bye, boys!*

Buongiorno, **buonasera**, and **arrivederci** are used in more formal situations. **Arrivederla** is an even more formal alternative to **arrivederci**:

Buonasera, signora!   *Good evening, madam!*

The pronoun **a** is often used when saying goodbye:

A domani!   *See you tomorrow!*
A presto!   *See you soon!*
A giovedì!   *See you on Thursday!*

Exhortations

Many words and phrases can be used to give orders or offer encouragement. A verb is not always necessary:

Avanti!   *Come in!*
Su, coraggio!   *Come on!*
Fuori!   *Get out!*

Expressing attitudes and opinions

There are many exclamatory expressions used to express attitudes and opinions:

Per carità!   *God forbid!*
Neanche per sogno!   *No way!*

che

Used in exclamations, **che** can be followed directly by an adjective or a noun. The indefinite article is never used:

Che bello!   **How** *nice!*
Che bel giardino!   **What a** *nice garden!*
Che orecchini graziosi!   **What** *pretty earrings!*
Che uomo!   **What a** *man!*

come

Come is followed by a verb:

Com'è silenzioso!   **How** *quiet it is!*
Come sei stupido!   *You're so stupid!*
Come parla!   *What a way to talk!*

quanto

Quanto is an alternative to **come**:

Quant'è silenzioso!   **How** *quiet it is!*

When making exclamations about quantities, use **quanto/quanta**:

Quanto mangia!   **What a lot** *he eats!*

For numbers, use **quanti/quante**:

Quante macchine!   **What a lot of** *cars!*

| Word order

The subject

Word order in Italian is more flexible than in English. In particular, the subject of the sentence does not need to come at the beginning of the sentence. It is often placed at the end of the sentence, for example to show that new information is being added, or to show a contrast:

Ha chiamato **tuo fratello**   **Your brother** called
Sono arrivati **i tuoi amici**   **Your friends** have arrived
Ci vado **io**   I'll go

With negative sentences using **niente**, **nessuno**, etc., this is the most common word order. Note that **non** comes at the beginning of the sentence:

Non è successo **niente**   **Nothing** happened
Non verrà **nessuno**   **No one** will come

It is also very common with reflexive verbs:

Si è accesa **la luce**   **The light** came on
In questa fabbrica si fanno **le scarpe**   **Shoes** are made in this factory

In questions, the subject comes either at the beginning or at the end:

Lei è medico?/È medico **lei**?   Are **you** a doctor?
La sua storia è vera?/È vera **la sua storia**?   Is **his story** true?

With imperatives, the subject can be added at the end to show a contrast:

Vacci **tu**!   **You** go!

The object

It is common in spoken Italian for a direct object or an indirect object to to be duplicated, so that it appears both as a pronoun and as a noun phrase. The object noun phrase can come either at the end of the sentence or at the beginning:

L'ho fatto io **quel dolce**   *I made **that cake***

Quel dolce l'ho fatto io   *I made **that cake***

A Stefano non **gli** è andata bene   *It didn't work out **for Stefano***

Phrases with **di** and **a** can also be duplicated by **ne** and **ci** respectively, when these refer to things rather than people:

Non me **ne** intendo **di computer**   *I don't know anything **about computers***

A queste cose non **ci** pensi mai!   *You never think **about these things!***

Verb forms

Irregular verbs

This list includes all the irregular verbs that are in common use in Italian today. Those verbs which are given in capital letters are treated in full in the verb tables on *p. 233*. The other verbs listed form their tenses on the model of the verb which is given after it. The list also states if a verb forms its compound tenses with essere (*see p. 69* for more information).

Note that the prefix ri- (meaning 'again') can be used with almost any verb in Italian. Verbs beginning with this prefix have not been included here, unless the meaning is different from the basic form of the verb.

accadere *to happen* ➤ like cadere (compound tenses with essere)

accedere *to accede, to enter* ➤ like concedere (compound tenses with essere)

accendere *to light, to switch on* ➤ like rendere

accogliere *to welcome* ➤ like cogliere

accorgersi *to realize* ➤ like volgere (compound tenses with essere)

accorrere *to rush* ➤ like correre (compound tenses with essere)

addirsi *to be suitable* ➤ like dire (compound tenses with essere)

affliggere *to afflict* ➤ like leggere

aggiungere *to add* ➤ like piangere

alludere *to allude* ➤ like chiudere

ammettere *to admit* ➤ like mettere

ANDARE *to go*

ANNETTERE *to annex*

APPARIRE *to appear*

appartenere *to belong* ➤ like tenere (compound tenses with essere or avere)

appendere *to hang* ➤ like rendere

apprendere *to learn* ➤ like rendere

APRIRE *to open*

arrendersi to give up, to surrender ➤ like rendere (compound tenses with essere)

assalire to attack ➤ like salire (compound tenses with avere)

ASSISTERE to attend

assolvere to acquit ➤ like risolvere

ASSUMERE to assume, to take on

astenersi to abstain ➤ like tenere (compound tenses with essere)

attendere to await ➤ like rendere

attrarre to attract ➤ like trarre

AVERE to have

avvenire to happen ➤ like venire (compound tenses with essere)

avvolgere to wrap ➤ like volgere

BERE to drink

CADERE to fall

capovolgere to overturn ➤ like volgere

CHIEDERE to ask

CHIUDERE to close

COGLIERE to pick

coincidere to coincide ➤ like decidere

coinvolgere to involve ➤ like volgere

commettere to commit ➤ like mettere

commuovere to move ➤ like muovere

comparire to appear ➤ like apparire (compound tenses with essere)

compiacere to please ➤ like piacere (compound tenses with avere)

compiangere to feel sorry for ➤ like piangere

comporre to compose ➤ like porre

comprendere to include, to understand ➤ like rendere

comprimere to compress ➤ like esprimere

compromettere to compromise ➤ like mettere

CONCEDERE to grant

concludere to conclude ➤ like chiudere

concorrere to compete ➤ like correre

condividere to share ➤ like decidere

condurre to lead, to conduct ➤ like ridurre

confondere to mix up ➤ like fondere

connettere to connect ➤ like annettere

CONOSCERE *to know*

consistere *to consist* ➤ like assistere (compound tenses with essere)

contendere *to compete* ➤ like rendere

contenere *to contain* ➤ like tenere

contraddire *to contradict* ➤ like dire

contraffare *to disguise, to forge* ➤ like fare

contrapporre *to contrast* ➤ like porre

contrarre *to contract* ➤ like trarre

convenire *to be better* ➤ like venire (compound tenses with essere)

convergere *to converge* ➤ like spargere (compound tenses with essere)

convincere *to convince* ➤ like vincere

convivere *to live together* ➤ like vivere (compound tenses with avere)

coprire *to cover* ➤ like aprire

correggere *to correct* ➤ like leggere

CORRERE *to run*

corrispondere *to correspond* ➤ like rispondere

corrodere *to corrode* ➤ like rodere

corrompere *to corrupt* ➤ like rompere

cospargere *to sprinkle* ➤ like spargere

costringere *to force* ➤ like stringere

CRESCERE *to grow*

CUOCERE *to cook*

DARE *to give*

decadere *to decline* ➤ like cadere (compound tenses with essere)

DECIDERE *to decide*

decomporre *to decompose* ➤ like porre

decorrere *to have effect* ➤ like correre (compound tenses with essere)

dedurre *to deduce* ➤ like ridurre

deludere *to disappoint* ➤ like chiudere

deporre *to testify* ➤ like porre

deprimere *to depress* ➤ like esprimere

descrivere *to describe* ➤ like scrivere

desistere *to stop* ➤ like assistere

desumere to deduce ➤ like assumere

detenere to hold ➤ like tenere

detrarre to deduct ➤ like trarre

difendere to defend ➤ like rendere

diffondere to spread ➤ like fondere

dimettere to discharge ➤ like mettere

dipendere to depend ➤ like rendere (compound tenses with essere)

dipingere to paint ➤ like piangere

DIRE to say, to tell

DIRIGERE to direct

discendere to descend ➤ like scendere (compound tenses with essere)

discorrere to talk ➤ like correre

DISCUTERE to discuss

disdire to cancel ➤ like dire

disfare to undo ➤ like fare

disperdere to diperse ➤ like perdere

dispiacere to dislike, to be sorry ➤ like piacere (compound tenses with essere)

disporre to arrange ➤ like porre

dissolvere to dissolve ➤ like risolvere

dissuadere to dissuade ➤ like invadere

distendere to stretch out ➤ like rendere

DISTINGUERE to distinguish

distogliere to divert ➤ like togliere

distorcere to twist ➤ like torcere

distrarre to distract ➤ like trarre

distruggere to destroy ➤ like leggere

divenire to become ➤ like venire (compound tenses with essere)

divergere to diverge ➤ like spargere

dividere to divide ➤ like decidere

DOVERE must

eleggere to elect ➤ like leggere

eludere to avoid ➤ like chiudere

emergere to emerge ➤ like spargere (compound tenses with essere)

emettere to emit ➤ like mettere

equivalere to be equivalent ➤ like valere (compound tenses with essere or avere)

erodere to erode ➤ like rodere

escludere to exclude ➤ like chiudere

ESIGERE to demand

esistere to exist ➤ like assistere (compound tenses with essere)

ESPANDERE to expand

ESPELLERE to expel

esplodere to explode ➤ like rodere (compound tenses with essere)

esporre to expose, to exhibit ➤ like porre

ESPRIMERE to express

ESSERE to be

estendere to extend ➤ like rendere

estinguere to extinguish ➤ like distinguere

estrarre to extract ➤ like trarre

estromettere to expel ➤ like mettere

evadere to escape ➤ like invadere (compound tenses with essere or avere)

FARE to do, to make

fingere to pretend ➤ like piangere

FONDERE to melt

fraintendere to misunderstand ➤ like rendere

friggere to fry ➤ like leggere

giacere to lie ➤ like piacere (compound tenses with essere)

giungere to arrive ➤ like piangere (compound tenses with essere)

illudere to delude ➤ like chiudere

immergere to immerse ➤ like spargere

immettere to put in ➤ like mettere

imporre to impose ➤ like porre

imprimere to impress ➤ like esprimere

incidere to record, to engrave ➤ like decidere

includere to include, to enclose ➤ like chiudere

incorrere to meet ➤ like correre (compound tenses with essere)

indire to call ➤ like dire

indurre to induce ➤ like ridurre

infliggere to inflict ➤ like leggere

infrangere to break ➤ like piangere

insistere to insist, to persist ➤ like assistere

insorgere to arise, to rebel ➤ like scorgere (compound tenses with essere)

intendere to intend, to mean ➤ like rendere

interdire to ban ➤ like dire

interrompere to interrupt ➤ like rompere

intervenire to intervene ➤ like venire (compound tenses with essere)

intraprendere to begin ➤ like rendere

intrattenere to keep amused ➤ like tenere

intravedere to catch a glimpse of ➤ like vedere

introdurre to introduce ➤ like ridurre

intromettersi to interfere ➤ like mettere (compound tenses with essere)

INVADERE to invade

irrompere to burst in ➤ like rompere

iscrivere to enrol ➤ like scrivere

LEGGERE to read

mantenere to keep ➤ like tenere

METTERE to put

mordere to bite ➤ like perdere

MORIRE to die

mungere to milk ➤ like piangere

MUOVERE to move

NASCERE to be born

nascondere to hide ➤ like rispondere

NUOCERE to harm

occorrere to be necessary ➤ like correre (compound tenses with essere)

offendere to offend ➤ like rendere

offrire to offer ➤ like aprire

omettere to omit ➤ like mettere

opporre to oppose ➤ like porre

opprimere to oppress ➤ like esprimere

ottenere to obtain ➤ like tenere

PARERE to seem

percorerre to cover ➤ like correre

PERDERE to lose

permettere to allow ➤ like mettere

persistere *to persist* ≻ like assistere
persuadere *to persuade* ≻ like invadere
pervadere *to pervade* ≻ like invadere
pervenire *to arrive* ≻ like venire (compound tenses with essere)
PIACERE *to like*
PIANGERE *to cry*
PIOVERE *to rain*
porgere *to give* ≻ like scorgere
PORRE *to put*
POSSEDERE *to own*
POTERE *to be able*
predire *to foretell* ≻ like dire
predisporre *to prepare* ≻ like porre
prendere *to take* ≻ like rendere
prescrivere *to prescribe* ≻ like scrivere
presiedere *to chair* ≻ like possedere
presumere *to presume* ≻ like assumere
presupporre *to assume* ≻ like porre
pretendere *to expect* ≻ like rendere
prevalere *to prevail* ≻ like valere (compound tenses with essere
  or avere)
prevedere *to foresee* ≻ like vedere
prevenire *to prevent* ≻ like venire (compound tenses with avere)
produrre *to produce* ≻ like ridurre
promettere *to promise* ≻ like mettere
promuovere *to promote* ≻ like muovere
proporre *to propose* ≻ like porre
proteggere *to protect* ≻ like leggere
protrarre *to extend* ≻ like trarre
provenire *to come* ≻ like venire (compound tenses with essere)
provvedere *to see to* ≻ like vedere
pungere *to sting* ≻ like piangere
racchiudere *to hold* ≻ like chiudere
raccogliere *to pick, to pick up* ≻ like cogliere
radere *to shave off* ≻ like invadere
raggiungere *to reach* ≻ - like piangere
redigere *to edit* ≻ like esigere
reggere *to hold* ≻ like leggere
RENDERE *to give back*

reprimere to repress ➤ like esprimere

resistere to resist ➤ like assistere

respingere to turn down ➤ like piangere

RESTRINGERE to shrink

retrocedere to be relegated ➤ like concedere (compound tenses with essere or avere)

riassumere to summarize ➤ like assumere

riconoscere to recognize ➤ like conoscere

ridere to laugh ➤ like decidere

RIDURRE to reduce

RIEMPIRE to fill

RIMANERE to stay

rimpiangere to regret ➤ like piangere

rinchiudere to lock up ➤ like chiudere

rincorrere to run after ➤ like correre

rinvenire to come round ➤ like venire (compound tenses with essere)

riprodurre to reproduce ➤ like ridurre

risalire to go up, to date back ➤ like salire (compound tenses with essere)

riscuotere to draw (salary) ➤ like scuotere

RISOLVERE to solve

RISPONDERE to answer

ritenere to consider ➤ like tenere

ritrarre to portray ➤ like trarre

riuscire to manage ➤ like uscire (compound tenses with essere)

rivolgere to address ➤ like volgere

RODERE to gnaw

ROMPERE to break

SALIRE to go up, to come up

SAPERE to know

scadere to expire ➤ like cadere (compound tenses with essere)

scegliere to choose ➤ like cogliere

SCENDERE to go down, to come down

sciogliere to melt, to dissolve ➤ like cogliere

scommettere to bet ➤ like mettere

scomparire to disappear ➤ like apparire (compound tenses with essere)

scomporre to break down ➤ like porre

sconfiggere to defeat ➤ like leggere
sconvolgere to upset ➤ like volgere
scoprire to discover ➤ like aprire
SCORGERE to catch sight of
scorrere to flow ➤ like correre (compound tenses with essere)
SCRIVERE to write
SCUOTERE to shake
SEDERSI to sit down
sedurre to seduce ➤ like ridurre
SEPPELLIRE to bury
sfare to undo ➤ like fare
smettere to stop ➤ like mettere
soccorrere to help ➤ like correre
soddisfare to satisfy ➤ like fare
soffrire to suffer ➤ like aprire
sommergere to submerge ➤ like spargere
sopprimere to suppress ➤ like esprimere
sopraggiungere to arrive, to occur ➤ like piangere (compound tenses with essere)
sopravvivere to survive ➤ like vivere (compound tenses with essere)
sorgere to rise, to arise ➤ like scorgere (compound tenses with essere)
sorprendere to surprise ➤ like rendere
sorreggere to support ➤ like leggere
sorridere to smile ➤ like decidere
sospendere to suspend ➤ like rendere
sospingere to drive ➤ like piangere
sostenere to support ➤ like tenere
sottintendere to imply ➤ like rendere
sottomettere to subdue ➤ like mettere
sottoporre to subject ➤ like porre
sottoscrivere to to sign, to subscribe ➤ like scrivere
sottrarre to subtract ➤ like trarre
sovrapporre to superimpose ➤ like porre
sovrastare to dominate ➤ like stare
SPARGERE to scatter
SPEGNERE to put out
spendere to spend ➤ like rendere

spingere to push ➤ like piangere
sporgere to stick out ➤ like scorgere
STARE to be
stendere to spread out ➤ like rendere
storcere to twist ➤ like torcere
strafare to overdo it ➤ like fare
stravolgere to upset ➤ like volgere
STRINGERE to squeeze
succedere to happen ➤ like concedere (compound tenses with essere)
suddividere to subdivide ➤ like decidere
supporre to suppose ➤ like porre
svenire to faint ➤ like venire (compound tenses with essere)
svolgere to carry out ➤ like volgere
TACERE to be silent
tendere to stretch ➤ like rendere
TENERE to hold
tingere to dye ➤ like piangere
togliere to remove ➤ like cogliere
TORCERE to twist
tradurre to translate ➤ like ridurre
TRARRE to draw
trascorrere to spend (time) ➤ like correre
trascrivere to transcribe ➤ like scrivere
trasmettere to transmit ➤ like mettere
trattenere to keep ➤ like tenere
travolgere to run over ➤ like volgere
uccidere to kill ➤ like decidere
UDIRE to hear
ungere to grease ➤ like piangere
USCIRE to go out, to come out
VALERE to be worth
VEDERE to see
VENIRE to come
VINCERE to win
VIVERE to live
VOLERE to want
VOLGERE to turn

Regular verb tables

parlare *to speak*

present	future	past historic	gerund
parlo	parlerò	parlai	parlando
parli	parlerai	parlasti	
parla	parlerà	parlò	*past participle*
parliamo	parleremo	parlammo	parlato/parlata
parlate	parlerete	parlaste	
parlano	parleranno	parlarono	

perfect	conditional	present subjunctive	imperative
ho parlato	parlerei	parli	parla!
hai parlato	parleresti	parli	parli!
ha parlato	parlerebbe	parli	parlate!
abbiamo parlato	parleremmo	parliamo	
avete parlato	parlereste	parliate	
hanno parlato	parlerebbero	parlino	

pluperfect	imperfect	past subjunctive
avevo parlato	parlavo	parlassi
avevi parlato	parlavi	parlassi
aveva parlato	parlava	parlasse
avevamo parlato	parlavamo	parlassimo
avevate parlato	parlavate	parlaste
avevano parlato	parlavano	parlassero

Like parlare: most verbs ending in -are (but see the exceptions which follow).

cominciare *to start*

present	future	past historic	gerund
comincio	comincerò	cominciai	cominciando
cominci	comincerai	cominciasti	
comincia	comincerà	cominciò	*past participle*
cominciamo	cominceremo	cominciammo	cominciato/
cominciate	comincerete	cominciaste	cominciata
cominciano	cominceranno	cominciarono	

perfect	conditional	present subjunctive	imperative
ho cominciato	comincerei	cominci	comincia!
hai cominciato	cominceresti	cominci	cominci!
ha cominciato	comincerebbe	cominci	cominciat!
abbiamo cominciato	cominceremmo	cominciamo	
avete cominciato	comincereste	cominciate	
hanno cominciato	comincerebbero	comincino	

pluperfect	imperfect	past subjunctive
avevo cominciato	cominciavo	cominciassi
avevi cominciato	cominciavi	cominciassi
aveva cominciato	cominciava	cominciasse
avevamo cominciato	cominciavamo	cominciassimo
avevate cominciato	cominciavate	cominciaste
avevano cominciato	cominciavano	cominciassero

Like cominciare: all verbs ending in -ciare, e.g. baciare, bruciare, denunciare, lanciare.

mangiare to eat

present	future	past historic	gerund
mangio	mangerò	mangiai	mangiando
mangi	mangerai	mangiasti	
mangia	mangerà	mangiò	past participle
mangiamo	mangeremo	mangiammo	mangiato/mangiata
mangiate	mangerete	mangiaste	
mangiano	mangeranno	mangiarono	

perfect	conditional	present subjunctive	imperative
ho mangiato	mangerei	mangi	mangia!
hai mangiato	mangeresti	mangi	mangi!
ha mangiato	mangerebbe	mangi	
abbiamo mangiato	mangeremmo	mangiamo	
avete mangiato	mangereste	mangiate	
hanno mangiato	mangerebbero	mangino	

pluperfect	imperfect	past subjunctive
avevo mangiato	mangiavo	mangiassi
avevi mangiato	mangiavi	mangiassi
aveva mangiato	mangiava	mangiasse
avevamo mangiato	mangiavamo	mangiassimo
avevate mangiato	mangiavate	mangiaste
avevano mangiato	mangiavano	mangiassero

Like mangiare: all verbs ending in -giare, e.g. assaggiare, festeggiare, parcheggiare, viaggiare.

giocare to play

present	future	past historic	gerund
gioco	giocherò	giocai	giocando
giochi	giocherai	giocasti	
gioca	giocherà	giocò	past participle
giochiamo	giocheremo	giocammo	giocato/cominciata
giocate	giocherete	giocaste	
giocano	giocheranno	giocarono	

perfect	conditional	present subjunctive	imperative
ho giocato	giocherei	giochi	gioca!
hai giocato	giocheresti	giochi	giochi!
ha giocato	giocherebbe	giochi	giocate!
abbiamo giocato	giocheremmo	giochiamo	
avete giocato	giochereste	giochiate	
hanno giocato	giocherebbero	giochino	

pluperfect	imperfect	past subjunctive
avevo giocato	giocavo	giocassi
avevi giocato	giocavi	giocassi
aveva giocato	giocava	giocasse
avevamo giocato	giocavamo	giocassimo
avevate giocato	giocavate	giocaste
avevano giocato	giocavano	giocassero

Like giocare: all verbs ending in -care, e.g. cercare, dimenticare, leccare, toccare.

legare *to tie*

present	future	past historic	gerund
lego	legherò	legai	legando
leghi	legherai	legasti	
lega	legherà	legò	*past participle*
leghiamo	legheremo	legammo	legato/legata
legate	legherete	legaste	
legano	legheranno	legarono	

perfect	conditional	present subjunctive	imperative
ho legato	legherei	leghi	lega!
hai legato	legheresti	leghi	leghi!
ha legato	legherebbe	leghi	legate!
abbiamo legato	legheremmo	leghiamo	
avete legato	leghereste	leghiate	
hanno legato	legherebbero	leghino	

pluperfect	imperfect	past subjunctive
avevo legato	legavo	legassi
avevi legato	legavi	legassi
aveva legato	legava	legasse
avevamo legato	legavamo	legassimo
avevate legato	legavate	legaste
avevano legato	legavano	legassero

Like legare: all verbs ending in -gare, e.g. collegare, pagare, piegare, spiegare.

studiare *to study*

present	future	past historic	gerund
studio	studierò	studiai	studiando
studi	studierai	studiasti	
studia	studierà	studiò	*past participle*
studiamo	studieremo	studiammo	studiato/studiata
studiate	studierete	studiaste	
studiano	studieranno	studiarono	

perfect	conditional	present subjunctive	imperative
ho studiato	studierei	studi	studia!
hai studiato	studieresti	studi	studi!
ha studiato	studierebbe	studi	studiate!
abbiamo studiato	studieremmo	studiamo	
avete studiato	studiereste	studiate	
hanno studiato	studierebbero	studino	

pluperfect	imperfect	past subjunctive
avevo studiato	studiavo	studiassi
avevi studiato	studiavi	studiassi
aveva studiato	studiava	studiasse
avevamo studiato	studiavamo	studiassimo
avevate studiato	studiavate	studiaste
avevano studiato	studiavano	studiassero

Like studiare: most verbs ending in -iare (but not in -ciare or -giare), e.g. abbaiare, cambiare, lasciare, sbagliare. See also inviare.

inviare *to send*

present	future	past historic	gerund
invio	invierò	inviai	inviando
invii	invierai	inviasti	
invia	invierà	inviò	*past participle*
inviamo	invieremo	inviammo	inviato/inviata
inviate	invierete	inviaste	
inviano	invieranno	inviarono	

perfect	conditional	present subjunctive	imperative
ho inviato	invierei	invii	invia!
hai inviato	invieresti	invii	invii!
ha inviato	invierebbe	invii	inviate!
abbiamo inviato	invieremmo	inviamo	
avete inviato	inviereste	inviate	
hanno inviato	invierebbero	inviino	

pluperfect	imperfect	past subjunctive	
avevo inviato	inviavo	inviassi	
avevi inviato	inviavi	inviassi	
aveva inviato	inviava	inviasse	
avevamo inviato	inviavamo	inviassimo	
avevate inviato	inviavate	inviaste	
avevano inviato	inviavano	inviassero	

Like inviare: some verbs ending in -iare, e.g. avviare, sciare.

vendere *to sell*

present	future	past historic	gerund
vendo	venderò	vendei *or* vendetti	vendendo
vendi	venderai	vendesti	
vende	venderà	vendé *or* vendette	*past participle*
vendiamo	venderemo	vendemmo	venduto/venduta
vendete	venderete	vendeste	
vendono	venderanno	venderono *or* vendettero	

perfect	conditional	present subjunctive	imperative
ho venduto	venderei	venda	vendi!
hai venduto	venderesti	venda	venda!
ha venduto	venderebbe	venda	vendete!
abbiamo venduto	venderemmo	vendiamo	
avete venduto	vendereste	vendiate	
hanno venduto	venderebbero	vendano	

pluperfect	imperfect	past subjunctive	
avevo venduto	vendevo	vendessi	
avevi venduto	vendevi	vendessi	
aveva venduto	vendeva	vendesse	
avevamo venduto	vendevamo	vendessimo	
avevate venduto	vendevate	vendeste	
avevano venduto	vendevano	vendessero	

Like vendere: some verbs ending in -ere, e.g. battere, credere, ricevere, ripetere. A few verbs ending in –ere, e.g. temere, are stressed on the second-last syllable. This affects the infinitive only.

finire to finish

present	future	past historic	gerund
finisco	finirò	finii	finendo
finisci	finirai	finisti	
finisce	finirà	finì	*past participle*
finiamo	finiremo	finimmo	finito/finita
finite	finirete	finiste	
finiscono	finiranno	finirono	

perfect	conditional	present subjunctive	imperative
ho finito	finirei	finisca	finisci!
hai finito	finiresti	finisca	finisca!
ha finito	finirebbe	finisca	finite!
abbiamo finito	finiremmo	finiamo	
avete finito	finireste	finiate	
hanno finito	finirebbero	finiscano	

pluperfect	imperfect	past subjunctive	
avevo finito	finivo	finissi	
avevi finito	finivi	finissi	
aveva finito	finiva	finisse	
avevamo finito	finivamo	finissimo	
avevate finito	finivate	finiste	
avevano finito	finivano	finissero	

Like finire: most verbs ending in -ire, e.g. capire, colpire, preferire, sparire.

sentire to hear, to feel

present	future	past historic	gerund
sento	sentirò	sentii	sentendo
senti	sentirai	sentisti	
sente	sentirà	sentì	*past participle*
sentiamo	sentiremo	sentimmo	sentito/sentita
sentite	sentirete	sentiste	
sentono	sentiranno	sentirono	

perfect	conditional	present subjunctive	imperative
ho sentito	sentirei	senta	senti!
hai sentito	sentiresti	senta	senta!
ha sentito	sentirebbe	senta	sentite!
abbiamo sentito	sentiremmo	sentiamo	
avete sentito	sentireste	sentiate	
hanno sentito	sentirebbero	sentano	

pluperfect	imperfect	past subjunctive	
avevo sentito	sentivo	sentissi	
avevi sentito	sentivi	sentissi	
aveva sentito	sentiva	sentisse	
avevamo sentito	sentivamo	sentissimo	
avevate sentito	sentivate	sentiste	
avevano sentito	sentivano	sentissero	

Like sentire: some verbs ending in -ire, e.g. avvertire, dormire, partire, seguire.

Irregular verb tables

andare *to go*

present	future	past historic	gerund
vado	andrò	andai	andando
vai	andrai	andasti	
va	andrà	andò	*past participle*
andiamo	andremo	andammo	andato/andata
andate	andrete	andaste	
vanno	andranno	andarono	

perfect	conditional	present subjunctive	imperative
sono andato/andata	andrei	vada	va'!
sei andato/andata	andresti	vada	*or*
è andato/andata	andrebbe	vada	vai!
siamo andati/andate	andremmo	andiamo	vada!
siete andati/andate	andreste	andiate	andate!
sono andati/andate	andrebbero	vadano	

pluperfect	imperfect	past subjunctive
ero andato/andata	andavo	andassi
eri andato/andata	andavi	andassi
era andato/andata	andava	andasse
eravamo andati/andate	andavamo	andassimo
eravate andati/andate	andavate	andaste
erano andati/andate	andavano	andassero

annettere *to annex*

present	future	past historic	gerund
annetto	annetterò	annettei	annettendo
annetti	annetterai	annettesti	
annette	annetterà	annetté	*past participle*
annettiamo	annetteremo	annettemmo	annesso/annessa
annettete	annetterete	annetteste	
annettono	annetteranno	annetterono	

perfect	conditional	present subjunctive	imperative
ho annesso	annetterei	annetta	annetti!
hai annesso	annetteresti	annetta	annetta!
ha annesso	annetterebbe	annetta	annettete!
abbiamo annesso	annetteremmo	annettiamo	
avete annesso	annettereste	annettiate	
hanno annesso	annetterebbero	annettano	

pluperfect	imperfect	past subjunctive
avevo annesso	annettevo	annettessi
avevi annesso	annettevi	annettessi
aveva annesso	annetteva	annettesse
avevamo annesso	annettevamo	annettessimo
avevate annesso	annettevate	annetteste
avevano annesso	annettevano	annettessero

apparire to appear

present	future	past historic	gerund
appaio	apparirò	apparvi	apparendo
appari	apparirai	apparisti	
appare	apparirà	apparve	*past participle*
appariamo	appariremo	apparimmo	apparso/apparsa
apparite	apparirete	appariste	
appaiono	appariranno	apparvero	

perfect	conditional	present subjunctive	imperative
sono apparso/	apparirei	appaia	appari!
apparsa	appariresti	appaia	appaia!
sei apparso/apparsa	apparirebbe	appaia	apparite!
è apparso/apparsa	appariremmo	appariamo	
siamo apparsi/	apparireste	appariate	
apparse	apparirebbero	appaiano	
siete apparsi/apparse	*imperfect*	*past subjunctive*	
sono apparsi/apparse	apparivo	apparissi	
	apparivi	apparissi	
pluperfect	appariva	apparisse	
ero apparso/apparsa	apparivamo	apparissimo	
eri apparso/apparsa	apparivate	appariste	
era apparso/apparsa	apparivano	apparissero	
eravamo apparsi/			
apparse			
eravate apparsi/			
apparse			
erano apparsi/			
apparse			

aprire to open

present	future	past historic	gerund
apro	aprirò	aprii	aprendo
apri	aprirai	apristi	
apre	aprirà	aprì	*past participle*
apriamo	apriremo	aprimmo	aperto/aperta
aprite	aprirete	apriste	
aprono	apriranno	aprirono	

perfect	conditional	present subjunctive	imperative
ho aperto	aprirei	apra	apri!
hai aperto	apriresti	apra	apra!
ha aperto	aprirebbe	apra	aprite!
abbiamo aperto	apriremmo	apriamo	
avete aperto	aprireste	apriate	
hanno aperto	aprirebbero	aprano	

pluperfect	imperfect	past subjunctive
avevo aperto	aprivo	aprissi
avevi aperto	aprivi	aprissi
aveva aperto	apriva	aprisse
avevamo aperto	aprivamo	aprissimo
avevate aperto	aprivate	apriste
avevano aperto	aprivano	aprissero

assistere to attend

present	future	past historic	gerund
assisto	assisterò	assistei *or* assistetti	assistendo
assisti	assisterai	assistesti	
assiste	assisterà	assisté *or* assistette	*past participle*
assistiamo	assisteremo	assistemmo	assistito/assistita
assistete	assisterete	assisteste	
assistono	assisteranno	assisterono *or* assistettero	

perfect	conditional	present subjunctive	imperative
ho assistito	assisterei	assista	assisti!
hai assistito	assisteresti	assista	assista!
ha assistito	assisterebbe	assista	assistete!
abbiamo assistito	assisteremmo	assistiamo	
avete assistito	assistereste	assistiate	
hanno assistito	assisterebbero	assistano	

pluperfect	imperfect	past subjunctive	
avevo assistito	assistevo	assistessi	
avevi assistito	assistevi	assistessi	
aveva assistito	assisteva	assistesse	
avevamo assistito	assistevamo	assistessimo	
avevate assistito	assistevate	assisteste	
avevano assistito	assistevano	assistessero	

assumere to assume, to take on

present	future	past historic	gerund
assumo	assumerò	assunsi	assumendo
assumi	assumerai	assumesti	
assume	assumerà	assunse	*past participle*
assumiamo	assumeremo	assumemmo	assunto/assunta
assumete	assumerete	assumeste	
assumono	assumeranno	assunsero	

perfect	conditional	present subjunctive	imperative
ho assunto	assumerei	assuma	assumi!
hai assunto	assumeresti	assuma	assuma!
ha assunto	assumerebbe	assuma	assumete!
abbiamo assunto	assumeremmo	assumiamo	
avete assunto	assumereste	assumiate	
hanno assunto	assumerebbero	assumano	

pluperfect	imperfect	past subjunctive	
avevo assunto	assumevo	assumessi	
avevi assunto	assumevi	assumessi	
aveva assunto	assumeva	assumesse	
avevamo assunto	assumevamo	assumessimo	
avevate assunto	assumevate	assumeste	
avevano assunto	assumevano	assumessero	

avere to have

present	future	past historic	gerund
ho	avrò	ebbi	avendo
hai	avrai	avesti	
ha	avrà	ebbe	*past participle*
abbiamo	avremo	avemmo	avuto/avuta
avete	avrete	aveste	
hanno	avranno	ebbero	

perfect	conditional	present subjunctive	imperative
ho avuto	avrei	abbia	abbi!
hai avuto	avresti	abbia	abbia!
ha avuto	avrebbe	abbia	abbiate!
abbiamo avuto	avremmo	abbiamo	
avete avuto	avreste	abbiate	
hanno avuto	avrebbero	abbiano	

pluperfect	imperfect	past subjunctive
avevo avuto	avevo	avessi
avevi avuto	avevi	avessi
aveva avuto	aveva	avesse
avevamo avuto	avevamo	avessimo
avevate avuto	avevate	aveste
avevano avuto	avevano	avessero

bere to drink

present	future	past historic	gerund
bevo	berrò	bevvi *or* bevetti	bevendo
bevi	berrai	bevesti	
beve	berrà	bevve *or* bevette	*past participle*
beviamo	berremo	bevemmo	bevuto/bevuta
bevete	berrete	beveste	
bevono	berranno	bevvero *or* bevettero	

perfect	conditional	present subjunctive	imperative
ho bevuto	berrei	beva	bevi!
hai bevuto	berresti	beva	beva!
ha bevuto	berrebbe	beva	bevete!
abbiamo bevuto	berremmo	beviamo	
avete bevuto	berreste	beviate	
hanno bevuto	berrebbero	bevano	

pluperfect	imperfect	past subjunctive
avevo bevuto	bevevo	bevessi
avevi bevuto	bevevi	bevessi
aveva bevuto	beveva	bevesse
avevamo bevuto	bevevamo	bevessimo
avevate bevuto	bevevate	beveste
avevano bevuto	bevevano	bevessero

cadere to fall

present	future	past historic	gerund
cado	cadrò	caddi	cadendo
cadi	cadrai	cadesti	
cade	cadrà	cadde	*past participle*
cadiamo	cadremo	cademmo	caduto/caduta
cadete	cadrete	cadeste	
cadono	cadranno	caddero	

perfect	conditional	present subjunctive	imperative
sono caduto/caduta	cadrei	cada	cadi!
sei caduto/caduta	cadresti	cada	cada!
è caduto/caduta	cadrebbe	cada	cadete!
siamo caduti/cadute	cadremmo	cadiamo	
siete caduti/cadute	cadreste	cadiate	
sono caduti/cadute	cadrebbero	cadano	

pluperfect	imperfect	past subjunctive
ero caduto/caduta	cadevo	cadessi
eri caduto/caduta	cadevi	cadessi
era caduto/caduta	cadeva	cadesse
eravamo caduti/cadute	cadevamo	cadessimo
eravate caduti/cadute	cadevate	cadeste
erano caduti/cadute	cadevano	cadessero

chiedere to ask

present	future	past historic	gerund
chiedo	chiederò	chiesi	chiedendo
chiedi	chiederai	chiedesti	
chiede	chiederà	chiese	*past participle*
chiediamo	chiederemo	chiedemmo	chiesto/chiesta
chiedete	chiederete	chiedeste	
chiedono	chiederanno	chiesero	

perfect	conditional	present subjunctive	imperative
ho chiesto	chiederei	chieda	chiedi!
hai chiesto	chiederesti	chieda	chieda!
ha chiesto	chiederebbe	chieda	chiedete!
abbiamo chiesto	chiederemmo	chiediamo	
avete chiesto	chiedereste	chiediate	
hanno chiesto	chiederebbero	chiedano	

pluperfect	imperfect	past subjunctive
avevo chiesto	chiedevo	chiedessi
avevi chiesto	chiedevi	chiedessi
aveva chiesto	chiedeva	chiedesse
avevamo chiesto	chiedevamo	chiedessimo
avevate chiesto	chiedevate	chiedeste
avevano chiesto	chiedevano	chiedessero

chiudere to close

present	future	past historic	gerund
chiudo	chiuderò	chiusi	chiudendo
chiudi	chiuderai	chiudesti	
chiude	chiuderà	chiuse	*past participle*
chiudiamo	chiuderemo	chiudemmo	chiuso/chiusa
chiudete	chiuderete	chiudeste	
chiudono	chiuderanno	chiusero	

perfect	conditional	present subjunctive	imperative
ho chiuso	chiuderei	chiuda	chiudi!
hai chiuso	chiuderesti	chiuda	chiuda!
ha chiuso	chiuderebbe	chiuda	chiudete!
abbiamo chiuso	chiuderemmo	chiudiamo	
avete chiuso	chiudereste	chiudiate	
hanno chiuso	chiuderebbero	chiudano	

pluperfect	imperfect	past subjunctive
avevo chiuso	chiudevo	chiudessi
avevi chiuso	chiudevi	chiudessi
aveva chiuso	chiudeva	chiudesse
avevamo chiuso	chiudevamo	chiudessimo
avevate chiuso	chiudevate	chiudeste
avevano chiuso	chiudevano	chiudessero

cogliere to pick

present	future	past historic	gerund
colgo	coglierò	colsi	cogliendo
cogli	coglierai	cogliesti	
coglie	coglierà	colse	*past participle*
cogliamo	coglieremo	cogliemmo	colto/colta
cogliete	coglierete	coglieste	
colgono	coglieranno	colsero	

perfect	conditional	present subjunctive	imperative
ho colto	coglierei	colga	cogli!
hai colto	coglieresti	colga	colga!
ha colto	coglierebbe	colga	cogliete!
abbiamo colto	coglieremmo	cogliamo	
avete colto	cogliereste	cogliate	
hanno colto	coglierebbero	colgano	

pluperfect	imperfect	past subjunctive
avevo colto	coglievo	cogliessi
avevi colto	coglievi	cogliessi
aveva colto	coglieva	cogliesse
avevamo colto	coglievamo	cogliessimo
avevate colto	coglievate	coglieste
avevano colto	coglievano	cogliessero

concedere to grant

present	future	past historic	gerund
concedo	concederò	concessi	concedendo
concedi	concederai	concedesti	
concede	concederà	concesse	*past participle*
concediamo	concederemo	concedemmo	concesso/concessa
concedete	concederete	concedeste	
concedono	concederanno	concessero	

perfect	conditional	present subjunctive	imperative
ho concesso	concederei	conceda	concedi!
hai concesso	concederesti	conceda	conceda!
ha concesso	concederebbe	conceda	concedete!
abbiamo concesso	concederemmo	concediamo	
avete concesso	concedereste	concediate	
hanno concesso	concederebbero	concedano	

pluperfect	imperfect	past subjunctive	
avevo concesso	concedevo	concedessi	
avevi concesso	concedevi	concedessi	
aveva concesso	concedeva	concedesse	
avevamo concesso	concedevamo	concedessimo	
avevate concesso	concedevate	concedeste	
avevano concesso	concedevano	concedessero	

conoscere to know

present	future	past historic	gerund
conosco	conoscerò	conobbi	conoscendo
conosci	conoscerai	conoscesti	
conosce	conoscerà	conobbe	*past participle*
conosciamo	conosceremo	conoscemmo	conosciuto/
conoscete	conoscerete	conosceste	conosciuta
conoscono	conosceranno	conobbero	

perfect	conditional	present subjunctive	imperative
ho conosciuto	conoscerei	conosca	conosci!
hai conosciuto	conosceresti	conosca	conosca!
ha conosciuto	conoscerebbe	conosca	conoscete!
abbiamo conosciuto	conosceremmo	conosciamo	
avete conosciuto	conoscereste	conosciate	
hanno conosciuto	conoscerebbero	conoscano	

pluperfect	imperfect	past subjunctive	
avevo conosciuto	conoscevo	conoscessi	
avevi conosciuto	conoscevi	conoscessi	
aveva conosciuto	conosceva	conoscesse	
avevamo conosciuto	conoscevamo	conoscessimo	
avevate conosciuto	conoscevate	conosceste	
avevano conosciuto	conoscevano	conoscessero	

correre to run

present	future	past historic	gerund
corro	correrò	corsi	correndo
corri	correrai	corresti	
corre	correrà	corse	past participle
corriamo	correremo	corremmo	corso/corsa
correte	correrete	correste	
corrono	correranno	corsero	

perfect	conditional	present subjunctive	imperative
ho corso	correrei	corra	corri!
hai corso	correresti	corra	corra!
ha corso	correrebbe	corra	correte!
abbiamo corso	correremmo	corriamo	
avete corso	correreste	corriate	
hanno corso	correrebbero	corràno	

pluperfect	imperfect	past subjunctive	
avevo corso	correvo	corressi	
avevi corso	correvi	corressi	
aveva corso	correva	corresse	
avevamo corso	correvamo	corressimo	
avevate corso	correvate	correste	
avevano corso	correvano	corressero	

The compound tenses of correre can also be conjugated with essere. See p. 74 for more information.

crescere to grow

present		imperfect	past subjunctive
cresco	era cresciuto/cresciuta	crescevo	crescessi
cresci	eravamo cresciuti/cresciute	crescevi	crescessi
cresce		cresceva	crescesse
cresciamo	eravate cresciuti/cresciute	crescevamo	crescessimo
crescete		crescevate	cresceste
crescono	erano cresciuti/cresciute	crescevano	crescessero

perfect	future	past historic	gerund
sono cresciuto/cresciuta	crescerò	crebbi	crescendo
sei cresciuto/cresciuta	crescerai	crescesti	
è cresciuto/cresciuta	crescerà	crebbe	past participle
siamo cresciuti/cresciute	cresceremo	crescemmo	cresciuto/cresciuta
siete cresciuti/cresciute	crescerete	cresceste	
sono cresciuti/cresciute	cresceranno	crebbero	

	conditional	present subjunctive	imperative
	crescerei	cresca	cresci!
	cresceresti	cresca	cresca!
	crescerebbe	cresca	crescete!
	cresceremmo	cresciamo	
pluperfect	crescereste	cresciate	
ero cresciuto/cresciuta	crescerebbero	crescano	
eri cresciuto/cresciuta			

cuocere *to cook*

present	*future*	*past historic*	*gerund*
cuocio	cuocerò	cossi	cuocendo
cuoci	cuocerai	cuocesti	
cuoce	cuocerà	cosse	*past participle*
cuociamo	cuoceremo	cuocemmo	cotto/cotta
cuocete	cuocerete	cuoceste	
cuociono	cuoceranno	cossero	

perfect	*conditional*	*present subjunctive*	*imperative*
ho cotto	cuocerei	cuocia	cuoci!
hai cotto	cuoceresti	cuocia	cuocia!
ha cotto	cuocerebbe	cuocia	cuocete!
abbiamo cotto	cuoceremmo	cuociamo	
avete cotto	cuocereste	cuociate	
hanno cotto	cuocerebbero	cuociano	

pluperfect	*imperfect*	*past subjunctive*
avevo cotto	cuocevo	cuocessi
avevi cotto	cuocevi	cuocessi
aveva cotto	cuoceva	cuocesse
avevamo cotto	cuocevamo	cuocessimo
avevate cotto	cuocevate	cuoceste
avevano cotto	cuocevano	cuocessero

dare *to give*

present	*future*	*past historic*	*gerund*
do	darò	diedi *or* detti	dando
dai	darai	desti	
dà	darà	diede *or* dette	*past participle*
diamo	daremo	demmo	dato/data
date	darete	deste	
danno	daranno	diedero *or* dettero	

perfect	*conditional*	*present subjunctive*	*imperative*
ho dato	darei	dia	da'! *or* dai!
hai dato	daresti	dia	dia!
ha dato	darebbe	dia	date!
abbiamo dato	daremmo	diamo	
avete dato	dareste	diate	
hanno dato	darebbero	diano	

pluperfect	*imperfect*	*past subjunctive*
avevo dato	davo	dessi
avevi dato	davi	dessi
aveva dato	dava	desse
avevamo dato	davamo	dessimo
avevate dato	davate	deste
avevano dato	davano	dessero

decidere to decide

present	future	past historic	gerund
decido	deciderò	decisi	decidendo
decidi	deciderai	decidesti	
decide	deciderà	decise	*past participle*
decidiamo	decideremo	decidemmo	deciso/decisa
decidete	deciderete	decideste	
decidono	decideranno	decisero	

perfect	conditional	present subjunctive	imperative
ho deciso	deciderei	decida	decidi!
hai deciso	decideresti	decida	decida!
ha deciso	deciderebbe	decida	decidete!
abbiamo deciso	decideremmo	decidiamo	
avete deciso	decidereste	decidiate	
hanno deciso	deciderebbero	decidano	

pluperfect	imperfect	past subjunctive
avevo deciso	decidevo	decidessi
avevi deciso	decidevi	decidessi
aveva deciso	decideva	decidesse
avevamo deciso	decidevamo	decidessimo
avevate deciso	decidevate	decideste
avevano deciso	decidevano	decidessero

dire to say, to tell

present	future	past historic	gerund
dico	dirò	dissi	dicendo
dici	dirai	dicesti	
dice	dirà	disse	*past participle*
diciamo	diremo	dicemmo	detto/detta
dite	direte	diceste	
dicono	diranno	dissero	

perfect	conditional	present subjunctive	imperative
ho detto	direi	dica	di'!
hai detto	diresti	dica	dica!
ha detto	direbbe	dica	dite!
abbiamo detto	diremmo	diciamo	
avete detto	direste	diciate	
hanno detto	direbbero	dicano	

pluperfect	imperfect	past subjunctive
avevo detto	dicevo	dicessi
avevi detto	dicevi	dicessi
aveva detto	diceva	dicesse
avevamo detto	dicevamo	dicessimo
avevate detto	dicevate	diceste
avevano detto	dicevano	dicessero

dirigere to direct

present	*future*	*past historic*	*gerund*
dirigo	dirigerò	diressi	dirigendo
dirigi	dirigerai	dirigesti	
dirige	dirigerà	diresse	*past participle*
dirigiamo	dirigeremo	dirigemmo	diretto/diretta
dirigete	dirigerete	dirigeste	
dirigono	dirigeranno	diressero	

perfect	*conditional*	*present subjunctive*	*imperative*
ho diretto	dirigerei	diriga	dirigi!
hai diretto	dirigeresti	diriga	diriga!
ha diretto	dirigerebbe	diriga	dirigete!
abbiamo diretto	dirigeremmo	dirigiamo	
avete diretto	dirigereste	dirigiate	
hanno diretto	dirigerebbero	dirigano	

pluperfect	*imperfect*	*past subjunctive*	
avevo diretto	dirigevo	dirigessi	
avevi diretto	dirigevi	dirigessi	
aveva diretto	dirigeva	dirigesse	
avevamo diretto	dirigevamo	dirigessimo	
avevate diretto	dirigevate	dirigeste	
avevano diretto	dirigevano	dirigessero	

discutere to discuss

present	*future*	*past historic*	*gerund*
discuto	discuterò	discussi	discutendo
discuti	discuterai	discutesti	
discute	discuterà	discusse	*past participle*
discutiamo	discuteremo	discutemmo	discusso/discussa
discutete	discuterete	discuteste	
discutono	discuteranno	discussero	

perfect	*conditional*	*present subjunctive*	*imperative*
ho discusso	discuterei	discuta	discuti!
hai discusso	discuteresti	discuta	discuta!
ha discusso	discuterebbe	discuta	discutete!
abbiamo discusso	discuteremmo	discutiamo	
avete discusso	discutereste	discutiate	
hanno discusso	discuterebbero	discutano	

pluperfect	*imperfect*	*past subjunctive*	
avevo discusso	discutevo	discutessi	
avevi discusso	discutevi	discutessi	
aveva discusso	discuteva	discutesse	
avevamo discusso	discutevamo	discutessimo	
avevate discusso	discutevate	discuteste	
avevano discusso	discutevano	discutessero	

distinguere to distinguish

present	future	past historic	gerund
distinguo	distinguerò	distinsi	distinguendo
distingui	distinguerai	distinguesti	
distingue	distinguerà	distinse	past participle
distinguiamo	distingueremo	distinguemmo	distinto/distinta
distinguete	distinguerete	distingueste	
distinguono	distingueranno	distinsero	

perfect	conditional	present subjunctive	imperative
ho distinto	distinguerei	distingua	distingui!
hai distinto	distingueresti	distingua	distingua!
ha distinto	distinguerebbe	distingua	distinguete!
abbiamo distinto	distingueremmo	distinguiamo	
avete distinto	distinguereste	distinguiate	
hanno distinto	distinguerebbero	distinguano	

pluperfect	imperfect	past subjunctive
avevo distinto	distinguevo	distinguessi
avevi distinto	distinguevi	distinguessi
aveva distinto	distingueva	distinguesse
avevamo distinto	distinguevamo	distinguessimo
avevate distinto	distinguevate	distingueste
avevano distinto	distinguevano	distinguessero

dovere must

present	future	past historic	gerund
devo	dovrò	dovetti	dovendo
devi	dovrai	dovesti	
deve	dovrà	dovette	past participle
dobbiamo	dovremo	dovemmo	dovuto/dovuta
dovete	dovrete	doveste	
devono	dovranno	dovettero	

perfect	conditional	present subjunctive
ho dovuto	dovrei	deva
hai dovuto	dovresti	deva
ha dovuto	dovrebbe	deva
abbiamo dovuto	dovremmo	dobbiamo
avete dovuto	dovreste	dobbiate
hanno dovuto	dovrebbero	devano

pluperfect	imperfect	past subjunctive
avevo dovuto	dovevo	dovessi
avevi dovuto	dovevi	dovessi
aveva dovuto	doveva	dovesse
avevamo dovuto	dovevamo	dovessimo
avevate dovuto	dovevate	doveste
avevano dovuto	dovevano	dovessero

esigere to demand

present	future	past historic	gerund
esigo	esigerò	esigei *or* esigetti	esigendo
esigi	esigerai	esigesti	
esige	esigerà	esigé *or* esigette	past participle
esigiamo	esigeremo	esigemmo	esatto/esatta
esigete	esigerete	esigeste	
esigono	esigeranno	esigero *or* esigettero	

perfect	conditional	present subjunctive	imperative
ho esatto	esigerei	esiga	esigi!
hai esatto	esigeresti	esiga	esiga!
ha esatto	esigerebbe	esiga	esigete!
abbiamo esatto	esigeremmo	esigiamo	
avete esatto	esigereste	esigiate	
hanno esatto	esigerebbero	esigano	

pluperfect	imperfect	past subjunctive
avevo esatto	esigevo	esigessi
avevi esatto	esigevi	esigessi
aveva esatto	esigeva	esigesse
avevamo esatto	esigevamo	esigessimo
avevate esatto	esigevate	esigeste
avevano esatto	esigevano	esigessero

espandere to expand

present	future	past historic	gerund
espando	espanderò	espandei	espandendo
espandi	espanderai	espandesti	
espande	espanderà	espandette	past participle
espandiamo	espanderemo	espandemmo	espanso/espansa
espandete	espanderete	espandeste	
espandono	espanderanno	espandettero	

perfect	conditional	present subjunctive	imperative
ho espanso	espanderei	espanda	espandi!
hai espanso	espanderesti	espanda	espanda!
ha espanso	espanderebbe	espanda	espandete!
abbiamo espanso	espanderemmo	espandiamo	
avete espanso	espandereste	espandiate	
hanno espanso	espanderebbero	espandano	

pluperfect	imperfect	past subjunctive
avevo espanso	espandevo	espandessi
avevi espanso	espandevi	espandessi
aveva espanso	espandeva	espandesse
avevamo espanso	espandevamo	espandessimo
avevate espanso	espandevate	espandeste
avevano espanso	espandevano	espandessero

espellere to expel

present	future	past historic	gerund
espello	espellerò	espulsi	espellendo
espelli	espellerai	espellesti	
espelle	espellerà	espulse	*past participle*
espelliamo	espelleremo	espellemmo	espulso/espulsa
espellete	espellerete	espelleste	
espellono	espelleranno	espulsero	

perfect	conditional	present subjunctive	imperative
ho espulso	espellerei	espella	espelli!
hai espulso	espelleresti	espella	espella!
ha espulso	espellerebbe	espella	espellete!
abbiamo espulso	espelleremmo	espelliamo	
avete espulso	espellereste	espelliate	
hanno espulso	espellerebbero	espellano	

pluperfect	imperfect	past subjunctive	
avevo espulso	espellevo	espellessi	
avevi espulso	espellevi	espellessi	
aveva espulso	espelleva	espellesse	
avevamo espulso	espellevamo	espellessimo	
avevate espulso	espellevate	espelleste	
avevano espulso	espellevano	espellessero	

esprimere to express

present	future	past historic	gerund
esprimo	esprimerò	espressi	esprimendo
esprimi	esprimerai	esprimesti	
esprime	esprimerà	espresse	*past participle*
esprimiamo	esprimeremo	esprimemmo	espresso/espressa
esprimete	esprimerete	esprimeste	
esprimono	esprimeranno	espressero	

perfect	conditional	present subjunctive	imperative
ho espresso	esprimerei	esprima	esprimi!
hai espresso	esprimeresti	esprima	esprima!
ha espresso	esprimerebbe	esprima	esprimete!
abbiamo espresso	esprimeremmo	esprimiamo	
avete espresso	esprimereste	esprimiate	
hanno espresso	esprimerebbero	esprimano	

pluperfect	imperfect	past subjunctive	
avevo espresso	esprimevo	esprimessi	
avevi espresso	esprimevi	esprimessi	
aveva espresso	esprimeva	esprimesse	
avevamo espresso	esprimevamo	esprimessimo	
avevate espresso	esprimevate	esprimeste	
avevano espresso	esprimevano	esprimessero	

essere to be

present	future	past historic	gerund
sono	sarò	fui	essendo
sei	sarai	fosti	
è	sarà	fu	*past participle*
siamo	saremo	fummo	stato/stata
siete	sarete	foste	
sono	saranno	furono	

perfect	conditional	present subjunctive	imperative
sono stato/stata	sarei	sia	sii!
sei stato/stata	saresti	sia	sia!
è stato/stata	sarebbe	sia	siate!
siamo stati/state	saremmo	siamo	
siete stati/state	sareste	siate	
sono stati/state	sarebbero	siano	

pluperfect	imperfect	past subjunctive
ero stato/stata	ero	fossi
eri stato/stata	eri	fossi
era stato/stata	era	fosse
eravamo stati/state	eravamo	fossimo
eravate stati/state	eravate	foste
erano stati/state	erano	fossero

fare to do, to make

present	future	past historic	gerund
faccio	farò	feci	facendo
fai	farai	facesti	
fa	farà	fece	*past participle*
facciamo	faremo	facemmo	fatto/fatta
fate	farete	faceste	
fanno	faranno	fecero	

perfect	conditional	present subjunctive	imperative
ho fatto	farei	faccia	fa'! or fai!
hai fatto	faresti	faccia	faccia!
ha fatto	farebbe	faccia	fate!
abbiamo fatto	faremmo	facciamo	
avete fatto	fareste	facciate	
hanno fatto	farebbero	facciano	

pluperfect	imperfect	past subjunctive
avevo fatto	facevo	facessi
avevi fatto	facevi	facessi
aveva fatto	faceva	facesse
avevamo fatto	facevamo	facessimo
avevate fatto	facevate	faceste
avevano fatto	facevano	facessero

fondere *to melt*

present	future	past historic	gerund
fondo	fonderò	fusi	fondendo
fondi	fonderai	fondesti	
fonde	fonderà	fuse	*past participle*
fondiamo	fonderemo	fondemmo	fuso/fusa
fondete	fonderete	fondeste	
fondono	fonderanno	fusero	

perfect	conditional	present subjunctive	imperative
ho fuso	fonderei	fonda	fondi!
hai fuso	fonderesti	fonda	fonda!
ha fuso	fonderebbe	fonda	fondete!
abbiamo fuso	fonderemmo	fondiamo	
avete fuso	fondereste	fondiate	
hanno fuso	fonderebbero	fondano	

pluperfect	imperfect	past subjunctive	
avevo fuso	fondevo	fondessi	
avevi fuso	fondevi	fondessi	
aveva fuso	fondeva	fondesse	
avevamo fuso	fondevamo	fondessimo	
avevate fuso	fondevate	fondeste	
avevano fuso	fondevano	fondessero	

invadere *to invade*

present	future	past historic	gerund
invado	invaderò	invasi	invadendo
invadi	invaderai	invadesti	
invade	invaderà	invase	*past participle*
invadiamo	invaderemo	invademmo	invaso/invasa
invadete	invaderete	invadeste	
invadono	invaderanno	invasero	

perfect	conditional	present subjunctive	imperative
ho invaso	invaderei	invada	invadi!
hai invaso	invaderesti	invada	invada!
ha invaso	invaderebbe	invada	invadete!
abbiamo invaso	invaderemmo	invadiamo	
avete invaso	invadereste	invadiate	
hanno invaso	invaderebbero	invadano	

pluperfect	imperfect	past subjunctive	
avevo invaso	invadevo	invadessi	
avevi invaso	invadevi	invadessi	
aveva invaso	invadeva	invadesse	
avevamo invaso	invadevamo	invadessimo	
avevate invaso	invadevate	invadeste	
avevano invaso	invadevano	invadessero	

leggere to read

present	*future*	*past historic*	*gerund*
leggo	leggerò	lessi	leggendo
leggi	leggerai	leggesti	
legge	leggerà	lesse	*past participle*
leggiamo	leggeremo	leggemmo	letto/letta
leggete	leggerete	leggeste	
leggono	leggeranno	lessero	

perfect	*conditional*	*present subjunctive*	*imperative*
ho letto	leggerei	legga	leggi!
hai letto	leggeresti	legga	legga!
ha letto	leggerebbe	legga	leggete!
abbiamo letto	leggeremmo	leggiamo	
avete letto	leggereste	leggiate	
hanno letto	leggerebbero	leggano	

pluperfect	*imperfect*	*past subjunctive*	
avevo letto	leggevo	leggessi	
avevi letto	leggevi	leggessi	
aveva letto	leggeva	leggesse	
avevamo letto	leggevamo	leggessimo	
avevate letto	leggevate	leggeste	
avevano letto	leggevano	leggessero	

mettere to put

present	*future*	*past historic*	*gerund*
metto	metterò	misi	mettendo
metti	metterai	mettesti	
mette	metterà	mise	*past participle*
mettiamo	metteremo	mettemmo	messo/messa
mettete	metterete	metteste	
mettono	metteranno	misero	

perfect	*conditional*	*present subjunctive*	*imperative*
ho messo	metterei	metta	metti!
hai messo	metteresti	metta	metta!
ha messo	metterebbe	metta	mettete!
abbiamo messo	metteremmo	mettiamo	
avete messo	mettereste	mettiate	
hanno messo	metterebbero	mettano	

pluperfect	*imperfect*	*past subjunctive*	
avevo messo	mettevo	mettessi	
avevi messo	mettevi	mettessi	
aveva messo	metteva	mettesse	
avevamo messo	mettevamo	mettessimo	
avevate messo	mettevate	metteste	
avevano messo	mettevano	mettessero	

morire to die

present	future	past historic	gerund
muoio	morirò	morii	morendo
muori	morirai	moristi	
muore	morirà	morì	past participle
moriamo	moriremo	morimmo	morto/morta
morite	morirete	moriste	
muoiono	moriranno	morirono	

perfect	conditional	present subjunctive	imperative
sono morto/morta	morirei	muoia	muori!
sei morto/morta	moriresti	muoia	muoia!
è morto/morta	morirebbe	muoia	morite!
siamo morti/morte	moriremmo	moriamo	
siete morti/morte	morireste	moriate	
sono morti/morte	morirebbero	muoiano	

pluperfect	imperfect	past subjunctive
ero morto/morta	morivo	morissi
eri morto/morta	morivi	morissi
era morto/morta	moriva	morisse
eravamo morti/morte	morivamo	morissimo
eravate morti/morte	morivate	moriste
erano morti/morte	morivano	morissero

muovere to move

present	future	past historic	gerund
muovo	muoverò	mossi	muovendo
muovi	muoverai	muovesti	
muove	muoverà	mosse	past participle
muoviamo	muoveremo	muovemmo	mosso/mossa
muovete	muoverete	muoveste	
muovono	muoveranno	mossero	

perfect	conditional	present subjunctive	imperative
ho mosso	muoverei	muova	muovi!
hai mosso	muoveresti	muova	muova!
ha mosso	muoverebbe	muova	muovete!
abbiamo mosso	muoveremmo	muoviamo	
avete mosso	muovereste	muoviate	
hanno mosso	muoverebbero	muovano	

pluperfect	imperfect	past subjunctive
avevo mosso	muovevo	muovessi
avevi mosso	muovevi	muovessi
aveva mosso	muoveva	muovesse
avevamo mosso	muovevamo	muovessimo
avevate mosso	muovevate	muoveste
avevano mosso	muovevano	muovessero

nascere to be born

present	future	past historic	gerund
nasco	nascerò	nacqui	nascendo
nasci	nascerai	nascesti	
nasce	nascerà	nacque	*past participle*
nasciamo	nasceremo	nascemmo	nato/nata
nascete	nascerete	nasceste	
nascono	nasceranno	nacquero	

perfect	conditional	present subjunctive
sono nato/nata	nascerei	nasca
sei nato/nata	nasceresti	nasca
è nato/nata	nascerebbe	nasca
siamo nati/nate	nasceremmo	nasciamo
siete nati/nate	nascereste	nasciate
sono nati/nate	nascerebbero	nascano

pluperfect	imperfect	past subjunctive
ero nato/nata	nascevo	nascessi
eri nato/nata	nascevi	nascessi
era nato/nata	nasceva	nascesse
eravamo nati/nate	nascevamo	nascessimo
eravate nati/nate	nascevate	nasceste
erano nati/nate	nascevano	nascessero

nuocere to harm

present	future	past historic	gerund
nuoccio	nuocerò	nocqui	nuocendo
nuoci	nuocerai	nuocesti	
nuoce	nuocerà	nocque	*past participle*
nuociamo	nuoceremo	nuocemmo	nuociuto/nuociuta
nuocete	nuocerete	nuoceste	
nuocciono	nuoceranno	nocquero	

perfect	conditional	present subjunctive	imperative
ho nuociuto	nuocerei	nuoccia	nuoci!
hai nuociuto	nuoceresti	nuoccia	nuoccia!
ha nuociuto	nuocerebbe	nuoccia	nuocete!
abbiamo nuociuto	nuoceremmo	nuociamo	
avete nuociuto	nuocereste	nuociate	
hanno nuociuto	nuocerebbero	nuocciano	

pluperfect	imperfect	past subjunctive
avevo nuociuto	nuocevo	nuocessi
avevi nuociuto	nuocevi	nuocessi
aveva nuociuto	nuoceva	nuocesse
avevamo nuociuto	nuocevamo	nuocessimo
avevate nuociuto	nuocevate	nuoceste
avevano nuociuto	nuocevano	nuocessero

parere to seem

present	future	past historic	gerund
pare	parrà	parve	parendo
paiono	parranno	parvero	

perfect	conditional	present subjunctive	past participle
è parso	parrebbe	paia	parso/parsa
sono parsi	parrebbero	paiano	

pluperfect	imperfect	past subjunctive	
era parso	pareva	paresse	
erano parsi	parevano	paressero	

perdere to lose

present	future	past historic	gerund
perdo	perderò	persi	perdendo
perdi	perderai	perdesti	
perde	perderà	perse	past participle
perdiamo	perderemo	perdemmo	perso/persa
perdete	perderete	perdeste	
perdono	perderanno	persero	

perfect	conditional	present subjunctive	imperative
ho perso	perderei	perda	perdi!
hai perso	perderesti	perda	perda!
ha perso	perderebbe	perda	perdete!
abbiamo perso	perderemmo	perdiamo	
avete perso	perdereste	perdiate	
hanno perso	perderebbero	perdano	

pluperfect	imperfect	past subjunctive	
avevo perso	perdevo	perdessi	
avevi perso	perdevi	perdessi	
aveva perso	perdeva	perdesse	
avevamo perso	perdevamo	perdessimo	
avevate perso	perdevate	perdeste	
avevano perso	perdevano	perdessero	

piacere to like

present	future	past historic	gerund
piaccio	piacerò	piacqui	piacendo
piaci	piacerai	piacesti	
piace	piacerà	piacque	*past participle*
piacciamo	piaceremo	piacemmo	piaciuto/piaciuta
piacete	piacerete	piaceste	
piacciono	piaceranno	piacquero	

perfect	conditional	present subjunctive
sono piaciuto/ piaciuta	piacerei	piaccia
sei piaciuto/piaciuta	piaceresti	piaccia
è piaciuto/piaciuta	piacerebbe	piaccia
siamo piaciuti/ piaciute	piaceremmo	piacciamo
siete piaciuti/ piaciute	piacereste	piacciate
sono piaciuti/ piaciute	piacerebbero	piacciano

	imperfect	past subjunctive
	piacevo	piacessi
	piacevi	piacessi
	piaceva	piacesse
pluperfect	piacevamo	piacessimo
ero piaciuto/piaciuta	piacevate	piaceste
eri piaciuto/piaciuta	piacevano	piacessero
era piaciuto/piaciuta		
eravamo piaciuti/ piaciute		
eravate piaciuti/ piaciute		
erano piaciuti/ piaciute		

piangere to cry

present	future	past historic	gerund
piango	piangerò	piansi	piangendo
piangi	piangerai	piangesti	
piange	piangerà	pianse	*past participle*
piangiamo	piangeremo	piangemmo	pianto/pianta
piangete	piangerete	piangeste	
piangono	piangeranno	piansero	*imperative*
			piangi!

perfect	conditional	present subjunctive	pianga!
ho pianto	piangerei	pianga	piangete!
hai pianto	piangeresti	pianga	
ha pianto	piangerebbe	pianga	
abbiamo pianto	piangeremmo	piangiamo	
avete pianto	piangereste	piangiate	
hanno pianto	piangerebbero	piangano	

pluperfect	imperfect	past subjunctive
avevo pianto	piangevo	piangessi
avevi pianto	piangevi	piangessi
aveva pianto	piangeva	piangesse
avevamo pianto	piangevamo	piangessimo
avevate pianto	piangevate	piangeste
avevano pianto	piangevano	piangessero

piovere to rain

present	future	past historic	gerund
piove	pioverà	piovve	piovendo

perfect	conditional	present subjunctive	past participle
è piovuto	pioverebbe	piova	piovuto

pluperfect	imperfect	past subjunctive	
era piovuto	pioveva	piovesse	

porre to put

present	future	past historic	gerund
pongo	porrò	posi	ponendo
poni	porrai	ponesti	
pone	porrà	pose	past participle
poniamo	porremo	ponemmo	posto/posta
ponete	porrete	poneste	
pongono	porranno	posero	

perfect	conditional	present subjunctive	imperative
ho posto	porrei	ponga	poni!
hai posto	porresti	ponga	ponga!
ha posto	porrebbe	ponga	ponete!
abbiamo posto	porremmo	poniamo	
avete posto	porreste	poniate	
hanno posto	porrebbero	pongano	

pluperfect	imperfect	past subjunctive	
avevo posto	ponevo	ponessi	
avevi posto	ponevi	ponessi	
aveva posto	poneva	ponesse	
avevamo posto	ponevamo	ponessimo	
avevate posto	ponevate	poneste	
avevano posto	ponevano	ponessero	

possedere to own

present	future	past historic	gerund
possiedo	possiederò	possedei *or*	possedendo
possiedi	possiederai	possedetti	
possiede	possiederà	possedesti	*past participle*
possediamo	possiederemo	possedè *or*	posseduto/posseduta
possedete	possiederete	possedette	
possiedono	possiederanno	possedemmo	
		possedeste	
perfect	*conditional*	possederono *or*	
ho posseduto	possiederei	possedettero	
hai posseduto	possiederesti		
ha posseduto	possiederebbe	*present subjunctive*	*imperative*
abbiamo posseduto	possiederemmo	possieda	possiedi!
avete posseduto	possiedereste	possieda	possieda!
hanno posseduto	possiederebbero	possieda	possedete!
		possediamo	
pluperfect	*imperfect*	possediate	
avevo posseduto	possedevo	possiedano	
avevi posseduto	possedevi		
aveva posseduto	possedeva	*past subjunctive*	
avevamo posseduto	possedevamo	possedessi	
avevate posseduto	possedevate	possedessi	
avevano posseduto	possedevano	possedesse	
		possedessimo	
		possedeste	
		possedessero	

potere to be able

present	future	past historic	gerund
posso	potrò	potei	potendo
puoi	potrai	potesti	
può	potrà	poté	*past participle*
possiamo	potremo	potemmo	potuto/potuta
potete	potrete	poteste	
possono	potranno	poterono	
perfect	*conditional*	*present subjunctive*	
ho potuto	potrei	possa	
hai potuto	potresti	possa	
ha potuto	potrebbe	possa	
abbiamo potuto	potremmo	possiamo	
avete potuto	potreste	possiate	
hanno potuto	potrebbero	possano	
pluperfect	*imperfect*	*past subjunctive*	
avevo potuto	potevo	potessi	
avevi potuto	potevi	potessi	
aveva potuto	poteva	potesse	
avevamo potuto	potevamo	potessimo	
avevate potuto	potevate	poteste	
avevano potuto	potevano	potessero	

rendere to give back

present	future	past historic	gerund
rendo	renderò	resi	rendendo
rendi	renderai	rendesti	
rende	renderà	rese	*past participle*
rendiamo	renderemo	rendemmo	reso/resa
rendete	renderete	rendeste	
rendono	renderanno	resero	

perfect	conditional	present subjunctive	imperative
ho reso	renderei	renda	rendi!
hai reso	renderesti	renda	renda!
ha reso	renderebbe	renda	rendete!
abbiamo reso	renderemmo	rendiamo	
avete reso	rendereste	rendiate	
hanno reso	renderebbero	rendano	

pluperfect	imperfect	past subjunctive
avevo reso	rendevo	rendessi
avevi reso	rendevi	rendessi
aveva reso	rendeva	rendesse
avevamo reso	rendevamo	rendessimo
avevate reso	rendevate	rendeste
avevano reso	rendevano	rendessero

restringere to shrink

present	future	past historic	gerund
restringo	restringerò	restrinsi	restringendo
restringi	restringerai	restringesti	
restringe	restringerà	restrinse	*past participle*
restringiamo	restringeremo	restringemmo	ristretto/ristretta
restringete	restringerete	restringeste	
restringono	restringeranno	restrinsero	

perfect	conditional	present subjunctive	imperative
ho ristretto	restringerei	restringa	restringi!
hai ristretto	restringeresti	restringa	restringa!
ha ristretto	restringerebbe	restringa	restringete!
abbiamo ristretto	restringeremmo	restringiamo	
avete ristretto	restringereste	restringiate	
hanno ristretto	restringerebbero	restringano	

pluperfect	imperfect	past subjunctive
avevo ristretto	restringevo	restringessi
avevi ristretto	restringevi	restringessi
aveva ristretto	restringeva	restringesse
avevamo ristretto	restringevamo	restringessimo
avevate ristretto	restringevate	restringeste
avevano ristretto	restringevano	restringessero

ridurre to reduce

present	future	past historic	gerund
riduco	ridurrò	ridussi	riducendo
riduci	ridurrai	riducesti	
riduce	ridurrà	ridusse	past participle
riduciamo	ridurremo	riducemmo	ridotto/ridotta
riducete	ridurrete	riduceste	
riducono	ridurranno	ridussero	

perfect	conditional	present subjunctive	imperative
ho ridotto	ridurrei	riduca	riduci!
hai ridotto	ridurresti	riduca	riduca!
ha ridotto	ridurrebbe	riduca	riducete!
abbiamo ridotto	ridurremmo	riduciamo	
avete ridotto	ridurreste	riduciate	
hanno ridotto	ridurrebbero	riducano	

pluperfect	imperfect	past subjunctive
avevo ridotto	riducevo	riducessi
avevi ridotto	riducevi	riducessi
aveva ridotto	riduceva	riducesse
avevamo ridotto	riducevamo	riducessimo
avevate ridotto	riducevate	riduceste
avevano ridotto	riducevano	riducessero

riempire to fill

present	future	past historic	gerund
riempio	riempirò	riempii	riempiendo
riempi	riempirai	riempisti	
riempie	riempirà	riempì	past participle
riempiamo	riempiremo	riempimmo	riempito/riempita
riempite	riempirete	riempiste	
riempiono	riempiranno	riempirono	

perfect	conditional	present subjunctive	imperative
ho riempito	riempirei	riempia	riempi!
hai riempito	riempiresti	riempia	riempia!
ha riempito	riempirebbe	riempia	riempite!
abbiamo riempito	riempiremmo	riempiamo	
avete riempito	riempireste	riempiate	
hanno riempito	riempirebbero	riempiano	

pluperfect	imperfect	past subjunctive
avevo riempito	riempivo	riempissi
avevi riempito	riempivi	riempissi
aveva riempito	riempiva	riempisse
avevamo riempito	riempivamo	riempissimo
avevate riempito	riempivate	riempiste
avevano riempito	riempivano	riempissero

rimanere to stay

present	future	past historic	gerund
rimango	rimarrò	rimasi	rimanendo
rimani	rimarrai	rimanesti	
rimane	rimarrà	rimase	*past participle*
rimaniamo	rimarremo	rimanemmo	rimasto/rimasta
rimanete	rimarrete	rimaneste	
rimangono	rimarranno	rimasero	

perfect	conditional	present subjunctive	imperative
sono rimasto/rimasta	rimarrei	rimanga	rimani!
sei rimasto/rimasta	rimarresti	rimanga	rimanga!
è rimasto/rimasta	rimarrebbe	rimanga	rimanete!
siamo rimasti/rimaste	rimarremmo	rimaniamo	
siete rimasti/rimaste	rimarreste	rimaniate	
sono rimasti/rimaste	rimarrebbero	rimangano	

pluperfect	imperfect	past subjunctive	
ero rimasto/rimasta	rimanevo	rimanessi	
eri rimasto/rimasta	rimanevi	rimanessi	
era rimasto/rimasta	rimaneva	rimanesse	
eravamo rimasti/rimaste	rimanevamo	rimanessimo	
eravate rimasti/rimaste	rimanevate	rimaneste	
erano rimasti/rimaste	rimanevano	rimanessero	

risolvere to solve

present	future	past historic	gerund
risolvo	risolverò	risolsi	risolvendo
risolvi	risolverai	risolvesti	
risolve	risolverà	risolse	*past participle*
risolviamo	risolveremo	risolvemmo	risolto/risolta
risolvete	risolverete	risolveste	
risolvono	risolveranno	risolsero	

perfect	conditional	present subjunctive	imperative
ho risolto	risolverei	risolva	risolvi!
hai risolto	risolveresti	risolva	risolva!
ha risolto	risolverebbe	risolva	risolvete!
abbiamo risolto	risolveremmo	risolviamo	
avete risolto	risolvereste	risolviate	
hanno risolto	risolverebbero	risolvano	

pluperfect	imperfect	past subjunctive	
avevo risolto	risolvevo	risolvessi	
avevi risolto	risolvevi	risolvessi	
aveva risolto	risolveva	risolvesse	
avevamo risolto	risolvevamo	risolvessimo	
avevate risolto	risolvevate	risolveste	
avevano risolto	risolvevano	risolvessero	

rispondere to answer

present	future	past historic	gerund
rispondo	risponderò	risposi	rispondendo
rispondi	risponderai	rispondesti	
risponde	risponderà	rispose	
rispondiamo	risponderemo	rispondemmo	*past participle*
rispondete	risponderete	rispondeste	risposto/risposta
rispondono	risponderanno	risposero	

perfect	conditional	present subjunctive	imperative
ho risposto	risponderei	risponda	rispondi!
hai risposto	risponderesti	risponda	risponda!
ha risposto	risponderebbe	risponda	rispondete!
abbiamo risposto	risponderemmo	rispondiamo	
avete risposto	rispondereste	rispondiate	
hanno risposto	risponderebbero	rispondano	

pluperfect	imperfect	past subjunctive
avevo risposto	rispondevo	rispondessi
avevi risposto	rispondevi	rispondessi
aveva risposto	rispondeva	rispondesse
avevamo risposto	rispondevamo	rispondessimo
avevate risposto	rispondevate	rispondeste
avevano risposto	rispondevano	rispondessero

rodere to gnaw

present	future	past historic	gerund
rodo	roderò	rosi	rodendo
rodi	roderai	rodesti	
rode	roderà	rose	
rodiamo	roderemo	rodemmo	*past participle*
rodete	roderete	rodeste	roso/rosa
rodono	roderanno	rosero	

perfect	conditional	present subjunctive	imperative
ho roso	roderei	roda	rodi!
hai roso	roderesti	roda	roda!
ha roso	roderebbe	roda	rodete!
abbiamo roso	roderemmo	rodiamo	
avete roso	rodereste	rodiate	
hanno roso	roderebbero	rodano	

pluperfect	imperfect	past subjunctive
avevo roso	rodevo	rodessi
avevi roso	rodevi	rodessi
aveva roso	rodeva	rodesse
avevamo roso	rodevamo	rodessimo
avevate roso	rodevate	rodeste
avevano roso	rodevano	rodessero

rompere to break

present	future	past historic	gerund
rompo	romperò	ruppi	rompendo
rompi	romperai	rompesti	
rompe	romperà	ruppe	*past participle*
rompiamo	romperemo	rompemmo	rotto/rotta
rompete	romperete	rompeste	
rompono	romperanno	ruppero	

perfect	conditional	present subjunctive	imperative
ho rotto	romperei	rompa	rompi!
hai rotto	romperesti	rompa	rompa!
ha rotto	romperebbe	rompa	rompete!
abbiamo rotto	romperemmo	rompiamo	
avete rotto	rompereste	rompiate	
hanno rotto	romperebbero	rompano	

pluperfect	imperfect	past subjunctive	
avevo rotto	rompevo	rompessi	
avevi rotto	rompevi	rompessi	
aveva rotto	rompeva	rompesse	
avevamo rotto	rompevamo	rompessimo	
avevate rotto	rompevate	rompeste	
avevano rotto	rompevano	rompessero	

salire to go up, to come up

present	future	past historic	gerund
salgo	salirò	salii	salendo
sali	salirai	salisti	
sale	salirà	salì	*past participle*
saliamo	saliremo	salimmo	salito/salita
salite	salirete	saliste	
salgono	saliranno	salirono	

perfect	conditional	present subjunctive	imperative
sono salito/salita	salirei	salga	sali!
sei salito/salita	saliresti	salga	salga!
è salito/salita	salirebbe	salga	salite!
siamo saliti/salite	saliremmo	saliamo	
siete saliti/salite	salireste	saliate	
sono saliti/salite	salirebbero	salgano	

pluperfect	imperfect	past subjunctive	
ero salito/salita	salivo	salissi	
eri salito/salita	salivi	salissi	
era salito/salita	saliva	salisse	
eravamo saliti/salite	salivamo	salissimo	
eravate saliti/salite	salivate	saliste	
erano saliti/salite	salivano	salissero	

sapere to know

present	future	past historic	gerund
so	saprò	seppi	sapendo
sai	saprai	sapesti	
sa	saprà	seppe	*past participle*
sappiamo	sapremo	sapemmo	saputo/saputa
sapete	saprete	sapeste	
sanno	sapranno	seppero	

perfect	conditional	present subjunctive	imperative
ho saputo	saprei	sappia	sappi!
hai saputo	sapresti	sappia	sappia!
ha saputo	saprebbe	sappia	sappiate!
abbiamo saputo	sapremmo	sappiamo	
avete saputo	sapreste	sappiate	
hanno saputo	saprebbero	sappiano	

pluperfect	imperfect	past subjunctive
avevo saputo	sapevo	sapessi
avevi saputo	sapevi	sapessi
aveva saputo	sapeva	sapesse
avevamo saputo	sapevamo	sapessimo
avevate saputo	sapevate	sapeste
avevano saputo	sapevano	sapessero

scendere to go down, to come down

present	future	past historic	gerund
scendo	scenderò	scesi	scendendo
scendi	scenderai	scendesti	
scende	scenderà	scese	*past participle*
scendiamo	scenderemo	scendemmo	sceso/scesa
scendete	scenderete	scendeste	
scendono	scenderanno	scesero	

perfect	conditional	present subjunctive	imperative
sono sceso/scesa	scenderei	scenda	scendi!
sei sceso/scesa	scenderesti	scenda	scenda!
è sceso/scesa	scenderebbe	scenda	scendete!
siamo scesi/scese	scenderemmo	scendiamo	
siete scesi/scese	scendereste	scendiate	
sono scesi/scese	scenderebbero	scendano	

pluperfect	imperfect	past subjunctive
ero sceso/scesa	scendevo	scendessi
eri sceso/scesa	scendevi	scendessi
era sceso/scesa	scendeva	scendesse
eravamo scesi/scese	scendevamo	scendessimo
eravate scesi/scese	scendevate	scendeste
erano scesi/scese	scendevano	scendessero

scorgere to catch sight of

present	future	past historic	gerund
scorgo	scorgerò	scorsi	scorgendo
scorgi	scorgerai	scorgesti	
scorge	scorgerà	scorse	past participle
scorgiamo	scorgeremo	scorgemmo	scorto/scorta
scorgete	scorgerete	scorgeste	
scorgono	scorgeranno	scorsero	

perfect	conditional	present subjunctive	imperative
ho scorto	scorgerei	scorga	scorgi!
hai scorto	scorgeresti	scorga	scorga!
ha scorto	scorgerebbe	scorga	scorgete!
abbiamo scorto	scorgeremmo	scorgiamo	
avete scorto	scorgereste	scorgiate	
hanno scorto	scorgerebbero	scorgano	

pluperfect	imperfect	past subjunctive	
avevo scorto	scorgevo	scorgessi	
avevi scorto	scorgevi	scorgessi	
aveva scorto	scorgeva	scorgesse	
avevamo scorto	scorgevamo	scorgessimo	
avevate scorto	scorgevate	scorgeste	
avevano scorto	scorgevano	scorgessero	

scrivere to write

present	future	past historic	gerund
scrivo	scriverò	scrissi	scrivendo
scrivi	scriverai	scrivesti	
scrive	scriverà	scrisse	past participle
scriviamo	scriveremo	scrivemmo	scritto/scritta
scrivete	scriverete	scriveste	
scrivono	scriveranno	scrissero	

perfect	conditional	present subjunctive	imperative
ho scritto	scriverei	scriva	scrivi!
hai scritto	scriveresti	scriva	scriva!
ha scritto	scriverebbe	scriva	scrivete!
abbiamo scritto	scriveremmo	scriviamo	
avete scritto	scrivereste	scriviate	
hanno scritto	scriverebbero	scrivano	

pluperfect	imperfect	past subjunctive	
avevo scritto	scrivevo	scrivessi	
avevi scritto	scrivevi	scrivessi	
aveva scritto	scriveva	scrivesse	
avevamo scritto	scrivevamo	scrivessimo	
avevate scritto	scrivevate	scriveste	
avevano scritto	scrivevano	scrivessero	

scuotere to shake

present	future	past historic	gerund
scuoto	scuoterò	scossi	scuotendo
scuoti	scuoterai	scuotesti	
scuote	scuoterà	scosse	*past participle*
scuotiamo	scuoteremo	scuotemmo	scosso/scossa
scuotete	scuoterete	scuoteste	
scuotono	scuoteranno	scossero	

perfect	conditional	present subjunctive	imperative
ho scosso	scuoterei	scuota	scuoti!
hai scosso	scuoteresti	scuota	scuota!
ha scosso	scuoterebbe	scuota	scuotete!
abbiamo scosso	scuoteremmo	scuotiamo	
avete scosso	scuotereste	scuotiate	
hanno scosso	scuoterebbero	scuotano	

pluperfect	imperfect	past subjunctive	
avevo scosso	scuotevo	scuotessi	
avevi scosso	scuotevi	scuotessi	
aveva scosso	scuoteva	scuotesse	
avevamo scosso	scuotevamo	scuotessimo	
avevate scosso	scuotevate	scuoteste	
avevano scosso	scuotevano	scuotessero	

sedersi to sit down

present	future	past historic	gerund
mi siedo	mi siederò	mi sedei *or* sedetti	sedendo
ti siedi	ti siederai	ti sedesti	
si siede	si siederà	si sedè *or* sedette	*past participle*
ci sediamo	ci siederemo	ci sedemmo	seduto/seduta
vi sedete	vi siederete	vi sedeste	
si siedono	si siederanno	si sederono *or* si sedettero	

perfect	conditional	present subjunctive	imperative
mi sono seduto/seduta	mi siederei	mi sieda	siediti!
ti sei seduto/seduta	ti siederesti	ti sieda	si sieda!
si è seduto/seduta	si siederebbe	si sieda	sedetevi!
ci siamo seduti/sedute	ci siederemmo	ci sediamo	
vi siete seduti/sedute	vi siedereste	vi sediate	
si sono seduti/sedute	si siederebbero	si siedano	

pluperfect	imperfect	past subjunctive	
mi ero seduto/seduta	mi sedevo	mi sedessi	
ti eri seduto/seduta	ti sedevi	ti sedessi	
si era seduto/seduta	si sedeva	si sedesse	
ci eravamo seduti/sedute	ci sedevamo	ci sedessimo	
vi eravate seduti/sedute	vi sedevate	vi sedeste	
si erano seduti/sedute	si sedevano	si sedessero	

seppellire to bury

present	future	past historic	gerund
seppellisco	seppellirò	seppellii	seppellendo
seppellisci	seppellirai	seppellisti	
seppellisce	seppellirà	seppellì	*past participle*
seppelliamo	seppelliremo	seppellimmo	sepolto/sepolta
seppellite	seppellirete	seppelliste	
seppelliscono	seppelliranno	seppellirono	

perfect	conditional	present subjunctive	imperative
ho sepolto	seppellirei	seppellisca	seppellisci!
hai sepolto	seppelliresti	seppellisca	seppellisca!
ha sepolto	seppellirebbe	seppellisca	seppellite!
abbiamo sepolto	seppelliremmo	seppelliamo	
avete sepolto	seppellireste	seppelliate	
hanno sepolto	seppellirebbero	seppelliscano	

pluperfect	imperfect	past subjunctive	
avevo sepolto	seppellivo	seppellissi	
avevi sepolto	seppellivi	seppellissi	
aveva sepolto	seppelliva	seppellisse	
avevamo sepolto	seppellivamo	seppellissimo	
avevate sepolto	seppellivate	seppelliste	
avevano sepolto	seppellivano	seppellissero	

spargere to scatter

present	future	past historic	gerund
spargo	spargerò	sparsi	spargendo
spargi	spargerai	spargesti	
sparge	spargerà	sparse	*past participle*
spargiamo	spargeremo	spargemmo	sparso/sparsa
spargete	spargerete	spargeste	
spargono	spargeranno	sparsero	

perfect	conditional	present subjunctive	imperative
ho sparso	spargerei	sparga	spargi!
hai sparso	spargeresti	sparga	sparga!
ha sparso	spargerebbe	sparga	spargete!
abbiamo sparso	spargeremmo	spargiamo	
avete sparso	spargereste	spargiate	
hanno sparso	spargerebbero	spargano	

pluperfect	imperfect	past subjunctive	
avevo sparso	spargevo	spargessi	
avevi sparso	spargevi	spargessi	
aveva sparso	spargeva	spargesse	
avevamo sparso	spargevamo	spargessimo	
avevate sparso	spargevate	spargeste	
avevano sparso	spargevano	spargessero	

spegnere to put out

present	future	past historic	gerund
spengo	spegnerò	spensi	spegnendo
spegni	spegnerai	spegnesti	
spegne	spegnerà	spense	*past participle*
spegniamo	spegneremo	spegnemmo	spento/spenta
spegnete	spegnerete	spegneste	
spengono	spegneranno	spensero	*imperative*

perfect	conditional	present subjunctive	spegni!
ho spento	spegnerei	spenga	spenga!
hai spento	spegneresti	spenga	spegnete!
ha spento	spegnerebbe	spenga	
abbiamo spento	spegneremmo	spegniamo	
avete spento	spegnereste	spegniate	
hanno spento	spegnerebbero	spengano	

pluperfect	imperfect	past subjunctive
avevo spento	spegnevo	spegnessi
avevi spento	spegnevi	spegnessi
aveva spento	spegneva	spegnesse
avevamo spento	spegnevamo	spegnessimo
avevate spento	spegnevate	spegneste
avevano spento	spegnevano	spegnessero

stare to be

present	future	past historic	gerund
sto	starò	stetti	stando
stai	starai	stesti	
sta	starà	stette	*past participle*
stiamo	staremo	stemmo	stato/stata
state	starete	steste	
stanno	staranno	stettero	

perfect	conditional	present subjunctive	imperative
sono stato/stata	starei	stia	sta'! or stai!
sei stato/stata	staresti	stia	stia!
è stato/stata	starebbe	stia	state!
siamo stati/state	staremmo	stiamo	
siete stati/state	stareste	stiate	
sono stati/state	starebbero	stiano	

pluperfect	imperfect	past subjunctive
ero stato/stata	stavo	stessi
eri stato/stata	stavi	stessi
era stato/stata	stava	stesse
eravamo stati/state	stavamo	stessimo
eravate stati/state	stavate	steste
erano stati/state	stavano	stessero

stringere to squeeze

present	future	past historic	gerund
stringo	stringerò	strinsi	stringendo
stringi	stringerai	stringesti	
stringe	stringerà	strinse	*past participle*
stringiamo	stringeremo	stringemmo	stretto/stretta
stringete	stringerete	stringeste	
stringono	stringeranno	strinsero	

perfect	conditional	present subjunctive	imperative
ho stretto	stringerei	stringa	stringi!
hai stretto	stringeresti	stringa	stringa!
ha stretto	stringerebbe	stringa	stringete!
abbiamo stretto	stringeremmo	stringiamo	
avete stretto	stringereste	stringiate	
hanno stretto	stringerebbero	stringano	

pluperfect	imperfect	past subjunctive
avevo stretto	stringevo	stringessi
avevi stretto	stringevi	stringessi
aveva stretto	stringeva	stringesse
avevamo stretto	stringevamo	stringessimo
avevate stretto	stringevate	stringeste
avevano stretto	stringevano	stringessero

tacere to be silent

present	future	past historic	gerund
taccio	tacerò	tacqui	tacendo
taci	tacerai	tacesti	
tace	tacerà	tacque	*past participle*
tacciamo	taceremo	tacemmo	taciuto/taciuta
tacete	tacerete	taceste	
tacciono	taceranno	tacquero	

perfect	conditional	present subjunctive	imperative
ho taciuto	tacerei	taccia	taci!
hai taciuto	taceresti	taccia	taccia!
ha taciuto	tacerebbe	taccia	tacete!
abbiamo taciuto	taceremmo	tacciamo	
avete taciuto	tacereste	tacciate	
hanno taciuto	tacerebbero	tacciano	

pluperfect	imperfect	past subjunctive
avevo taciuto	tacevo	tacessi
avevi taciuto	tacevi	tacessi
aveva taciuto	taceva	tacesse
avevamo taciuto	tacevamo	tacessimo
avevate taciuto	tacevate	taceste
avevano taciuto	tacevano	tacessero

tenere to hold

present	future	past historic	gerund
tengo	terrò	tenni	tenendo
tieni	terrai	tenesti	
tiene	terrà	tenne	*past participle*
teniamo	terremo	tenemmo	tenuto/tenuta
tenete	terrete	teneste	
tengono	terranno	tennero	

perfect	conditional	present subjunctive	imperative
ho tenuto	terrei	tenga	tieni!
hai tenuto	terresti	tenga	tenga!
ha tenuto	terrebbe	tenga	tenete!
abbiamo tenuto	terremmo	teniamo	
avete tenuto	terreste	teniate	
hanno tenuto	terrebbero	tengano	

pluperfect	imperfect	past subjunctive
avevo tenuto	tenevo	tenessi
avevi tenuto	tenevi	tenessi
aveva tenuto	teneva	tenesse
avevamo tenuto	tenevamo	tenessimo
avevate tenuto	tenevate	teneste
avevano tenuto	tenevano	tenessero

torcere to twist

present	future	past historic	gerund
torco	torcerò	torsi	torcendo
torci	torcerai	torcesti	
torce	torcerà	torse	*past participle*
torciamo	torceremo	torcemmo	torto/torta
torcete	torcerete	torceste	
torcono	torceranno	torsero	

perfect	conditional	present subjunctive	imperative
ho torto	torcerei	torca	torci!
hai torto	torceresti	torca	torca!
ha torto	torcerebbe	torca	torcete!
abbiamo torto	torceremmo	torciamo	
avete torto	torcereste	torciate	
hanno torto	torcerebbero	torcano	

pluperfect	imperfect	past subjunctive
avevo torto	torcevo	torcessi
avevi torto	torcevi	torcessi
aveva torto	torceva	torcesse
avevamo torto	torcevamo	torcessimo
avevate torto	torcevate	torceste
avevano torto	torcevano	torcessero

trarre *to draw*

present	future	past historic	gerund
traggo	trarrò	trassi	traendo
trai	trarrai	traesti	
trae	trarrà	trasse	*past participle*
traiamo	trarremo	traemmo	tratto/tratta
traete	trarrete	traeste	
traggono	trarranno	trassero	

perfect	conditional	present subjunctive	imperative
ho tratto	trarrei	tragga	trai!
hai tratto	trarresti	tragga	tragga!
ha tratto	trarrebbe	tragga	traete!
abbiamo tratto	trarremmo	traiamo	
avete tratto	trarreste	traiate	
hanno tratto	trarrebbero	traggano	

pluperfect	imperfect	past subjunctive
avevo tratto	traevo	traessi
avevi tratto	traevi	traessi
aveva tratto	traeva	traesse
avevamo tratto	traevamo	traessimo
avevate tratto	traevate	traeste
avevano tratto	traevano	traessero

udire *to hear*

present	future	past historic	gerund
odo	udirò	udii	udendo
odi	udirai	udisti	
ode	udirà	udì	*past participle*
udiamo	udiremo	udimmo	udito/udita
udite	udirete	udiste	
odono	udiranno	udirono	

perfect	conditional	present subjunctive	imperative
ho udito	udirei	oda	odi!
hai udito	udiresti	oda	oda!
ha udito	udirebbe	oda	udite!
abbiamo udito	udiremmo	udiamo	
avete udito	udireste	udiate	
hanno udito	udirebbero	odano	

pluperfect	imperfect	past subjunctive
avevo udito	udivo	udissi
avevi udito	udivi	udissi
aveva udito	udiva	udisse
avevamo udito	udivamo	udissimo
avevate udito	udivate	udiste
avevano udito	udivano	udissero

uscire to go out, to come out

present	future	past historic	gerund
esco	uscirò	uscii	uscendo
esci	uscirai	uscisti	
esce	uscirà	uscì	*past participle*
usciamo	usciremo	uscimmo	uscito/uscita
uscite	uscirete	usciste	
escono	usciranno	uscirono	

perfect	conditional	present subjunctive	imperative
sono uscito/uscita	uscirei	esca	esci!
sei uscito/uscita	usciresti	esca	esca!
è uscito/uscita	uscirebbe	esca	uscite!
siamo usciti/uscite	usciremmo	usciamo	
siete usciti/uscite	uscireste	usciate	
sono usciti/uscite	uscirebbero	escano	

pluperfect	imperfect	past subjunctive	
ero uscito/uscita	uscivo	uscissi	
eri uscito/uscita	uscivi	uscissi	
era uscito/uscita	usciva	uscisse	
eravamo usciti/uscite	uscivamo	uscissimo	
eravate usciti/uscite	uscivate	usciste	
erano usciti/uscite	uscivano	uscissero	

valere to to be worth

present	future	past historic	gerund
valgo	varrò	valsi	valendo
vali	varrai	valesti	
vale	varrà	valse	*past participle*
valiamo	varremo	valemmo	valso/valsa
valete	varrete	valeste	
valgono	varranno	valsero	

perfect	conditional	present subjunctive	imperative
sono valso/valsa	varrei	valga	vali!
sei valso/valsa	varresti	valga	valga!
è valso/valsa	varrebbe	valga	valete!
siamo valsi/valse	varremmo	valiamo	
siete valsi/valse	varreste	valiate	
sono valsi/valse	varrebbero	valgano	

pluperfect	imperfect	past subjunctive	
ero valso/valsa	valevo	valessi	
eri valso/valsa	valevi	valessi	
era valso/valsa	valeva	valesse	
eravamo valsi/valse	valevamo	valessimo	
eravate valsi/valse	valevate	valeste	
erano valsi/valse	valevano	valessero	

vedere to see

present	future	past historic	gerund
vedo	vedrò	vidi	vedendo
vedi	vedrai	vedesti	
vede	vedrà	vide	past participle
vediamo	vedremo	vedemmo	visto/vista
vedete	vedrete	vedeste	
vedono	vedranno	videro	

perfect	conditional	present subjunctive	imperative
ho visto	vedrei	veda	vedi!
hai visto	vedresti	veda	veda!
ha visto	vedrebbe	veda	vedete!
abbiamo visto	vedremmo	vediamo	
avete visto	vedreste	vediate	
hanno visto	vedrebbero	vedano	

pluperfect	imperfect	past subjunctive
avevo visto	vedevo	vedessi
avevi visto	vedevi	vedessi
aveva visto	vedeva	vedesse
avevamo visto	vedevamo	vedessimo
avevate visto	vedevate	vedeste
avevano visto	vedevano	vedessero

venire to come

present	future	past historic	gerund
vengo	verrò	venni	venendo
vieni	verrai	venisti	
viene	verrà	venne	past participle
veniamo	verremo	venimmo	venuto/venuta
venite	verrete	veniste	
vengono	verranno	vennero	

perfect	conditional	present subjunctive	imperative
sono venuto/venuta	verrei	venga	vieni!
sei venuto/venuta	verresti	venga	venga!
è venuto/venuta	verrebbe	venga	venite!
siamo venuti/venute	verremmo	veniamo	
siete venuti/venute	verreste	veniate	
sono venuti/venute	verrebbero	vengano	

pluperfect	imperfect	past subjunctive
ero venuto/venuta	venivo	venissi
eri venuto/venuta	venivi	venissi
era venuto/venuta	veniva	venisse
eravamo venuti/venute	venivamo	venissimo
eravate venuti/venute	venivate	veniste
erano venuti/venute	venivano	venissero

vincere to win

present	future	past historic	gerund
vinco	vincerò	vinsi	vincendo
vinci	vincerai	vincesti	
vince	vincerà	vinse	*past participle*
vinciamo	vinceremo	vincemmo	vinto/vinta
vincete	vincerete	vinceste	
vincono	vinceranno	vinsero	

perfect	conditional	present subjunctive	imperative
ho vinto	vincerei	vinca	vinci!
hai vinto	vinceresti	vinca	vinca!
ha vinto	vincerebbe	vinca	vincete!
abbiamo vinto	vinceremmo	vinciamo	
avete vinto	vincereste	vinciate	
hanno vinto	vincerebbero	vincano	

pluperfect	imperfect	past subjunctive	
avevo vinto	vincevo	vincessi	
avevi vinto	vincevi	vincessi	
aveva vinto	vinceva	vincesse	
avevamo vinto	vincevamo	vincessimo	
avevate vinto	vincevate	vinceste	
avevano vinto	vincevano	vincessero	

vivere to live

present	future	past historic	gerund
vivo	vivrò	vissi	vivendo
vivi	vivrai	vivesti	
vive	vivrà	visse	*past participle*
viviamo	vivremo	vivemmo	vissuto/vissuta
vivete	vivrete	viveste	
vivono	vivranno	vissero	

perfect	conditional	present subjunctive	imperative
sono vissuto/vissuta	vivrei	viva	vivi!
sei vissuto/vissuta	vivresti	viva	viva!
è vissuto/vissuta	vivrebbe	viva	vivete!
siamo vissuti/vissute	vivremmo	viviamo	
siete vissuti/vissute	vivreste	viviate	
sono vissuti/vissute	vivrebbero	vivano	

pluperfect	imperfect	past subjunctive	
ero vissuto/vissuta	vivevo	vivessi	
eri vissuto/vissuta	vivevi	vivessi	
era vissuto/vissuta	viveva	vivesse	
eravamo vissuti/vissute	vivevamo	vivessimo	
eravate vissuti/vissute	vivevate	viveste	
erano vissuti/vissute	vivevano	vivessero	

volere to want

present	future	past historic	gerund
voglio	vorrò	volli	volendo
vuoi	vorrai	volesti	
vuole	vorrà	volle	*past participle*
vogliamo	vorremo	volemmo	voluto/voluta
volete	vorrete	voleste	
vogliono	vorranno	vollero	

perfect	conditional	present subjunctive	
ho voluto	vorrei	voglia	
hai voluto	vorresti	voglia	
ha voluto	vorrebbe	voglia	
abbiamo voluto	vorremmo	vogliamo	
avete voluto	vorreste	vogliate	
hanno voluto	vorrebbero	vogliano	

pluperfect	imperfect	past subjunctive	
avevo voluto	volevo	volessi	
avevi voluto	volevi	volessi	
aveva voluto	voleva	volesse	
avevamo voluto	volevamo	volessimo	
avevate voluto	volevate	voleste	
avevano voluto	volevano	volessero	

volgere to turn

present	future	past historic	gerund
volgo	volgerò	volsi	volgendo
volgi	volgerai	volgesti	
volge	volgerà	volse	*past participle*
volgiamo	volgeremo	volgemmo	volto/volta
volgete	volgerete	volgeste	
volgono	volgeranno	volsero	

perfect	conditional	present subjunctive	imperative
ho volto	volgerei	volga	volgi!
hai volto	volgeresti	volga	volga!
ha volto	volgerebbe	volga	volgete!
abbiamo volto	volgeremmo	volgiamo	
avete volto	volgereste	volgiate	
hanno volto	volgerebbero	volgano	

pluperfect	imperfect	past subjunctive	
avevo volto	volgevo	volgessi	
avevi volto	volgevi	volgessi	
aveva volto	volgeva	volgesse	
avevamo volto	volgevamo	volgessimo	
avevate volto	volgevate	volgeste	
avevano volto	volgevano	volgessero	

Glossary of grammatical terms

*Words in **bold** letters are defined in a separate entry in the glossary.*

Active: In a sentence with an active verb, the **subject** of the verb performs the action, e.g. *Sam* (subject) *identified* (verb) *the suspect* (as opposed to the passive construction *The suspect was identified by Sam*, where *the suspect* is the subject but is not doing the identifying). Cf. **Passive**.

Adjective: A word that describes a **noun** or **pronoun**, giving information about its shape, colour, size, etc., e.g. *triangular, red, large* in 'a *triangular* sign', 'the *red* dress', 'it is *large*'.

Adverb: A word expressing the manner, frequency, time, place, or extent of an action, e.g. *slowly* and *often* in 'Sue walked *slowly*', 'He *often* stumbled'. Adverbs can also be used with sentences, e.g. 'Sue *probably* went home', **adjectives**, e.g. 'Sue is *very* tall', and other adverbs, e.g. 'Sue left *extremely* early'.

Adverbial phrase: A phrase which does the same job as an adverb, e.g. *with care* (Italian 'con cura').

Agreement: Words are said to agree when they are put in the correct form in relation to another word. In Standard English and in Italian, a singular noun or pronoun has to have a singular verb, e.g. *he goes* (Italian 'lui va'), and a plural noun or pronoun has to have a plural verb, e.g. *they go* (Italian 'loro vanno'). In

Italian, **adjectives** also agree in **number** and **gender** with the **nouns** they go with, e.g. *case antiche* (English 'old houses').

Article: see **Definite article**, **Indefinite article**.

Auxiliary verb: In English, a verb which functions together with another verb to form a particular **tense** of the other verb, or to form the **passive**, a question, or a **negative**. In Italian there are two auxiliary verbs, *avere* and *essere*, which are used to form **compound tenses** and the **passive**.

Cardinal numbers: Cardinal numbers are the numbers used when counting. In English they are *one*, *two*, *three*, etc. (Italian 'uno', 'due', 'tre', etc.). Cf. **Ordinal numbers**.

Comparative: The form of an **adjective** or **adverb** used when comparing one thing with another, to express a greater degree of a quality, e.g. *cheaper, more expensive, more precisely* (Italian 'più economico', 'più caro', 'più precisamente'. Cf. **Superlative**.

Compound noun: A noun created by putting two or more existing words together, e.g. *bookshop, sofa bed, self-control*.

Compound tense: a **tense** which is formed using an **auxiliary verb**. In Italian, the compound tenses include

274 | Glossary of grammatical terms

the **perfect**, the **pluperfect**, and the **future perfect**.

Conditional: A verb form which expresses what would happen, or would have happened, under certain conditions. English normally uses *if* with a form of *would* to express this notion: *If I won the lottery... I would buy a car. / If I had won... I would have bought....* In Italian there are two conditional tenses: present and past.

Conjugations: The three main patterns of regular verbs in Italian. They can be recognized from their infinitive forms ending in -are, -ere, and -ire respectively, e.g. *mandare*, *vendere*, and *finire*.

Conjunction: A word whose function is to join sentences or phrases, e.g. 'Rachel *and* David', 'I'll go to the cinema *or* meet my friend for dinner', 'They left *because* it was late'.

Definite article: In English, the word *the*, which is used with a noun and implies that the thing mentioned has already been mentioned or is common knowledge, e.g. '*the* book on *the* table'. Cf. **Indefinite article**.

Demonstrative: A word indicating the person or thing referred to, e.g. *this*, *that*, *these*, *those* in '*this* book' (Italian '*questo* libro'), '*that* house' (Italian '*quella* casa'), '*these* books' (Italian '*questi* libri'), '*those* houses' (Italian '*quelle* case').

Diminutive endings: Endings which are added to nouns to express the idea of 'smallness'. There are two common diminutive endings in Italian: -ino and -etto.

Direct object: A word or group of words which is immediately affected

by the action indicated by the verb, e.g. 'James saw *the rabbit*'. Cf. **Indirect object**.

Feminine: see **Gender**.

Future: The future **tense** is used when the time of the event described has not yet happened. English uses the auxiliary verbs *shall* and *will* to express this notion, e.g. *They will be pleased* (Italian 'saranno contenti').

Future perfect: A **tense** used to say what *will have happened* by a certain time in the future. In English it can be recognized by the presence of *will have* or *shall have*, e.g. *They will have already left* (Italian 'saranno già partiti').

Gender: In some languages, nouns and pronouns are divided into grammatical classes called genders. The gender of a noun or pronoun can affect the form of words such as verbs or adjectives that accompany it and may need to **agree** with it in gender. Italian has two genders, **masculine** and **feminine**.

Gerund: The form of a verb that ends in -ing, e.g. *reading*. In Italian the gerund ends in -ando or -endo.

Imperative: The form of the verb used to express a command, e.g. *come* in 'Come here!'

Imperfect: An Italian tense that refers to a continuous or habitual action in the past, e.g. *fumavo* (English 'I was smoking, I used to smoke').

Impersonal verb: A verb which in English has *it* as its subject, where *it* does not refer to anything that has been mentioned, e.g. *It's nice to be here*. In Italian these verbs have no explicit subject, and can usually be used only in the third person singular, e.g. *piove* (English 'it's raining').

Indefinite article: In English, the word *a/an*, which introduces a noun phrase and implies that the thing mentioned is non-specific, e.g. 'she bought *a* book'. Cf. **Definite article**.

Indicative: The form of a verb used to express a simple statement of fact, when an event is considered to be definitely taking place or to have taken place, e.g. 'He *fell asleep*' (Italian 'si è addormentato'). Cf. **Subjunctive**.

Indirect object: A word or phrase referring to the person who receives the **direct object**, e.g. *the driver* in the sentences 'She gave the ticket to *the driver*' and 'She gave *the driver* the ticket'. Cf. **Direct object**.

Infinitive: The basic form of the verb, e.g. *laugh, damage, be*. It is not bound to a particular subject or tense and in English is often preceded by *to* or by another verb, e.g. 'I want *to see* her', 'She came *to see* me', 'Let me *see*'. Italian infinitives end in *-are, -ere, -ire*, or *-rre*.

Interrogative: A sentence or clause that asks a question, e.g. *Is the taxi waiting?, Where is the hotel?*

Intonation: The use of the pitch of the voice to convey meaning.

Intransitive verb: A verb not taking a **direct object**, e.g. *slept* in 'He *slept* well' (Italian 'ha dormito bene'). Cf. **Transitive verb**.

Irregular verb: In English, a verb such as *sing* which does not follow one of the usual **conjugations** of the language. There are many irregular verbs in Italian. Cf. **Regular verb**.

Masculine: see **Gender**.

Negative: A negative sentence asserts that something is not the case, for example by using *not* in English. Cf. **Affirmative**.

Noun: A word that identifies a person, e.g. *teenager*, a physical object, e.g. *computer*, or an abstract notion, e.g. *beauty*.

Number: Whether a word is **singular** or **plural**.

Object: See **Direct object**, **Indirect object**.

Ordinal numbers: Ordinal numbers are used to talk about the order of things, for example in time or on a list. In English the ordinal numbers are *first, second, third*, etc. (Italian 'primo', 'secondo', 'terzo', etc.). Cf. **Cardinal numbers**.

Past participle: In English, a word formed from a verb and used as an adjective or to form **compound tenses**. The English past participle ends in *-ed*, e.g. *finished* (Italian 'finito').

Partitive article: A small word in Italian which is placed before nouns to express an indefinite number or quantity, e.g. 'dell'acqua' (English 'some water').

Passive: The form of the verb used when the individual referred to by the **subject** undergoes (rather than performs) the action, e.g. 'The student *was nominated* for an award'. Cf. **Active**.

Past historic: An Italian tense that refers to something that happened in the past. It is generally used to talk about events in the relatively distant past, e.g. *partì* (English 'he left').

Perfect: An Italian tense that refers to something that happened in the past. The perfect is generally used to talk about events in the fairly recent past, or that have had some kind of effect on the present, e.g. *ha finito* (English 'he finished, he has finished').

Person: Person forms are the grammatical forms that refer to or agree with the speaker and other individuals addressed or mentioned, e.g. *I, we* (first person pronouns), *you* (second person pronoun), *he, she, it, they* (third person pronouns).

Personal pronoun: A **pronoun** that refers to a person or to people known to the speaker, e.g. *I, she, they* (Italian 'io', 'lei', 'loro').

Plural: A word or form referring to more than one person or object, e.g. *children, books, we, are*. Cf. **Singular**.

Possessive: An adjective or pronoun indicating possession, e.g. *my, mine* (Italian 'il mio').

Prefix: An element that is added to the beginning of a word to change its meaning or grammatical form, e.g. *re-* in *reread* (Italian 'rileggere').

Preposition: A word that precedes a noun or pronoun, expressing its relationship to another word in the sentence. This relationship can be to do with position, e.g. 'The book is *on* the table', time, e.g. 'He arrived *in* March', or it may have a purely grammatical function in the sentence, e.g. 'Wait *for* me'.

Present: The present **tense** is used when the time of the event described includes the time of utterance, e.g. *lives* in 'Peter *lives* in London'. Cf. **Past**.

Progressive: A verb form indicating that an action or process is or was ongoing, e.g. 'He *is waiting*', 'She *was laughing*'.

Pronoun: A word that substitutes for a noun or noun phrase, e.g. *them* in 'Children don't like *them*' (instead of 'Children don't like *vegetables*').

Reflexive pronoun: A pronoun that is the object of the verb, but refers back to the subject of the sentence in denoting the same individual, e.g. *herself* in 'She hurt *herself*' (Italian '*si* è fatta male'). Cf. also **Reflexive verb**.

Reflexive verb: A **verb** where the object is the same person or thing as the subject. In English they can be recognized by the presence of *myself, yourself, himself*, etc., e.g. 'She *wrapped herself* in a blanket'.

Regular verb: A verb such as *laugh* which follows one of the usual **conjugations**. Most regular verbs in Italian end in *-are*. Cf. **Irregular verb**.

Relative pronoun: A pronoun (*who, whose, which*, or *that*) used to refer back to a person or thing in the preceding part of the sentence, e.g. 'Peter lost the book *that/which* he bought'.

Singular: A word or form referring to just one person or thing, e.g. *child, book, I, is*. Cf. **Plural**.

Stress: The **syllable** of a word receiving relatively greater force or emphasis than the other(s) is said to be the stressed syllable, e.g. *ci̱ty* (Italian 'citta̱').

Subject: The subject of a sentence is generally the noun or pronoun that causes the action of the verb, e.g.

'*Alison* fed her cats'. In English all verbs must have an explicit subject. In Italian this is not always necessary because the ending of the verb shows what the subject is, e.g. *studio* (English '*I* study').

Subjunctive: A special form of the verb that expresses doubt, unlikelihood, or desire. The subjunctive is not very common in modern English, and often forms with **let**, **should**, etc. do the same job, e.g. '*Let* there *be* light!', 'It's rare that this *should happen*'. In Italian the subjunctive is very common. There are four tenses of the subjunctive in Italian: present, past, perfect, and pluperfect. Cf. **Indicative**.

Superlative: The form of an **adjective** or **adverb** used when comparing one thing with another to express the greatest degree of a quality, e.g. *the biggest* (Italian 'il più grande'), *the most beautiful* (Italian 'il più bello'). Cf. **Comparative**.

Syllable: A unit of pronunciation that is normally less than a word but greater than a single sound, e.g. *abracadabra* has five syllables: *a-bra-ca-da-bra*.

Tense: The form of the verb which indicates the time of the action, e.g. 'Anna *smokes*' (present tense), 'Anna *smoked*' (past tense).

Verb: A word that expresses an action, process, or state of affairs, e.g. 'He *closed* the door' (Italian 'Ha chiuso la porta'), 'They *laugh*' (Italian 'ridono'), 'We *were* at home' (Italian '*Eravamo* a casa').

Index

Italics are used to denote an Italian word in the Index.

Italics are used to denote an Italian word in the Index.

Italics are used to denote an Italian word in the Index.

Italics are used to denote an Italian word in the Index.

Italics are used to denote an Italian word in the Index.